JECT MODELING AND
DESIGN STRATEGIES

ADVANCES IN OBJECT TECHNOLOGY SERIES

Dr. Richard S. Wiener
Series Editor

Editor
Journal of Object-Oriented Programming
Report on Object Analysis and Design
SIGS Publications, Inc.
New York, New York

and

Department of Computer Science
University of Colorado
Colorado Springs, Colorado

Additional volumes in preparation

OBJECT MODELING AND DESIGN STRATEGIES

Tips and Techniques

SANJIV GOSSAIN

COPUBLISHED BY THE PRESS SYNDICATE OF THE UNIVERSITY OF CAMBRIDGE AND SIGS BOOKS
The Pitt Building, Trumpington Street, Cambridge CB2 1RP, United Kingdom

CAMBRIDGE UNIVERSITY PRESS
The Edinburgh Building, Cambridge CB2 2RU, UK   http: //www.cup.cam.ac.uk
40 West 20th Street, New York, NY 10011-4211, USA   http: ///www.cup.org
10 Stamford Road, Oakleigh, Melbourne 3166, Australia

SIGS Books & Multimedia   http: //www.sigs.com
71 West 23rd Street, third floor
New York, NY 10010

First published in 1998

Printed in the United States of America

Typeset in ITC Century and Helvetica

A catalog record for this book is available from
the British Library

Library of Congress Cataloging-in-Publication Data is available

ISBN 0-521-64822-X paperback

FOR MY PARENTS

Whose love and understanding
has made me who I am.

CONTENTS

About the Author

Sanjiv Gossain is CTO of Cambridge Technology Partners. He is a regular contributor to object-oriented magazines and has spoken at numerous conferences. Sanjiv has been involved in object technology for ten years, and he holds a Ph.D. in object-oriented development and reuse.

FOREWORD

AFTER MORE THAN 30 YEARS of object-oriented programming, the object-oriented approach has finally become irresistible only in the age of the World Wide Web. The prospect of widespread reuse, more flexible systems, and massively reduced system maintenance costs was never quite enough to drive the average corporate IT manager toward the top of the object water chute. But the Web has changed everything. The corporate need for network enabled business means that soon thousands of developers will be writing Java, which is (quite circumstantially as it happens) a true object-oriented language. The danger now is that all these developers might not only get the seats of their pants very wet on the slide but that many may drown on reaching the bottom—dragging their managers and users down with them. The trouble is that it is no use delivering objects that do not have stable, comprehensible interfaces. If you do that, all the advantages of objects evaporate. Thus, as I have argued elsewhere, systems analysis and design become far more important than ever before. They become, in many respects, THE critical development activities, along with requirements engineering and project management.

There are many books on object-oriented analysis and design methods. Sanjiv Gossain complements these works nicely with this commentary, which is full of the sort of useful and practical advice so often omitted from such tomes. He covers many of the stages of development using an approach synthesized from several methods, with the influence of two data-driven methods (Shlaer/Mellor and OMT) shining through most clearly. Useful ideas from other methods are cleverly woven in to this fabric. Sanjiv's approach is refreshingly critical. For example, he soundly debunks many of the myths surrounding the currently fashionable +use cases and design patterns. This book is also slightly unusual among books on object-oriented methods in paying some attention to the process as well as to mere notation: a trait that other authors on the subject would do well to emulate. The useful tips on system design in the final chapter will benefit any developer considering how best to implement an object model. Most valuable of all is the emphasis on and discussion of system architecture: another critical factor for the success of IT organizations migrating to object technology. I may not agree with absolutely everything Sanjiv says in this book, but I do believe it will be of great value to those developers approaching their initiatory object-oriented projects. Here is the chance to learn from someone who has ridden the water chute and swum successfully ashore to tell the tale.

IAN GRAHAM
London, May 1997

PREFACE

Background

I must have read some 20 different books on object-oriented methods over the last 3 years. Each had something valid to say on the subject and contributed a different view on the topic. In fact, I have used many of the ideas they presented on projects even if I was not using that particular method. There was, however, always something missing. The method needed some interpretation, some extra ideas to make it usable in practice. From the examples and the discussion in the book describing the method, it was not always evident if I was doing "the right thing at the right time" or if there was perhaps a "better" way to do certain things. From discussions with friends and colleagues within the object community I learned that this has largely been their experience also. Much of this was because some of the methods were very new and had only been tried on a few projects, and hence there was a lack of experience in the method.

An object-oriented method is fine for getting started, helping one understand the concepts, and for providing an initial framework in which to think and understand a problem; but the content of a book on an object-oriented method is by no means sufficient for building a real, working system. I have been involved in the construction of a number of object systems across a variety of application areas, and more interestingly, across many different types of systems. My roles on projects have meant my being responsible for object models used for building real-time and embedded systems as well as systems in the business world, typically deployed on client–server architectures.

Methods used range from ad hoc methods (i.e., no method) and formal textbook methods (Shlaer/Mellor and Object Modeling Technique [OMT]) to "roll-your-own methods" (making the best use of other methods and adapting them to existing working practice). I have no allegiance to any one method although I naturally have preferences. I believe in having a method and following that method if you are using it. Not everything is covered by a method, however, and there will always be times when techniques, approaches, and what I call strategies are needed to augment one's favorite method, be it OMT, Shlaer/Mellor, Martin/Odell, or whatever.

I have been distilling the various techniques and approaches espoused in numerous methods into a set of core strategies that I use on a regular basis. These strategies have been presented at numerous conferences and seminars, and I have incorporated much of the feedback from attendees in order to continually improve the strategies. Regular usage of the core strategies also contributes to their improvement. They are essentially a set of useful ideas based on real-world experiences that have assisted me in designing object systems.

This Book

The goal of this book is to get beyond the method hype and help the practicing object-oriented modeler, manager, and architect understand how to use object-oriented concepts *in practice*. This text describes techniques, strategies, and tools for modeling real-world problems using object technology. It also addresses some of the harder issues faced when designing and implementing object systems by providing a series of practical techniques that the object-oriented designer will find helpful in making some of the difficult decisions.

A pragmatic approach is taken in these descriptions in which the primary purpose is to "get the job done." As a result, there are strategies and tactics drawn from a number of different methods. Where these are mixed and matched I have tried to give consideration to how these can be integrated into any of the current methods.

The text looks at the different techniques and processes used in understanding problem domains, and aims to provide a compendium of guidelines for the practitioner. The examples used are founded in real-world experience drawn from a variety of application areas ranging from telecommunications to financial trading. Information of particular interest to the client–server business world and distributed -systems design is presented in a separate chapter devoted to those topics.

These strategies are highlighted throughout the text using the following format:

    📖   This symbol and paragraph describe a single, practically useful strategy that I hope will aid you in developing your object systems.

This is not a text describing another object-oriented method or describing how to manage object-oriented projects. There are numerous other books for that. In order to place the ideas in context, however, there will be some discussion on object-oriented methods and on some management issues, particularly those that are influenced by the techniques and strategies contained within.

I have tried to indicate where strategies are more closely tied to a particular method. I hope that you will be able to return to this book in the future, and use the techniques as consultation material during your object-oriented projects.

Target Audience

This text is aimed at the practitioner. After reading this book the object-oriented practitioner should have a better understanding of how to best use object technology *in practice*, and be able to use the techniques described here in *real projects*.

The object-oriented novice should find this book valuable in providing a framework in which he or she can understand the many different aspects of the technology. The novice should also find it useful in correlating some of the more academic, method-related texts to how object-oriented technology is actually used.

In writing this book I have assumed the reader is familiar with object concepts. Words such as encapsulation, polymorphism, and inheritance should not be frightening for the reader! It will certainly help with the reader's understanding if he or she has read at least one text on an object-oriented method.

Structure of the Text

Chapter 1 begins with a look at objects in industry: some of the benefits that have been achieved by corporations, followed by an examination of the state of the object industry today and its prospect for the next few years. This chapter closes with a description of some of the lessons learned in industry.

The purpose of chapter 2 is to provide a big picture of the object-oriented world by focusing on some of the more popular themes associated with object technology; it also examines whether there is any substance to the hyperbole surrounding objects in the media. Topics such as object methods, business objects, use cases, and modeling the real world are addressed.

The object-oriented development process in which most of these strategies have been used is then described. The purpose of this is to place into context the strategies described during the remaining chapters.

Chapter 2 also introduces two philosophies of design—elaboration and translation. These are two fundamentally different ways of looking at development and are themes that are revisited during the course of the text.

The subject of chapter 3 is the modeling of system structure. A number of strategies that can assist in this process are described. Some of the areas the strategies address are system partitioning, working with domain experts, finding objects and attributes, attribute placement, modeling associations, and modeling rules.

The behavioral properties of a domain must be modeled in addition to its structure. This is the subject of chapter 4. Using techniques from a number of different methods, the practicalities of identifying and modeling system behavior are presented. Some novel ways of looking at object communication and some strategies to help in deciding on roles and responsibilities are described.

Chapter 5 addresses the increasingly popular subject of architecture. The success of an object-based system can often be dependent on constructing a sound architecture that provides the right blend of vision with pragmatism; therefore, the importance of the architect in the success of an object system is highlighted along with a description of the role.

The process of designing an architecture—magic to many —is detailed and generalized to apply to most system architectures. A four- layer model for systems based on reusable services is also described. The chapter aims at providing some useful tips and techniques that the reader can take back to his or her project and use when designing and architecture for a system.

The two philosophies of design introduced in chapter 2— transformation and elaboration—offer different viewpoints. In chapter 6 we revisit these approaches and examine their view of design. The two approaches have different philosophies but common goals.

Even though design in the two paradigms can take on different forms, some of the activities undertaken are the same. In both cases objects in the analysis must be represented in some way in the design paradigm, relationships in the object models must be mapped to some design construct, and the designer must decide how to support attributes in the design. For each of these decisions there are a number of alternatives. Each must be considered in the light of a number of criteria. Chapter 6 provides a discussion of the issues that must be addressed in designing object systems.

Chapter 7 looks at two key issues involved in building object-oriented client–server systems—namely, object distribution and accessing legacy systems.

The final chapter is a collection of strategies built around putting the whole thing together and making it work. Areas addressed include project management, requirements traceability, allocating tasks among a team, and working in workshops.

Appendix A briefly describes the notation used on diagrams, whereas Appendix B is a collection of all the strategies found throughout the text. I hope this latter Appendix can be used to provide a quick reference while you are fully immersed in projects.

In this book I have tried to provide more of a collection of ideas that are grouped together into sections rather than a step-by-step walk-through of logically organized topics. Therefore, there may be times when you, as a reader, may find yourself referring from one chapter to another to relate back to an earlier issue. This is my fault. There are so many dependencies and interrelationships in the ideas presented here that I believe an iterative approach to reading this book is the best one!

The ideas presented here have worked for me. I hope that you find them as useful in your day-to-day work as I have.

SANJIV GOSSAIN
London, England

ACKNOWLEDGMENTS

I T IS NOT EVERY DAY that one decides to write a book. This is my first, and I hope not my last, but as I write this sentence it feels like it might be. There are so many people without whose involvement, direct or indirect, this text would not exist today. I would like to thank them.

First, my thanks to Bruce Anderson, who bears the responsibility for my being introduced to object orientation.

My exposure to the world of real-time embedded systems at Nokia Telecommunications provided a sound base for understanding what it takes to construct object systems. Thanks to all my colleagues of that time, including Andy and Emma Molloy, Andy Lauder, David Rutter, Taneli Vuorinen, and Laszlo Huray.

My friends at Project Technology, a family more than a company, introduced me to the translational paradigm and the world of consulting. Thanks to all, especially Kent Mingus, Marc Balcer, Michael Lee, Neil Lang, Phil Ryals, Rod Montrose, Sally Shlaer, and, of course, Stephen Mellor.

I would also like to recognize the substantial input of ideas and practices from my colleagues at my current place of employ, Cambridge Technology Partners. Thanks to David Levine for continually being curious and helping me retain my (somewhat limited) analytical side. Thanks also to my colleagues at Cambridge who have been responsive to being used as a testing ground for ideas and to those who have reviewed my writing: Aad Nales, Carla Glassman, David Levine, Kevin O'Connor, and Sally Davis. Thanks also to Mickey Smith for taking me to Lansing and introducing me to the human side of object stuff and the Wall, and to Bill Seibel for giving me even more new challenges in parallel to writing this book.

I am indebted to Tanvi Chawla, a great friend and architect extraordinaire, for the rapid production of the sketches in chapter 5. Much appreciated!

Also thanks to others, either friends or colleagues or both: to David Riches for his useful comments on various versions of the book, Sajida Malik for keeping me down to earth, Luis Torres for regular doses of sound advice; thanks also to those who were willing to listen me talk about objects: Libby Wright, Masood Chaudhry, Rajiv Mahajan, and Raj Mistry at Cambridge. Thanks also to Amrit Virdee , Mrugesh and Rehana Mehta, Nasar Khan, Pavlos Papachristos, and Sukhbir Nehra for their continual encouragement.

Thanks to the editorial staff at SIGS Publications, especially Peter Arnold, and my appreciation to the anonymous reviewers who provided numerous valuable comments, which have improved the content of the book.

Most of all, thanks to my family—my mother and father; Priya, Savita, Ajay, Anousha, and Sachin; and, of course, my wife, Serena—for sticking by me and putting up with me for so many years.

CHAPTER 1

OBJECTS: TODAY, TOMORROW, AND SOME LESSONS LEARNED

RATHER THAN PROVIDE yet another detailed introduction to objects through definitions, examples, notations, and methods, this chapter provides only a brief introduction to the technology through some of the benefits objects have to offer. This should place into context why object technology is so attractive as a software-development paradigm.

We then examine how and why object technology is on the brink of being accepted by mainstream business and industry as the software-development technology of choice. This is done through an assessment of the state of the marketplace (looking at objects today) and examining what the future holds for object orientation (taking a brief glimpse at tomorrow). This is followed by a look at some high-level lessons learned over my last 9 years of using object technology.

1.1 Objects: The Benefits

What began as a programming paradigm has now moved firmly into the methods and business processing arena. Starting out as concepts in programming through Simula67, the world of object-oriented programming moved to object-oriented design (Booch, 1986), and then further up the life cycle to object-oriented analysis (Shlaer & Mellor, 1988). And has now moved into the area of object-oriented business-process reengineering (Jacobson, 1995). Based on the wide applicability

1

of the concepts, the potential for objects to transform much of what we do is quite profound.

A large part of the rationale of the move to object orientation comes from the purported benefits the technology can offer. They include the following:

- reusability
- easier maintenance
- rapid development
- improved productivity
- seamlessness in development

In much of the media, however, these benefits have been overhyped and expectations set so high that reality could never come close. As a result, some of the earlier organizations adopting objects suffered some negative experiences with the technology. These experiences were principally in the areas of productivity and reuse. Expectations were set for improvements in productivity practically overnight, as well as for a set of reusable objects that came as a natural consequence of using objects. Such expectations now seem ridiculous to many, but the continued hype of objects must be tempered with practical experiences that ensure there is no belief in Brooks' (1987) silver bullet.

It is important to stress that benefits in productivity have been made by companies using object technology, with Swiss Bank Corporation being a notable example (*Computing*, 1994). Reuse is providing benefits for some organizations, although this has largely been attributable to overcoming the numerous nontechnical barriers, rather than the power of objects.

What follows are some of the real benefits that I have observed, experienced by corporations who have made the commitment to objects.

1.1.1 Better Mapping Between the Business and Software

The most obvious benefit is one of the most powerful. When brought into an organization objects transform the "black art" of software development into a process that is visible to all outside the usual development community. It is possible for the business to read, understand, and participate in the development of object models. Object software represents business concepts directly. The software community thus has the opportunity to respond to changes in the business much more rapidly.

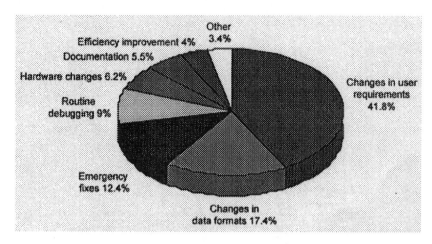

Figure 1.1. Breakdown of maintenance costs. From Lientz and Swanson (1989).

This mapping has the potential to improve other nontechnical areas, such as the improved communication between the user community and information technology (IT; Horan & Gossain, 1995), and improved communication between the business community and IT. The strong mapping between business and objects has proven to be so successful that object techniques are now being used as a core aspect of some business engineering activities (Jacobson, 1995).

1.1.2 Coping with Change (Maintainability)

Lientz and Swanson (1989) examined the breakdown of maintenance costs for over 500 major projects. As the pie chart of Figure 1.1 shows, "changes in user requirements" are the primary reason for maintenance. Such a statistic reflects the dynamic nature of the modern business environment.

The major paradigm of the 1990s is change (Peters, 1987), and the ability of the software community to adapt to change will be a key to its success. It is precisely the ability to cope with change that is one of the major strengths of object orientation.

The second largest reason for maintenance costs, as indicated in Figure 1.1, is change in data formats. Objects encapsulate data and thus offer great benefits in building systems that are resilient to changes in implementation. A change in a data format should mean a change that only affects the storage of data in a class (which is hidden from all its clients), and the methods of that class. Therefore the

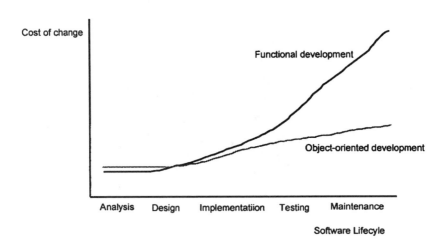

Figure 1.2. Cost of change through the life cycle.

implementation may change, but the interface to the external world does not. Again, change is localized.

Emergency fixes in procedural code can still produce unexpected behavior, and in many cases this creates more bugs than the fixes would solve. I would assert, however, that this is less likely to occur in a well-engineered object-oriented system because changes would be located either within objects, or through different routing of messages. They would thus be more traceable than in procedural code.

It is well known in the software engineering community that the cost of change increases the further along one is in the development life cycle (Figure 1.2). In development of procedural code using structured methods there is a dramatic increase when entering implementation. The cost of change escalates rapidly from here on. In object-oriented development, however, the cost of change only increases slightly. This is because the notion of encapsulation and abstraction allow for localization of changes in a good object-oriented design.

Considering that up to 80% of information systems (IS) budgets are dedicated to maintenance (Gagliardi, 1994), the use of object-oriented techniques can provide great savings. The ease by which object-oriented software can be extended and modified (extensibility) is also included as part of this benefit.

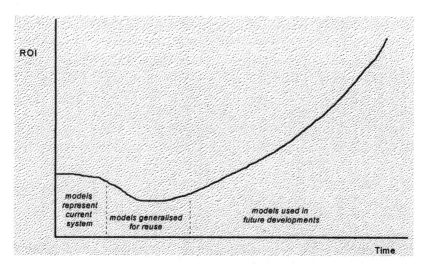

Figure 1.3. ROI of reusable designs.

1.1.3 Improved Productivity and Quality Through the Reuse of Existing Components

The benefits of reuse are long term. Even a small percentage of saving through reuse can result in potentially enormous financial savings for large organizations, and perhaps more important, can mean competitive advantage in the marketplace. In certain markets, a 5% increase in productivity can mean a distinct competitive advantage as it can lessen the time to market.

Much of the effort in this area has focused on the reuse of code. The benefits of using class libraries, generic containers, and the like are certainly worth striving for but these are small-scale savings when compared to the benefits that can be obtained through the reuse of frameworks and designs.

Figure 1.3 shows how reuse can provide handsome returns on investment when it is at the level of designs, as opposed to code. The graph depicts the return on investment (ROI) in a set of models developed as part of an application. The dip in the curve reflects the period when the models are generalized for reuse. Once the models have been generalized they provide large returns on the investment.

In many organizations reuse of code has taken place during development. In such scenarios reuse has been achieved through individual programmers "scavenging" for code from previous projects and from other developers. In many cases the introduction of a systematic reuse effort has only had a small effect and has not formalized the scavenging. Part of this is because reuse, to be successful, requires a shift in mind-set for all involved, from developers to project management to corporate management, and also requires a focus throughout the life cycle. A reuse-enabled software-development process that supports such a shift is a prerequisite for successful reuse.

1.2 Caveats

As with any new paradigm, there are a number of caveats that should be noted.

1.2.1 Organizational Impact and Culture

The introduction of objects into an organization and its effect on the software-development process and organization culture should not be underestimated. An organization that currently supports a software process geared for some variant of structured methodology needs to develop itself and begin to focus on iteration, sharing of components, and more group-oriented development activities. The impact on culture should not be underestimated.

The impact on the organization also occurs at the managerial level, not just at the levels of analysts and developers. Managers need to be reeducated on objects to fully appreciate the impact on their work.

1.2.2 Skill Set

Moving to objects requires a "paradigm shift." With this comes the need for a change in approach to software development and also a change in skill set. Many organizations, with a large number of staff experienced in COBOL, are daunted by the prospect of having to retrain and reskill their analysts and programmers into the object paradigm. An average of a 6-month learning curve to become proficient in object-think is widely quoted. Fortunately, there are now large numbers of education and training companies providing the necessary education, training, and mentoring needed.

Moving to object orientation also requires software development communities to "open up" their analysis-and-design process by involving nontechnical people in

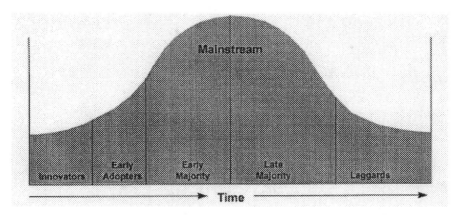

Figure 1.4. The Technology Adoption Life Cycle.

the process. Analysts need to involve people from the business domain throughout the process, and in some cases this can be a major sticking point.

1.2.3 Immaturity of the Technology

This is a concern for large, blue-chip, conservative organizations who resist the move to objects for fear that the technology is immature. As a number of case studies and experience reports have shown, however, object technology is being used to deliver large-scale mission-critical projects around the world. Three years ago the immaturity of the technology was a reasonable concern. This is no longer the case.

Whatever your view on object orientation, whether you are a novice or an expert, the benefits of object technology are so overwhelming that the object movement has now gained such momentum that it really cannot be ignored. If an organization wants to remain competitive and use software technology as a part of retaining that competitiveness, then it must embrace object orientation.

1.3 Objects Today and Tomorrow

In his book *Crossing the Chasm*, Geoffrey Moore (1991) describes how a major challenge for high-tech marketing is the crossing of a chasm between two segments of the well-known Technology Adoption Life Cycle (Figure 1.4).

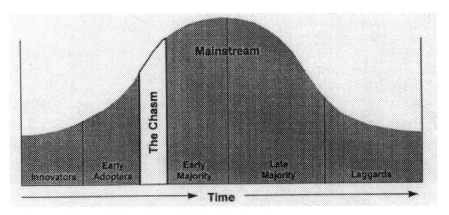

Figure 1.5. Moore's revised Technology Adoption Life Cycle. From Moore (1991).

Based on the real-world experiences of many companies, Moore revised this well-known bell-curve (see Figure 1.5) to more accurately reflect the challenges faced by organizations marketing to the high-tech sector, and has thus introduced the aforementioned chasm. Moore introduced a number of cracks, and of course the chasm, to more accurately reflect the possibility of companies falling into these hazards as they promote their technology.

The chasm is seen as a major pitfall for corporations wishing to make the strategically important move from the Early Adopters of a technology to the mainstream market where the bulk of the revenue lies.

1.3.1 Objects and the Technology Adoption Life Cycle

Although Moore's discussion centers on the marketing of technology, I feel the curve applies equally well to the adoption of object technology as it moves from the Early Adopters to the Early Majority. I believe object technology is on the brink of entering the mainstream. Some may argue that objects have already gone mainstream, but as surveys from popular object conferences have shown, many large organizations are still carrying out pilots and learning the impact of the technology. The years 1996 and 1997 will be the time when objects come into their own and are accepted by the Early Majority. Orfali et al. (1995), for example, predict that object-based middleware (Object Request Brokers) will become ubiquitous by early 1997.

In the late 1980s the world of objects was the sole property of the Innovators. The focus was on the technology and the programming languages. The only companies really using objects were small, innovative, technologically aware organizations acting as visionaries who believed in the technology.

Objects moved from the Innovators to the Early Adopters in the early 1990s as telecommunications companies and merchant banks engaged on large object-oriented projects. Both of these vertical markets are typical early adopters as they readily employ leading-edge technologies to provide them with a strategic advantage over their competitors in increasingly competitive markets. The world of telecommunications is becoming more and more deregulated and merchant banks operate in a high-risk trading world. As such, both need the assistance of technology to give them an edge over the competitors.

There are now signs that the Early Majority are adopting object technology through some major initiatives. Moore tells us that the Early Majority is a group of pragmatists who are "hard to win over but loyal once won" (Moore, 1991, p. 43). They are a group that like to see competition to encourage an open market place and lower costs, and are in it for the long haul. Pragmatists want evidence of success and need convincing that the technology they are buying is proven.

The recent work in standardization and method merging, the improving maturity of tools, and CORBA indicates that object technology is on the brink of acceptance by the mainstream. The move from pilot applications to production applications is a key indicator. Typically, more and more companies are past testing the technology through pilots and learning experiments and are now developing mission-critical applications using objects. Objects are now seen as an essential next step in the software-development world and no longer considered a revolutionary way to develop software. Evolution is the word of today.

1.3.2 The Whole Product

In order for object technology to successfully cross the chasm into the mainstream, it must be seen as a complete "whole product" (to use Moore's terminology once again). Figure 1.6 shows a diagrammatic representation of the whole product when related to objects. As the diagram shows there are six aspects to the whole product for object technology. In order for the pragmatists of the mainstream to feel comfortable and be convinced that objects are ready for the mainstream the "whole" product has to be available. Let us examine each aspect in turn.

Figure 1.6. The "whole product" for object technology.

1.3.2.1 Tools and Methods

This area is of most concern for the pragmatists, as it is probably the most prominent. The recent joining of prominent methodologists Grady Booch (1994) and James Rumbaugh et al. (1991) at the same organization (Rational) will lead to a unified method that aims to combine the best of both methods. This coupled with the more recent merging of Objective Systems and Rational now means that Ivar Jacobson has now also joined Booch and Rumbaugh and this will lead to a unified method from all three methodologists. As Booch (1996b, p. 94) points out:

> What we are doing in the unified method is far more than simply consolidating the Booch, Objectory, and OMT methods. Consolidation is certainly our first step . . . we've gone beyond unification and have tried to address more advanced modeling issues.

In addition to these leading methodologists joining forces there is also considerable work among other methodologists that will lead to some commonality across methods. The COMMA (Common Object Methodology Metamodel Architecture) project looks to construct a common meta-model of a number of the leading methodologies. As Henderson-Sellers (1994, p. 28) points out:

> For widespread success object technology requires not only solid methodological support for software development but also some identifiable

core that provides the lingua franca for practicing object technologists.
. . . COMMA-compliant methodologies could then be derived from this
higher level abstraction core methodology.

The work on COMMA seems to be following on with work on OPEN (Object-oriented Process, Environment, and Notation) from Henderson-Sellers and Graham
(1996), which is an additional unification effort that aims to build on the work of
numerous other methodologies to provide a full life-cycle process, including reuse
strategies and legacy systems.

At this time it is still too early to be able to predict the fate of the OPEN initiative, or the success of the unified method, but both are steps that will undoubtedly improve the acceptability of objects as a mainstream technology.

CASE tools (computer-aided software engineering), forever the overhyped
drawing package, are finally beginning to provide real support for methods. Tools
such as ParadigmPlus, Rational ROSE, and SELECT Enterprise provide very good
support for the more popular methods. In the area of code generation, tools such as
BridgePoint, can generate 100% *application* code for those using the Shlaer-Mellor
method (Lato & Parks, 1995). Examples such as these are another aspect of the convincing maturity of object-oriented methods and tools.

1.3.2.2 Languages and Environments

A few years ago Smalltalk was seen as being incapable of providing the necessary
features needed to deliver large production systems. Commonly cited issues such
as the lack of support for team development and poor performance no longer
apply. The advent of excellent products such as Object Technology International's
ENVY/Developer, the improvements in Smalltalk implementations, and the numerous systems written in Smalltalk are testimony to the industrial-strength environment Smalltalk is now becoming. Smalltalk is no longer seen as a purist or
research-only environment as systems serving 1,000+ users prove (Love, 1993).

C++ is now more mature and stable and more and more products offer a
Smalltalk-like development environment: a far cry from the simple editors and
debuggers of the late 1980s and early 1990s. Object COBOL, the current dark horse
of the language race, will feature prominently during 1997 and 1998.

The rapid rise in popularity of Java, an object-oriented programming language,
and the other object-related aspects of the Internet, will also aid in the acceptability of objects.

For the client–server world, a number of new second-generation development
environments are now all object oriented. This eclectic mix of products features

tools that were originally mainframe based but have now gone object oriented (such as NatStar and ObjectStar), and a number of tools developed as object oriented from their conception (such as Forté and Dynasty). All of these 4GL (4th-generation language)- type tools have object orientation as their unifying paradigm and claim to be industrial-strength, object-oriented, application-development environments.

All in all the availability of better development environments also facilitates pragmatist confidence in objects as a technology worth investing.

1.3.2.3 Training and Education

You only have to look at the magazine advertisements (in the *Journal of Object-Oriented Programming*, for example) to find numerous education companies providing introductory object education, migration consulting, training ,and consulting in object-oriented business-engineering, training on object-oriented languages, and courses on multiple object methods. Any company wishing to become conversant in object technology has a myriad of training sources available. Such wide availability means quality education can be attained through obtaining references, pursuing personal recommendations, and thus organizing a comprehensive education program for staff.

It should also be pointed out that it is too easy to reduce the education and training time required for moving to objects, because of the cost and the time investment. The importance of education in objects cannot be overstated. A number of project teams find themselves having severe difficulties late into a project due to a lack of understanding of the subject matter or the approach being taken. A lack of training and education in object orientation can lead to the failure of a project.

1.3.2.4 Standards

The world of object standards has come a long way since the formation of the Object Management Group (OMG). Their efforts won't be completed until some time in 1997, but the majority of the standards will be defined or will have appeared in products this year. CORBA and Active-X are the two dominant object-interoperability standards. CORBA 2.0 has long been announced and there are a number of CORBA 2.0-compliant products available. CORBA to Active-X interoperability is the only area of concern, but this is being addressed by vendors.

As mentioned earlier, there is also some notion of standardization through the combining of efforts of numerous prominent methodologists in unifying methods and in working on a common meta-model architecture for object methods. Those companies wishing to wait for standards to emerge in the object arena need wait only a little longer as the days of the standards "wars" getting in the way of large-scale integration projects are numbered.

1.3.2.5 Professional Services

The large consulting firms and systems integrators are now using objects in their development projects, some more as the norm than the exception. After many companies' early foray into objects, usually on the back of internal projects, systems integrators now have in-house expertise in object systems. Companies such as Cambridge Technology Partners, Andersen Consulting, SHL Systemhouse, and so on all have object-delivery capabilities. Specialist Object consultancies, such as Knowledge Systems Corporation and The Object People, are themselves growing at very fast rates in response to large demands.

1.3.2.6 Case Studies and Experiences

Perhaps most important of all for the pragmatists is the availability of case studies and experience reports from real projects. There are now hundreds of systems successfully delivered using object technology in a variety of domains as wide ranging as manufacturing, insurance, banking and finance, software development, and transportation. Reports of such projects are available in books (Harmon & Taylor,1993; Love, 1993; Meyer & Nerson,1993) as well as in conferences that now regularly feature experience reports. All this helps to build up the confidence of the pragmatist who wishes to use technology that has been proven and is providing benefits.

Those wishing to embark on the object-oriented path in earnest need to understand the real issues surrounding the technology when used on a project: What is different compared to how things were done previously, how does one migrate, how does one train, how does one organize for reuse? There are certainly a number of excellent books advising on such matters (Booch, 1995; Graham, 1995; McGibbon, 1996), but reports from actual projects carry a lot more weight.

It is important that we in the object community provide as wide a circulation as possible for these success stories so that they get coverage in the mass media. We must also ensure that they are not restricted to just "special issues" because that implies that object technology is "different." Success stories featuring objects should be covered just like any other article. After all, there are no special issues on "structured design," it's just the way it's done. Objects need to follow a similar route.

Examples that discuss object development in terms of some of the practical trade-offs that need to be made are also needed. Such articles and books aim to expose real issues and get beyond the hype surrounding objects. This book is aimed at being part of that group—books that help in making objects a practical reality based on experiences in the real world.

1.3.3 Beyond the Early Majority

Now that we can see that the "whole product" for object technology has emerged, we need to begin to think about the next stage in order that we may prepare for it. After the pragmatists come the conservatives of the Late Majority. This group likes to buy preassembled packages as discount-priced bundles. We are already seeing the availability of "domain objects," such as Person, Organization, Employment, and Postal Address, among others, from companies such as WorldFusion Software. There is now also an initiative underway to construct a core object model for the insurance industry by IBM, funded by a consortium of insurance companies (*Object Magazine*, 1995). Without commenting on the quality of such objects, both efforts certainly reflect a movement toward more "componentism" in the object world.

In the world of object-technology adoption, the conservatives will be the people who will use objects after libraries, frameworks, and components become much more widely available. As Moore (1991, p. 53) points out:

> We must use our experience with the pragmatist customer segment to identify all the issues that require service and then design solutions to these problems directly into the product.

It is difficult to estimate when the Late Majority will adopt objects, but we must ensure that we do use our experience with the pragmatists to the full. As Figure 1.5 shows, there is also a gap between the Early and Late majorities!

1.4 Lessons Learned

Through the exposure I have had in object development across a broad arena of application domains, I have compiled the top 10 lessons learned. This has not been an easy task as there have been so many lessons gained from practice, working with others, a failed project, learning from experts, and so on. I have given consideration to some of the more fundamental lessons I believe to be important, however. Here they are (in no particular order):

1. There really *is* such a thing as a paradigm shift. Everyone moves to objects at different speeds. Not everyone gets it.
2. Get as many different viewpoints as possible in the object-modeling process (both in developing the models and in reviewing progress).
3. Don't use CASE tools until the rate of change of the models begins to decrease.
4. Reuse needs to be supported *throughout* the software life cycle.
5. Architecture is key.
6. When making the transition, management education beforehand, and then continual buy-in during the transition, is essential.
7. Choose a project with *high* visibility for your first object project.
8. The method with the most market share isn't necessarily the best one for your organization.
9. Question methods—why, when, and why again.
10. Objects put "bad" designs up-front.

I should point out that these are some of the most high-level lessons to be learned. The detailed ones are to be found throughout the book in the form of strategies.

1.4.1 Paradigm Shift

There really is such a thing as a paradigm shift in moving to objects. People take varying amounts of time in going through this paradigm shift. Some people "get it" in days, for others it can take months; a few, sadly, never get it.

Much in the same way as management information systems (MIS) departments are having to re-skill their staff in order to be capable of developing client–server applications, moving to objects also requires reskilling. The shift to objects is perhaps harder to make, as it is a paradigm shift, not a straightforward reskilling. The difficult part, however, is that some people just do not manage the transition.

There is a wonderful paragraph from Kuhn (1970) in his book *The Structure of Scientific Revolutions*, which seems rather apt:

Though each may hope to convert the other to his way of seeing his science and its problems, neither may hope to prove his case. The competition between paradigms is not the sort of battle that can be resolved by proofs. . . . Before they can hope to communicate fully, one group or the other must experience the conversion that we have been calling a paradigm shift. Just because it is a transition between incommensurables, the transition between competing paradigms cannot be made a step at a time, forced by logic and neutral experience. Like a gestalt switch it must occur all at once or not at all. (Kuhn, 1970, pp. 147, 149)

The above quote concisely describes the notion of a paradigm shift. No matter how many seminars and tutorials are attended the paradigm shift has to be experienced. Although this phrase is over used and much derided by a number of commentators, this shift should be taken into consideration by management when transitioning people to the new technology. Learning object orientation is education, not training (Love, 1993).

1.4.2 Involvement in the Process

Throughout the object-modeling process get as many different views involved in the process as possible—people from the business, domain experts, users, modelers, developers, application support.

Using objects as your development paradigm can have a profound effect on the development process and the support of individuals from a variety of backgrounds. Objects brings the software- development process closer to nondevelopers.

The business sponsors of the application are able to feel involved in the process as they survey the models (see chapter 9). Domain experts can assist in reviews and in developing the models (see chapter 3). Users need to be involved heavily in the process, as they also have to feel ownership of the software (see chapter 3).

Using objects provides the software-development community of an organization with the opportunity to change the perception of software development from a backroom process, into an open process directly linked to the business.

A recent report by the Standish Group (1995) found that only 16% of IT projects were successful (completed on time, on budget with expected features). This report also found that some of the principal characteristics of successful projects was user involvement, business involvement, executive support, and smaller increments. It is therefore key that as many different views as possible are represented at appropriate stages in the projects life cycle.

1.4.3 CASE Tools

> Do not enter anything into a CASE tool until either the rate of change of the models begins to decrease, or the models begin to get too large to fit on a single large whiteboard. The best CASE tool early on is a whiteboard, some sticky yellow pads, and flip-charts.

It is very tempting and very easy to start entering your models into a CASE tool from day one. Don't! One should begin to enter object models into the tool when it is necessary to do so because the model is too large for a single whiteboard or if the model has stabilized to such a degree that you feel confident it won't change too radically.

Entering models into the tool too early can result in the tool slowing you down, and one ends up fighting the tool, rather than focusing on the important aspects of your modeling—understanding the problem domain.

A consultant friend of mine used to say that every morning he would come in to the office, take a look at his object models, and feel that he would want to make some changes. After a while the number of changes he wanted to make every morning would start to decrease. When the number of changes was down to a number he could easily use the CASE tool for, he would enter the model into the CASE tool.

1.4.4 Reuse

> Reuse needs to be supported throughout the software life cycle. Before a project begins you need to look for potential reuse into the project. During a project you need to constantly ask the question, "How can we build reuse into our objects?" After your project you need to identify reusable and potentially reusable components.

Reuse is a key selling point of object orientation and in many cases the major factor in an organization's move to objects. This is unfortunate as it is certainly not one of the major proven benefits of object orientation. Using object-oriented technology does not guarantee reuse. Reuse programs are fraught with difficulty and there are numerous hurdles that must be overcome in order to reach success. One of them relates to the life cycle.

Reuse is a complete life-cycle activity. It is not an after-the-fact stage of the process whereby reusable components are extracted from projects. It needs to be supported by a reuse-enabled life cycle.

Reuse is a topic that has been much written about, and much of the early experiences of corporations in organizing reuse programs have been documented. Management issues are well covered by Goldberg and Rubin (1995), with an all-around exposé adequately provided by Karlsson (1995). Some helpful, and humorous, anecdotes are provided by Tracz (1995). Every chapter of this book addresses reuse in some form or another.

1.4.5 Architecture

Architecture is key. Objects facilitate more flexible architectures. Before designing the system the architecture must be defined and then continually revisited throughout the process.

Objects allow us to describe, discuss, and reason about software architecture in a way that previous paradigms never did. This is not to say that architecture was not an issue until objects came around, but the spread of objects has been in step with the increasing awareness of architecture as an important aspect of system construction. It is the unique packaging of data and behavior into objects that allows us to discuss the architectural issues surrounding system construction. Thinking of subsystems and systems as objects allows us to apply object ideas to larger grain concepts.

Although it is true that objects are the building blocks of a system, merely following an object-oriented analysis-and-design method does not guarantee a "good" architecture.[1] Similarly, merely using C++ as the programming language does not mean one is writing object-oriented software. There are numerous issues, both technical and organizational, that must be addressed in producing a system architecture.

Each project must have an architect, who is responsible for ensuring the macro-structure of the system. It is important that the high-level architecture has been defined by the time design comes around. After that, as the design proceeds, the architecture must be continually revisited. It will, of course, change slightly, but the design should adhere to the principles of the architecture.

Architecture is addressed in considerably more detail in chapter 5.

---

[1]Booch (1996a) has recently been stating the importance of addressing architecture during the design process, such that he seems to have incorporated such processes into his method framework.

1.4.6 Management and Culture Change

> When making the transition, management education, and then buy-in, is essential. Managers at all levels need to be educated in order to fully appreciate the impact of objects.

Management needs to understand the full impact of object orientation. Particular areas that should be highlighted in any management education program have been identified by Meyer (1995) as follows:

- The benefits: what to expect, when to expect them, and what not to expect
- Effect on quality and productivity
- Effect on the software process
- The culture change that can result in using objects
- Role of reuse

In addition to the above I would also add that managers need to understand their role in the process more clearly. As pointed out in 1.4.2, objects provide the opportunity for management to have an input into the process. Advantage should be taken of this.

The need for leadership is another aspect worth mentioning at this point. It is important to distinguish between management and leadership. Using object technology, and learning from the projects taken up can require strong leadership.

1.4.7 The First Project

> When selecting your pilot project, choose one that has high visibility in the business community and one that will make a difference. Do not select a low-profile backroom project.

A popular way of introducing objects into an organization is to conduct a pilot project that will serve as a proof of concept for the technology, process, skill set, and so on. Many people take on board simple, low-risk applications for their pilot project. Although this is very tempting and certainly the safe option, it should not be followed. If you produced a pilot project of a simple back-room application using objects, and wished to demonstrate the benefits, who would care? How would you prove that objects were the way forward?

It is far more persuasive to select an application that will make a difference to the business. Such a project, when successful, will make the business sit up and take notice of this new technology. It will also set an example for others to follow and emulate. The team will also have more at stake and will work harder to achieve their goals.

Of course, when constructing this application one should do as much as possible to minimize risk, such as selecting a consulting organization to assist in mentoring and helping you through the difficult aspects of the development. Issues around migration are well addressed by Meyer (1995) and Graham (1995).

1.4.8 Choosing a Method

The method with most market share isn't necessarily the best one for your organization. Evaluate methods on their fitness for purpose, their support for a software process, and their fit into your organization.

Choosing a method is not an easy task. If we all chose a product based on market share we would all be using the Oracle database for our RDBMS, and using MS Windows on a personal computer (PC) as our operating system of choice. Unfortunately, many people use market share as their key differentiator when selecting a method, or nearly as bad, they choose a method based on a "meatball chart."[2]

Two other areas that deserve equal consideration:

Method is important. Process is just as important. This fact is not a well-known one in the software community. A "good" method is quite useless without the organizational support for activities that can contribute to the overall quality of the software-development program.

Organizational fit. Once selected, object methods are never used in isolation. They must be absorbed into existing organizational culture and adapted into organizational practices. Companies with a history in developing software in one paradigm will not manage the transition overnight.

Many organizations have merely chosen an object method and expected it to work without considering areas in which object-oriented development can differ

---

[2]This description, coined by Steve Mellor (I think), describes the method of comparing object-oriented methods based purely on features and documenting these on a grid, each "blob" on a grid being a meatball. The serious point it conveys is that just because a method may have more "features" than another doesn't mean it is more suitable for you.

from structured approaches. This has often slowed the transition to objects. Areas needing some attention include the following:

- the need for formal education in the object paradigm
- the impact of different team structures on projects
- will the culture of the existing organization be amenable to objects?
- the effect of the shift in emphasis on architectures that objects mandate
- the effect of the potential changes in the life cycle (depending on the method chosen)

1.4.9 Using Methods

Question methods—why, when, and why again. When using object methods, don't just blindly follow all the advice they provide.

When you have chosen your method, don't just blindly follow the advice provided. Learn from the experiences of others. Find out what works best, what are the useful techniques that can be exploited. Get on the mailing list for that method. Become part of the community and share your experiences with others.

Also, question the methods. Why are things done the way they are? When is it best to move away from the method guidelines? What techniques augment methods best? Then ask why again, maybe now the understanding will be better.

Object methods are evolving. We can all contribute to their evolution and provide feedback on what works, and more important, what does not. Methods are also discussed in chapter 2.

1.4.10 "Bad" Designs

Objects puts "bad" designs up front.

I learned this lesson early. Any serious flaws in an object-oriented system can be exposed early. An object system can be transparent in that it allows you to see the design quite easily. By focusing on the key abstractions and the key use cases the design of a system can be easily determined. A bad design is more easily visible in object design as the abstract classes and their interactions serve to act as a blueprint for the rest of the system.

1.5   Summary

This chapter has provided a perspective on object technology for today and tomorrow and has also examined some of the key lessons learned. We began by examining the principal purported benefits of objects:

- Improved productivity and quality through the reuse of existing components, both through the reuse of code and designs.
- Given that 80% of information systems' (IS) spending goes to maintenance, the ability of objects to cope with change and localize such changes has a major impact.
- Improved alignment between the business and software is an obvious but powerful benefit. It is now possible for the business to become involved in the process, and even begin to critique the models.

We also looked at some of the caveats of object technology:

- organizational impact, such as culture change, and a potentially different software process
- the need for new skills and the learning curve
- the relative immaturity of the technology

Crossing the Chasm by Geoffrey Moore (1991) was used as a framework with which to examine the object industry today, as it is on the brink of entering the mainstream. It is leaping over the chasm that separates the Early Adopters from the Early Majority on the Technology Adoption Life Cycle Curve. This is because object technology can now be seen as a "whole product."

The six aspects of object technology as a whole product were looked at in detail.

- *Tools and Methods:* The recent convergence in methods and successes in generating 100% of the application code.
- *Languages and Environments:* The increasing maturity of Smalltalk and C++ environments, and the emergence of Object COBOL will help gain acceptance by the Early Majority.
- *Professional Services:* These companies are now using object technology on projects very regularly.

- *Standards:* Recent advances in standards can only help the leap over the chasm.
- *Case Studies and Experience:* These are crucial to the acceptance of objects by the conservative Early Majority.
- *Training and Education:* There are a myriad of training-and-education companies providing object education.

Some of the top lessons learned in the use of object technology were presented. In summary form, and in no particular order, they are as follows:

1. There really is such a thing as a paradigm shift. Everyone moves to objects at different speeds. Not everyone gets it.
2. Get as many different views involved in the object-modeling process as possible (both in developing the models and in reviewing progress).
3. Don't use CASE tools until the rate of change of the models begins to decrease.
4. Reuse needs to be supported throughout the software life cycle.
5. Architecture is key.
6. When making the transition, management education beforehand, and then continual buy-in during the transition, is essential.
7. Choose a project with high visibility for your first object project.
8. The method with the most market share isn't necessarily the best one for your organization.
9. Question methods—why, when, and why again.
10. Objects put "bad" designs up front.

References

Booch, G. (1986). Object-oriented development. *IEEE Transactions on Software Engineering*, 12, 211–221.

Booch, G. (1994). *Object-Oriented Design With Applications*, 2nd edition. Redwood City, CA: Benjamin/Cummings.

Booch, G. (1996a). *Object Solutions: Managing the Object-Oriented Project.* Menlo Park, CA: Addison Wesley.

Booch, G. (1996b, April). Unification. *Object Magazine*, 6(*2*), 94–96.

Brooks, F. (1987, April). No silver bullet: Essence and accidents of software engineering, *IEEE Computer*.

Gagliardi, G. (1994). *Client/Server Computing: Killing the Mainframe Dinosaur and Slashing Runaway MIS Costs*. Englewood Cliffs, NJ: Prentice-Hall.

Goldberg, A., & Rubin, K. (1995). *Succeeding with Objects: Decision Frameworks for Project Management*. Reading, MA: Addison-Wesley.

Graham, I. (1995). *Migrating to Object Technology*. Wokingham, UK: Addison-Wesley.

Harmon, P., & Taylor, D. (1993). *Objects in Action: Commercial Applications of Object-Oriented Technologies*. Reading, MA: Addison-Wesley.

Horan, B., & Gossain, S. (1995). User-driven strategies for object-oriented development. *OOPSLA 1995 Tutorial*, Austin, TX.

Henderson-Sellers, B. (1994, Sept.–Oct.). COMMA: An architecture for method interoperability. *ROAD*, 1(*3*), 25–28.

Henderson-Sellers, B., & Graham, I. (1996). OPEN: Toward method convergence? *IEEE Computer*, 29(*4*), 86–89.

Jacobson, I. (1995). *The Object Advantage: Business Process Reengineering with Object Technology*. Reading, MA: Addison-Wesley.

Karlsson, E.A. (Ed.). (1995). *Software Reuse: A Holistic Approach*. Chichester, UK: Wiley.

Kuhn, T. (1970). *The Structure of Scientific Revolutions*. Chicago: University of Chicago Press.

Lato, K., & Parks, T. (1995). Automatic code generation at AT&T. *Object Magazine*, 5(*7*), 71–72, 74–75.

Lientz, & Swanson, (1989, April). Software maintenance. *Data Management*, 26–30.

Love, T. (1993). *Object Lessons*. New York: SIGS Books.

McGibbon, B. (1996). *Managing Your Move to Object Technology*. New York: SIGS Books.

Meyer, B. (1995). *Object Success: A Manager's Guide to Object-Orientation on the Corporation and Its Use for Reengineering the Software Process*. Hempstead, UK: Prentice-Hall, Hemel.

Meyer, B., & Nerson, J.M. (Eds.). (1993). *Object-Oriented Applications*. Hempstead, UK: Prentice-Hall, Hemel.

Moore., G. (1991). *Crossing the Chasm*. New York: Harper Business.

Object Magazine. (1995). IBM creating insurance industry class libraries. *Executive Brief, Object Magazine*, 5(7), 10.

Peters, T. (1987). *Thriving on Chaos*. New York: Vintage Books.

Rumbaugh, J., Blaha, M., Premerlani, W., Eddy, F., & Lorensen, W. (1991). *Object-Oriented Modeling and Design*. Englewood Cliffs, NJ: Prentice-Hall.

Shlaer, S., & Mellor, S. (1988). *Object-Oriented Systems Analysis: Modeling the World in Data*. Reading, MA: Prentice-Hall.

CHAPTER 2

THE BIG PICTURE

T HERE IS MUCH TALK surrounding objects in the software world today. Much of it is pure hyperbole. Some of it is real. This chapter presents the broader, larger picture that describes the more wide-reaching ideas that work in practice and have proven to be quite profound when used on projects. Many of these ideas also happen to be those that have been the greatest cause for concern for object projects, and in some cases have been responsible for the failure of projects because of misunderstanding or lack of experience.

We explore the object-oriented development process at a high level and identify key activities and work products. We close the chapter with a look at two very different development philosophies of object-oriented development that provide the basis for many of today's object-oriented methods. These two philosophies are presented in this "pragmatic" book because the object developer should be aware of which approach is being used on his or her project, as this will ultimately lead to some strategies being used rather than others. This shall become clearer throughout the book.

2.1 Myths and Magic

There are numerous myths surrounding object technology and its purported benefits. There is also a great deal of talk about the "magic" that surrounds the use of objects when it has been introduced successfully within a software-development organization. There is a great deal of hype surrounding the use of objects—some of it based on myths and some of it grounded in reality. So, what is myth and what is magic?[1]

2.1.1 Object Methods

The world of object methods has exploded since people started moving up the life cycle from object-oriented programming, to object-oriented design, and then to object-oriented analysis. Over the last 8 years, I have used over five different object-oriented methods (some more formal than others) on a variety of different projects in numerous application areas, ranging from medical instrumentation to database reporting. The methods used were OMT (Rumbaugh, Blaha, Premerlani, Eddy, & Lorensen, 1991), Shlaer-Mellor (1988, 1990), Booch (1994), and a couple of home-grown methods that were combinations of others (e.g., an OMT–Jacobson combination). All but one of the projects was successful, and each project had at least one team member who was new to object-oriented technology, with most having two to three novices. In every project the method was just one factor that was attributable to the project's success. In many cases it was not even the major factor. Such experiences led me to question the importance placed on methodology by many in the object-oriented world.

Each method used in these projects was augmented with, or supported by techniques borrowed from other methods or ideas learned from other successful developments. I call these techniques, *practices* or *strategies*. Each strategy is employed for a specific purpose, is reasonably method independent, and has a particular role in the object-development life cycle. Strategies can be either technical or nontechnical with specific examples including business views, service objects (technical), and object blitzing (nontechnical).[2]

Based on my experiences of methods and heavy incorporation of strategies I am now of the belief that the principal values of object-oriented methods are as follows:

- They can teach novices some of the basic thought processes behind object orientation. Whether they are using OMT, Booch, or whatever method does not matter a great deal at the early stages of their object-oriented experience.

---

[1]I have addressed technical and nontechnical issues. These are my own personal views based upon my own experiences.

[2]These strategies are described in later chapters.

- Object-oriented methods provide a series of intellectual tools through which one can understand a problem and design a solution. The methodical approach does vary from method to method, of course.
- Objects provide a means of expressing one's ideas through some notation.

Once a certain level of proficiency in object development is reached, it does not matter which method is used because the differences become more notational than semantic. A good method exposes the issues; how these issues are addressed and dealt with are the real challenges faced by the object-oriented designer. This is where experience and the object-oriented "bag of tricks" comes in.

Once the philosophical approach to development has been chosen, it is not the method used that is the most important aspect of the object approach but the set of techniques, strategies, and practices used within the broader context of a project. A published object-oriented method certainly provides structure and a framework in which to approach problem solving, but it in itself does not guarantee success.

Yet despite this consensus, most managers and potential users of object technology still persist in pinning their hopes of success on the method they are using in the belief that the selection of a method will ensure overnight success. I am always coming across people who are considering the move to object orientation, and their first thoughts concern looking for a method, thinking that once a method has been selected their problems will be solved and "perfect" software will be developed. Going object oriented is more than choosing a method!

A method provides a framework in which to think about problems and a notation in which to express those ideas. Although these are important aspects of system development, it is important to place them in context. For example, creating an object model provides a means of analyzing a system in order to understand and describe the principal objects in a system, their attributes, and their relationships. It does not matter if I am using OMT or Shlaer-Mellor, the objects can be found and represented equally well. Certainly, there might be variations in expression and support for certain constructs (e.g., OMT supports aggregation, whereas Shlaer-Mellor does not), but in essence from this perspective the methods are somewhat equal (these methods differ in other ways).

The above statements notwithstanding, *how* I find the object, *how* I determine what the attributes are, *how* I think about the problem, *how* I go about finding objects, *how* I decide which modeling construct to use, *how* I work with users to develop my object model . . . and so on are the things that do matter. There are strategies to address these issues. These strategies comprise the principal content of this book.

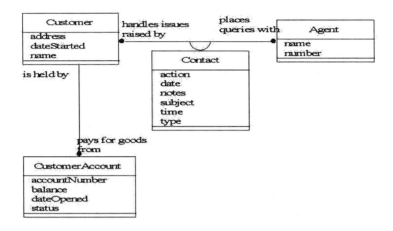

Figure 2.1. Part of a static model of a customer-management system.

2.1.2 Modeling the "Real World"

Objects model the real world. At least that's what we always hear. Well, this is true to some extent.

Objects don't model the real world, but model how we see the real world given the semantics of the modeling paradigm; that is, we model the world using objects, attributes, relationships, messages, events, and states. This model is then transformed into some specification that can be implemented, which is then employed using some form of programming language. This rather simplistic view is appealing as it means there is a correspondence between our model of the world and the eventual software implementation.

This seems fine, but it becomes a problem if we take the phrase "model the real world" too literally, as many people do, because then we run into trouble. An example would best describe the kind of trouble to which I am referring.

Consider the notion of a customers-management system. The object model extract shown in Figure 2.1 offers some key objects and relationships of the problem domain. This seems fine.

The static model (object structure model) captures the attributes and relationships of objects found in the problem domain and can be fairly accurate with respect to a model of the world outside. The dynamic interactions of objects do not model the real world precisely, however. We are limited by the semantics of the modeling paradigm. Novice modelers not realizing this can create "skew" models

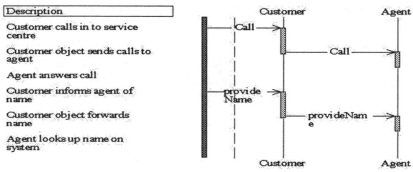

Figure 2.2. Partial confused object-interaction diagram of agent taking a call.

where there is confusion between the real world and the software system that will deal with the real world.

Figure 2.2 shows a portion of an object interaction diagram in which the modeler has confused the real-world customer with the Customer object modeled in the object model. As a result the Customer object is merely repeating the actions of the real-world customer. This is a typical point of confusion.

The real-world Customer is an actor, and the Customer object is merely the representation in the system. The real-world customer is outside the system boundary and initiates the events that trigger functionality within the system. Typically, the system representation of the real-world object is an object that responds to events to update its representation of the real-world object. It does not usually initiate activities. The real-world object can be "modeled" through defining a number of use cases (see section 2.1.3) in which that object participates.

> For real-world objects, create system representations of those objects that respond to events rather than initiate them. They should be maintaining a representation of the object, rather than initiating activities.

Interestingly, the issue around modeling the real world is a central topic of discussion by Cook and Daniels (1994), who base their methodology, Syntropy, around the construction of a series of models that move from a model of the real world (an Essential Model), to a model of the software (Specification Model), to an Implementation Model that describes how the objects execute and send messages.

The Essential Model does not have objects sending events to each other because in the real world objects do not send events to each other. Instead, events are simultaneously visible everywhere, and the goal of the model is to construct a model of the real world, and not to be limited by the semantics of the message-passing paradigm of object implementations.

There is some truth in objects modeling the real world, however. It is not a total myth. "Modeling the real world" should not be taken too literally, however. Objects represent concepts in the real world and as such make the models much more understandable to all concerned, bringing the software system "closer" to nonsystem professionals.

2.1.3 Use Cases

Whichever article or book you pick up on objects these days, use cases seem to be at the center of everything. As you will see, use cases also feature prominently in this text. They are one of the "magical" areas that brings systems to life for many involved in object development. The reason for their appeal is somewhat related to the overemphasis of many object methods on the static aspects of object modeling, which tend to neglect the functionality aspects of requirements gathering.

Use cases offer an attractive balance in that they provide a functional view of some system usage, which is immediately accessible to the users of the system. This is appealing because users can directly relate to the use case as they are essentially user centered. They are based around actors, and form a tangible requirement specification of system functionality at the initiation of some system event for which the users[3] are responsible.

It should be pointed out that use cases are not object-oriented, and have never claimed to be. They are functional abstractions that, when mapped to an object-oriented design, are provided by the interactions between objects. They are used to identify functionality rather than define object behavior, which is done by modeling the object interactions. Use cases and objects are orthogonal concepts.

The surge in interest in use cases has led to their usage being overemphasized by many methodologists. Some of the causes for concern surrounding use cases are as follows:

- What exactly is a use case? What is an actor? What is a scenario? Just finding, and agreeing on a common definition is problematic. Press articles don't always help: An article I read in a popular programmers' magazine

---

[3]The term "user" here is used loosely. An actor in a use-case can also be another object. This is especially true in systems that may not have human users.

was totally contradictory to the definition and usage of "use cases" as described in numerous articles by Jacobson (such as Jacobson, 1994). It is no wonder that so much confusion abounds in this area. My definition is the same as Jacobson's.

- Identifying objects using use cases can be dangerous. Use cases are functional in nature and therefore, identifying different control, entity, and interface objects for each use case, as suggested by Jacobson (1992), can lead to a set of fine-grained, ill-defined objects that are dedicated to the use cases from which they were derived. It is possible to identify good candidate objects from use cases, but it is easy to fall into the trap of creating too many functional objects. Some caution is needed. In fact, if you are just beginning to use use cases, it is best to avoid the notions of *extends* and *uses* until you have had some experience with simple use cases.

📖 Treat "extends" and "uses" as advanced features of use cases and do not use them until you feel comfortable working with simple use cases.

- Partitioning work among a team using use cases can be problematic. Giving work to one team based on a set of use cases and to another team based on a different set of use cases could mean that the data and behavior of objects being distributed across teams may lead to redundant work carried out by different teams, with individual teams having only partial views of objects. It can also lead to major integration issues, as the work of different teams has to be brought into synchronization.

- How do I know when I have identified enough use cases? This is an issue many grapple with as even the most simple of systems can lead to several hundred scenarios based on numerous use cases. One useful approach to enumerate the use cases is described in section 8.2.3. It is impossible, however, to address all use cases. The 80/20 rule can be usefully applied here.

📖 Attempt to define 80% of the use cases that you will need to meet the system's functionality. Striving for the remaining 20% will take longer than the extra effort deserves. The remaining use cases will most likely be identified later in the design process.

Given all the above caveats, I should perhaps outline some of the advantages of using use cases. These are listed on the following page.

- Users relate to use cases very well indeed.

- Business domain experts can understand and critique use cases easily, because they are written using natural language descriptions.

- Use cases are a natural next step for development practices that are derived from business-process modeling.

- Testing specifications can be grounded in use cases, and can provide a means of achieving end-to-end traceability from requirements that are specified while employing use cases through to implementation.

Use cases are an important and valuable concept that play a central role throughout the development process; they must, however, be used with caution.

2.1.4 Reuse

This is a topic about which people have written (and will continue to write) entire books. It is usually the first thing that comes to mind when people talk about objects and the automatic benefit they bring to an organization. Unfortunately, this is simply not true. *The myth of objects providing reuse for free, is unfortunately only hype. Objects encourage and facilitate reuse. Using objects does not automatically mean reuse.*

Reuse is not a new idea, it dates back as far as 1968, when the idea of reusable components was first put forward by McIlroy (1969). Since then the idea has gained increasing attention both within and outside the object community (Gaffney & Cruickshank, 1992; Griss, 1993; Meyer, 1994). The promise of objects has meant that software reuse is more achievable.

Embarking on grand plans of introducing reuse using repositories, business objects, class hierarchies, and the like are all doomed to failure without addressing the principal barriers to reuse, all of which are nontechnical. This is a lesson learned the hard way by many organizations.

Some of the major issues around reuse are as follows:

- the need for management commitment
- providing access to, and information about, available components
- documentation for supporting reusable components
- adequate incentives that reward those who reuse
- a software-development process that supports reuse

Some of the more challenging and vital areas for reuse within the object-oriented paradigm concern user-interface frameworks, domain-specific kits and frameworks (Gossain, 1990; Griss, 1995; O'Connor, 1995), and class libraries (Grossman, 1994; Meyer, 1994).

2.1.5 Business Objects

What started out as a programming paradigm has extended itself backward through design into analysis, and now into business modeling. Business-object models now seem to be de riguer in many organizations that have taken the bold step of embracing object technology. A number of grand-enterprise modeling activities have been initiated. Unfortunately, some are becoming unstuck as they are overambitious and attempt to model the whole enterprise as a one-off activity. Business models are achievable using objects. It is a myth, however, to suggest that they automatically arise from object developments, or can be created through single monolithic efforts.

Although the value of object-based models for business is not in question, grandiose plans of building corporate-wide business-object models are not achievable as a single effort. Business-object models should be built in small steps with well-bounded business areas having been identified previously and subsequently modeled. Object frameworks, which are essentially an implementation of a model of a problem domain, have shown us that domain knowledge evolves and grows as the understanding of the domain improves. For frameworks, this occurs over implementations of multiple applications: As many experts have observed, it is impossible to build a truly usable framework in a single effort (Gossain, 1990; Johnson, 1992). It seems fairly improbable therefore that a convincing business-object model of a domain can be built without validation and testing in the real world.

Something often overlooked that should be addressed is the need for a business case for constructing a business-object model. Why would one embark on modeling the business unless it could be related to some benefit to the business?

The business-object-modeling arena has now grown such that books on the topic are emerging, and an OMG Special Interest Group has been formed. Some of the work of the OMG is now moving toward defining standard object models for key areas such as those in the securities arena. This work involves numerous interested parties whose aim is to define a business-object model for a particular business area.

2.1.6 The Object Matrix

Use cases can be used to successfully elicit functional requirements. Mapping these requirements to the objects is a key activity in the early-development process, when attempting to understand how things will fit together and later, when actually designing the functionality of the application.

Typically, in projects I have been involved with, experienced object modelers begin to sketch an initial object model very early in the process; more to understand things themselves than to create a work-product of the analysis. This is usually a high-level object model that identifies the principal "players" in the domain. These initial coarse-grain objects[4] can be used as a means to map the functional requirements to objects. The object matrix is a simple but effective tool that can be used to achieve such a mapping.

Table 2.1 shows an example of part of an object matrix for a customer-management system. The principal objects are listed in column one, with titles of the use cases centered around those objects enumerated in the corresponding row.[5] So for the Customer object, the two main use cases are *Create a new customer* and *Query customer details*. This object will be the subject of those scenarios. This does not mean that the Customer object will not be involved in other scenarios, merely that it is perceived as the principal player in the use case.

The object matrix is a useful tool for eliciting functional requirements from users and experts and mapping them onto the objects. Listing the principal objects along the left we can then ask questions of experts and users, such as "So what other things do you need to be able to do to Accounts?" Having created business-process models prior to this stage, it is now possible to take those models, identify system functionality, and map that functionality to the object matrix.

The object matrix can be used to document system requirements and use cases and, as we shall see in chapter 4, it can be used as an input to dynamic modeling. In fact, the object matrix becomes a high-level road map of the requirements of the system that can be used throughout the development process.

---

[4]These objects are coarse-grain because these are high-level objects identified early in the process and also because they may be further partitioned into more objects later.

[5]Each use case will also have a detailed description, but that is part of another work product.

Table 2.1 PARTIAL OBJECT MATRIX DEPICTING AN OBJECT-FUNCTIONAL MAPPING

Customer	Create a new customer	Query customer details		
Account	Open a new account	Close an account	Suspend an account	
Order	Enter a new order	Check order status	Query order details	
Contact	Escalate contact to superior	Look up contact history		
Payment	Match payment to customer	Match payment to account	Enter payment details	Handle overdue payment
Agent	Sign-on	Sign-off	Mark self busy	Engage in action items

2.1.7 Cross-Functional Teams

Object analysis and design can be an excellent medium for bringing together individuals from different areas of an organization. Cross-functional teams representing views of users, the domain experts, and modelers are able to communicate and discuss modeling issues using the same vocabulary—that of the domain. Objects provide some magic in this area as they are built on the language of the domain.

Business-domain experts who may previously have been interested only in the end product of software development can now be actively involved throughout the whole modeling process, thus ensuring greater acceptance of the end system and contributing to a system that more closely meets their needs.

Workshop-based techniques have been used to great effect, more details of which are described in section 2.2. One of the primary reasons for their success has been the participation and contribution of all interested parties. Successful object projects are built on communication and collaboration among the development team and all those are involved in the project; hence the importance of cross-functional teams.

The notion of cross-functional teams is not new, and it is not dependent on the use of objects. The common vocabulary is only made possible by the use of objects, however.

📖   Involve users and domain experts equally throughout the system-
     development process.

2.2   The Object-Oriented Development Process

In order to place subsequent chapters into context, it is important to describe the overall object-oriented development process. The process, illustrated in Figure 2.3, is a generalization of the process used for a number of projects executed in exceptionally rapid time frames, and also for a few projects carried out in more "traditional" software-engineering environments with longer time frames. Such has been the nature of development that those projects that necessitated rapid time to market have followed an incremental delivery approach with smaller increments, whereas other longer term projects had much larger increments, and thereby bypassed the prototyping stage.

The gray box shown in Figure 2.3 indicates an area that is the core activity in the analysis, design, and implementation of increments. The length of time spent in this area will depend on the size of the increment. It is a time-boxed activity and applies especially to those projects described as having been completed rapidly. The diagram is similar to that proposed by Graham (1995), whose process model emanates from similar project environments. Graham's model, however, does not address reuse so explicitly and is more of a management-process model, unlike the development-process model of Figure 2.3. The process model should be applicable across multiple methods.

This process model encompasses a number of business- and organization-related activities that are outside the principal areas of discussion of this book. They are mentioned in order, however, to place into context the object-development activities, but no justification is provided for them. Examples include: cost–benefit analysis proposals, system-requirements proposals, and high-level technical architecture documentation. These are also activities that can vary from one organization to another.

For the description of each stage of the process model the main focus will be on those activities and work-products that are pertinent to object-oriented development.

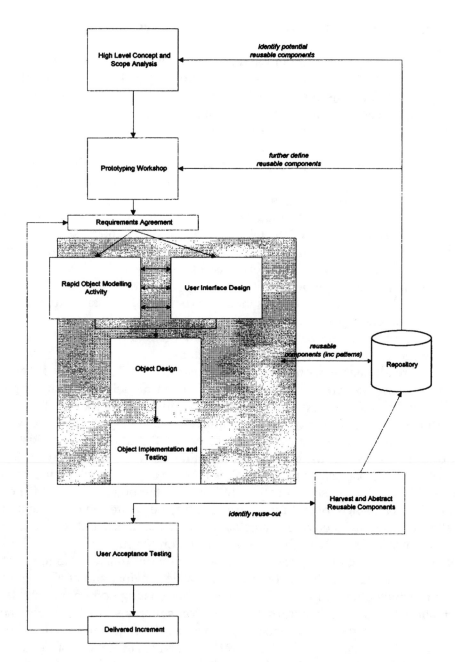

Figure 2.3. A high-level object-oriented process model.

2.2.1 High-Level Concept and Scope Analysis

The goal of this stage is to understand at a very high level the proposed system concept and scope. At this point the organization typically is exploring the business benefit for the construction of the application through a preliminary cost–benefit analysis (both quantitative and qualitative) as well as understanding the principal motivators for the application (such as loss of market share, new business area, etc.).

The length of this stage can vary from 1 to 3 weeks. A scope analysis need only be conducted by a small team of experienced individuals: technical architect, business analyst, object modelers, and project manager.

Business experts, users, and modelers get together for short, directed sessions to identify and explore some of the use cases of the system being scoped. The goal is to arrive at a set of preliminary use cases that will provide the basis for discussion of the application. At this stage each use case will be a short two- to three-sentence narration (which will be elaborated later).

From the discussion between users and experts, it is possible to construct a coarse-grain object model that serves to provide the beginnings of an understanding of the problem domain. This model, although it is at a high level, can also be verified with business experts during this stage. Typically, it will have mainly objects and relationships with a few of the most "obvious" attributes. I have often found that a short session on how to read an object model for domain experts is sufficient at this stage for experts to be able to critique the initial model.

As the initial functionality of the application is being determined and the objects identified, it is possible to begin to create the object matrix. List all the main objects on the left-hand side and examine each use case in turn. Identify which object each use case will affect. Consider the object for which it is most relevant, and list the use case in a cell in the row for that object. When it is not possible to identify a single object most directly affected, write the use case in multiple cells, but annotate each relevant cell to indicate that it is a multiple occurrence.

Reuse must begin early in the process. Based on the functionality of the application, search through the repository for any potential reusable components. At this stage the search will be fairly broad and wide-ranging, and components may include previous object models, documents, and existing code components. The search should also include external information sources so that any commercial class libraries, frameworks, or packages providing the requisite functionality may be identified. The goal of this initial search is to arrive at a set of components that may be candidates for reuse later in the process.

Other activities and work-products of this stage include the following:

- construction of a preliminary feasibility study
- identification of existing systems that will be affected by this system
- preliminary technical architecture

The principal object-related work-products from this stage are therefore

- initial use cases
- an initial high-level object model
- the object matrix
- a list of components that may be reused in this system

2.2.2 Prototyping Workshop

The primary goal of the prototyping stage is to generate an executable prototype of the system. As Carey (1990) points out, the prototype is meant to communicate a potential *sample* of the final system to the user and the business community:

> "Prototyping" is the process of quickly building a model of the final software system, which is used primarily as a communication tool to assess and meet the information needs of the user.

There are two extreme types of prototype (see Figure 2.4):

1. A *horizontal prototype* exhibits a wide number of features, but is limited in its functionality. Typically, there is little data, but a great deal of user-interface functionality.
2. A *vertical prototype* demonstrates a narrow piece of the system, but in greater detail. When connectivity to legacy systems is needed, this may also be demonstrated.

We have found that the most powerful prototypes are ones that demonstrate some functionality that the user can relate to. Nielsen (1993) also uses the term "scenario," which fits in very nicely with demonstrating some instance(s) of use cases. The intersection between a scenario and the two types of prototype is also indicated in Figure 2.4. Working with users to identify some functionality that takes them through some of their typical tasks and demonstrating that functionality by means of a prototype is a very powerful concept.

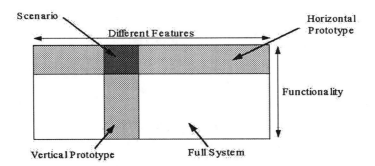

Figure 2.4. Horizontal and vertical prototypes.

The exact content of the prototype varies from system to system, but it is important that the prototype be executable. In this way the prototype acts as a proof of concept for the high-level system functionality and preliminary technical architecture. More important perhaps, it also acts as a preliminary indicator of user needs and an initial estimate for system complexity.

The length of time spent on the prototyping stage varies from one project to another. Two to four weeks is not unusual. The development of the prototype is not the only activity that takes place during this time, however, as there is also a considerable amount of work needed in further refining the cost–benefit analysis, additional object modeling will also need to be done.

During the prototyping stage, the following activities can also be carried out in addition to prototyping:

- Working with users and experts to define in more detail the use cases, object model, and the object matrix. The use cases identified in the earlier stage can be augmented if needed and can now be further defined in considerable detail, especially for those use cases that are part of the prototype.

- As the object model becomes more detailed, some more objects can be identified and explored for the coarse-grain object model. This is especially true for systems in which a horizontal prototype is developed, as this will uncover large areas of the system's features at a high level. For vertical prototypes, some extra discussion may uncover additional functionality, but I would not expect as broad an object model as with a horizontal prototype.

- The reuse repository will need to be examined again in the light of increasing knowledge about the system. It is possible that some of the reusable assets identified earlier will now be excluded from potential reuse in the system or that additional components will need to be considered. At this point it should also be possible to identify reusable assets that the system may produce for reuse in future systems.

- From the work with the users in identifying prototype functionality, some initial screens and screen flows will no doubt have been created. These can be used as an input into the next stage of the process.

- The technical, physical architecture of the system can now also be outlined in principle.

We can see from the preceding list that there are a number of useful activities aside from prototyping that can be carried out during this stage; the principal work-products are as follows:

1. further definition of use cases
2. further definition of the object model
3. further definition of the object matrix
4. further definition of components that may be reused in this system
5. identification of components that may be available from this system
6. initial screens
7. initial screen flow
8. the prototype itself

It is important to reiterate that the primary purpose of the prototyping stage is to demonstrate some system behavior to numerous interested parties. For systems in which there is little need for demonstrating such functionality, this stage can be omitted from the overall process.

2.2.3 Requirements Agreement

This is a small, but essential stage whose goal is to foster agreement on the scope of the increment to be delivered. It is a time when the analysis, design, implementation, and testing activities are planned, and when the major milestones are set. The object matrix is now at a level of detail where there is a detailed description of the functionality for each cell, and agreement between all parties on the semantics of the description. Once the requirements have been agreed on the modeling can formally begin.

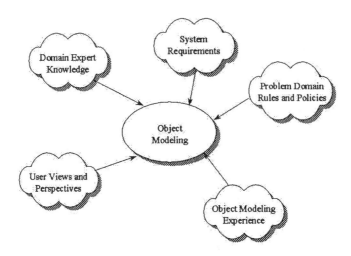

Figure 2.5. Inputs to the rapid object modeling activity.

2.2.4 Rapid Object Modeling Activity

As shown in Figure 2.3, this stage is conducted in parallel with User-Interface Design, which is an activity in which the user interface is specified through workshops with users (see section 2.2.5). Figure 2.5 shows the different inputs to the rapid object modeling activity.

Because the object-modeling and user-interface design phases are conducted in parallel there is a great deal of information flowing between the two activities, as shown in Figure 2.3. In fact, a number of the same people are involved in both activities.

Figure 2.6 illustrates the relative amount of time and effort spent on user-interface design and modeling during these two phases. One can see that early on, while the design of the user interface is occurring, the emphasis in the modeling is the construction of the object model and the use cases. Once the user -interface design has been completed, the focus shifts to the interactions and dynamics of the system. This is because the user interaction has now been defined and the modeling needs to shift to understanding how the objects interact to provide the expected functionality.

The detailed process for the rapid object modeling activity, which consists of the activities and principal work-products just described, is illustrated in Figure 2.7.

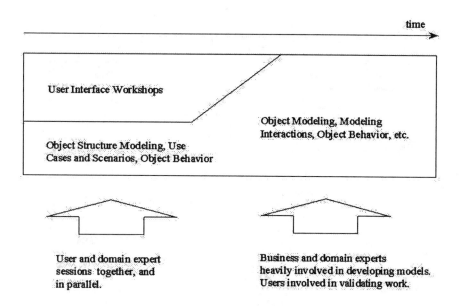

Figure 2.6. Details of modeling and user-interface design.

As can be seen in Figure 2.7, the rapid object modeling activity is an iterative and nonlinear process. As Parnas and Clements (1986) point out, those who wish to read the development documentation are interested in the end result, not in reliving the process of discovery. It is the process of discovery that this stage addresses. The details of each of the boxes indicated in will be addressed in chapters 3 and 4, and so are not described here.

Rather than create a multitude of work-products during this activity, there is a focus on a number of core deliverables. The work-products found to be most useful are part of most of the popular object methods: namely, an object-structure model depicting objects, attributes, and relationships (the notation used in this book is that of OMT [Object Modeling Technique]); object-interaction diagrams showing the interobject communication between objects in the context of a particular scenario (as in ObjectOry); object state models in which each object with interesting behavior has its life cycle represented by a finite state machine (as in Shlaer/Mellor); and object-communication model (from Shlaer/Mellor), which summarizes all of the interobject communication across a number of scenarios. There are also a number of secondary models created that are intermediate work-products from particular strategies. These are not always necessary, however, and are more for documenting work in progress than being actual deliverables.

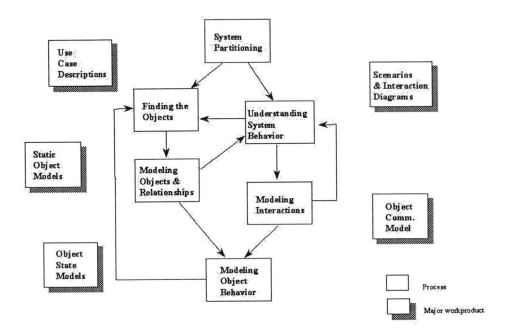

Figure 2.7. Rapid object modeling activity.

There are numerous participants in this stage of the process, but the principal ones are domain experts, users, business analysts, and object modelers. Some of the high-level themes of the rapid object modeling activity are as follows:

> *Object workshops*—there is a strong emphasis on collaborative exploration of the problem space with domain experts and users. Typically, short morning-long modeling sessions directed at specific areas are held with experts. These provide input to individual working or smaller sessions during which the lower level details of issues raised in morning sessions are examined. These are then fed back to experts in group sessions in an attempt to get some consensus and aim toward closure of these topics. The principles of Joint Application Design (JAD; August, 1991) are used quite effectively here.

> *Use cases*—these are used throughout the modeling processes. The initial use cases identified during the Scoping and Prototyping phases are now described in much more detail and are used to drive a scenario-based approach to creating the object-interaction diagrams.

> *Continual review*—a process of continual review is employed throughout the modeling activity. All models are reviewed by domain experts *and* users.

The principal object-related work-products from this stage are

1. object-structure model
2. use case descriptions
3. object-interaction diagrams
4. object state models
5. object-communication model
6. logical data model

2.2.5 User Interface Design

User-centered design is an approach to system design that involves users early in the development life cycle. It was introduced through the work of Hansen (1971) with his principle of "know the user" and has been transformed into working practice through the involvement of users in the design process of object-oriented systems (Horan & Gossain, 1995). These principles form the basis for the user-interface design process described here.

This user involvement during design is intended to lead to systems that

- are easier for experienced users to learn
- are easier for new users to learn
- allow for improved user productivity
- are based on user usage patterns

The process outlined in this text involves users from the early scoping-analysis activity through to the delivery of the system, where the final stage is User Acceptance Testing.

During user-interface design, the users are led through workshop sessions during which their tasks are explored and documented. Some business-process modeling may already have taken place during earlier phases, or prior to the high-level scope analysis, but now the focus is on user tasks and modeling these tasks. These work-products are used to provide input to the rapid object modeling activity being conducted in parallel.[6]

---

[6]The user design and object modeling activities are conducted in parallel in order to reduce the overall system-development time. These activities could certainly be conducted sequentially if time to development was not an important factor.

These models of user processes are then used to work with users to identify the interaction they will have with the system through the screens of the user interface. Screen design is conducted on whiteboards and flip-charts and the screen flow is also outlined in order to link the screens together for each task. Once the users have provided their input, these paper drawings can be used to create screens in the chosen user-interface development tool.[7] It is common that at this point the wishes of the users may have to be tempered somewhat in order to satisfy usability requirements and for the interface to conform to standard user-interface guidelines.

Once the screens have been designed they are shown to the users, who are led through their tasks with the screen designs and screen flow; at this point changes can be made. Sometimes, wholesale changes are required after users see their wishes transformed into real screens!

Once the screens have been agreed on in principle, screen specifications can be created, identifying fields and their contents, and the events generated from each screen with the appropriate data. This event information is used to drive the object-interaction modeling, as we shall see later in chapter 4. It is important to note that the user-interface design activity is not complete until users have "signed-off" on all screens and are happy with their look and with the screen flow.

Principal work-products from this stage are

1. user task models based on business-process models
2. screen specifications
3. screen flows to support business processes and use cases

2.2.6 Object Design

The inputs to the object-design process are all of the models created during the rapid object modeling activity and the screen-related work-products from user-interface design. The goal of this activity is to arrive at an implementable specification of the objects from the analysis. It is perfectly possible, and in some

---

[7]We have found that at design time, a user-interface development tool can be used to design the screen layout. The tool need not be object-oriented and need not be the tool to be used in development. For example, it could be Visual Basic during design, with development carried out in VisualWorks.

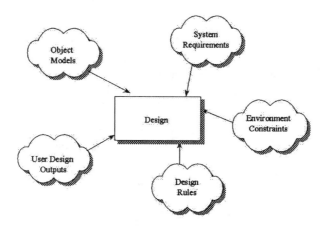

Figure 2.8. Inputs to the design process.

cases necessary, to transform the object models to a design model that is non-object-oriented.[8]

Figure 2.8 shows the inputs to the design process. We can see that the models produced are just one piece of the puzzle. Other important inputs are

- *System requirements.* These include data volatility issues, performance requirements, and user requirements.

- *Environment constraints.* These include the existing and future network infrastructure, corporate and industry standards that may need to be adhered to, and the technical architecture.

- *Design rules.* These represent the collective design experience from experts in the form of books on design patterns, software architectures, client–server configurations, and object distribution approaches.

As with the modeling activity, there is no formal step-by-step process to object design but rather a series of activities that are iterative and nonlinear. The overall design process is shown in Figure 2.9.

---

[8]I have been involved in two projects where a series of object models were used to understand a problem domain, but the actual design and implementation were in nonobject-oriented constructs. The first was designed so that the system could be implemented in assembler, while the second was mapped into a functional design implemented in C. In both cases there were legitimate technical reasons for such decisions.

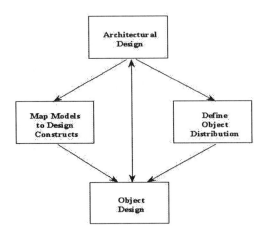

Figure 2.9. The design process.

The details of these activities are described in chapters 5 and 6, but it is important to stress the need for an architectural design activity at the beginning of this stage.

The use of objects has increased the awareness of the importance of architecture, and the experiences of system designers (both object oriented and nonobject oriented) has shown that a good architecture is the central theme of successful systems. One of the top 10 lessons learned, as described in chapter 1, was that architecture is key. As a result, the architecture should be set in place, or at least articulated at the commencement of the design stage. Failing to do so can lead to a system of objects that does not have a consistent structure to it. Such a system could be brittle, lack cohesion where needed, and be poorly designed such that changes cannot be made easily.

Some of the themes of this stage are as follows:

> *Object distribution*—objects will need to be distributed across the physical architecture, which may comprise multiple processes and/or machines. This will be driven by the architecture and will also affect the internal design of the clusters of objects that are found within the same distribution construct. The result is a series of object-distribution diagrams, showing object–class clusters and how they will be partitioned across the environment.

> *Use of design patterns*—in order to benefit from the micro-design experience of numerous others, the use of design patterns is an essential source

of ideas used to map the objects into microarchitectures (Gamma, Helm, Johnson, & Vlissides, 1994). This may require some transformation of existing models to conform to the pattern selected.

Mapping models to design—the objects of the models will not necessarily be implemented within an object-oriented design, and there is certainly no guarantee that there will be a one-to-one mapping between an object in the models to a class in an object-oriented design. This process must map the objects to some implementable constructs.

Reusing existing design constructs—where existing design models have been identified for reuse in this system, there may need to be an adjustment of the object models to allow for inclusion of these components.

Creating class specifications—every class needed in the implementation is specified down to the types of parameters, the definition of each method, and the types of private data members (instance variables). Taking the models as an input, and the decisions made with regard to object distribution and design patterns, precise class specifications can be written. This activity occurs in the Object Design activity of Figure 2.9.

Database design—if the project needs to access a database, the physical database model is created at this stage.

All of the above activities are detailed in later chapters. The principal work-products from this stage are

1. object distribution diagrams
2. object design templates
3. class specifications
4. database design and definition

Other important work-products created during design include

- system test plans
- acceptance test plans
- class test specifications

2.2.7 Object Implementation and Testing

During this stage the design is implemented in the programming language(s) of choice. The user interface is also implemented. Following the implementation, the testing is carried out. This includes testing at class level and within class clusters. This phase also includes integration and system testing.

2.2.8 User Acceptance Testing

Before a system is deemed complete it must be accepted by the user community. The users are invited to use the system by running scenarios with test data and ensuring that the system is acceptable for their needs. The scenarios should be wide-ranging and also include a great deal of exception cases in order to fully test the system. Any changes and bug fixes are identified and corrected before the system is accepted.

2.2.9 Harvest and Abstract Reusable Components

A critical activity of a reuse-enabled software process is the identification of potentially reusable components from a system. During earlier stages, components were identified, and there must now be a detailed review of the system to identify reusable components. Components consist of classes or groups of classes. There are two types of components that can be identified at this stage:

1. Those components that can be harvested from the system and included in the repository with little or no additional effort. These include scripts, task automaters, and so on.

2. Those components that need to be generalized to become reusable or new components that need to be created from existing application-specific components. This will typically include domain-specific components that need to be made reusable.

Once these have been identified, the resources from the project who were responsible for these components need to be provided with ample time to work on the components to bring them up to the levels of documentation, comments, and functionality required before they can be placed in the repository. Alternatively, members of the reuse organization need to carry out this work, after being transitioned by the project team members.

It is important to note that when deciding on which components to harvest from a system, the selection must be based on business need. Harvesting all possible components, without consideration to business need will lead to a repository full of components that no one needs and that no one can use.

All project-related documentation (proposals, models, design documents, etc.) should be placed into the repository as a matter of course. They may be useful in subsequent projects, both within the same domain and potentially in other domains.

2.2.10 The Repository

The *reuse repository* is a central resource for the whole development process. Because reuse requires support throughout the development process, it is important that the repository be searched for reusable components at each stage.

It is best to have two levels of repository. One should contain certified components that have undergone a qualification and selection criteria to ensure that they are adequately tested and documented. The other should contain those components that have not been certified. This is because there will be numerous components not yet certified that are not supported by the reuse organization. This second level should not only contain reusable code, but should also be the storage medium for previous business models, process models, analysis models, design models, and other documentation from past projects. It is a place for shared knowledge.

An easily accessible repository is the key to ensuring that the reuse process is adequately supported and that project participants have access to the organization's components.[9] It is also possible to monitor the access of reusable components to see which are most popular and also to begin to predict the organization's component needs.

There are numerous technologies that are being used to implement repositories, but access to them from a distributed organization has been the most problematic. One of the most attractive solutions is to provide World Wide Web access to the repository. With web browsers becoming more and more widespread because of the increasing popularity of the Internet, a web interface is becoming a more acceptable idea.

---

[9]There are a number of other essential concepts that need to be supported for reuse to work, including a review process for component access, reward programs, etc. These are outside the scope of the text. However, see section 2.1.4.

2.3 Development Philosophies

There are two principal development philosophies in the object world. They differ in their definition of analysis and their approach to design and implementation. This distinction fundamentally affects many of the object-oriented methods being used today. The distinction is important because it can affect the techniques and strategies used during modeling, and also because one approach requires a very different attitude to system development from the other. This will become clearer as you read the following two sections, and the discussion in section 2.3.3 should help to put things into perspective.

2.3.1 Elaborational Approach

This approach, based on *elaboration*, is probably the one with which the majority of readers are most familiar. It is the one espoused by most of the popular object methods. Object models are created, successively refined, and detail added until they become implementation-level models. There is no formal freezing of the analysis and there is no firm distinction between analysis and design.

Such an approach means that analysis follows a number of guidelines as opposed to rules, and as one proceeds further down the development life cycle, details are added to the models that allow for design decisions to be made and added. The process allows for careful, micro-controlled adjustments to the models to meet performance and other design constraints.

It is a relatively straightforward additive approach whereby the design activity follows analysis (see Figure 2.10) and is dedicated to the current system. The process is one of adding more detail to the same set of models, much in the same way as the Object Analysis and Design Reference Model proposed by the OMG.

The development process described in section 2.2 directly supports an elaborational approach. This approach is that followed by methodologies such as OMT, Booch, MOSES (Methodology for Object-Oriented Software Engineering of Systems) (Henderson-Sellers & Edwards, 1994), and SOMA (Semantic Object Modeling Approach) (Graham, 1995), among others.

2.3.2 Translational Approach

This approach, based on *translation*, features a different approach to "design" altogether. It is an intellectually appealing approach that is very analysis-centric.

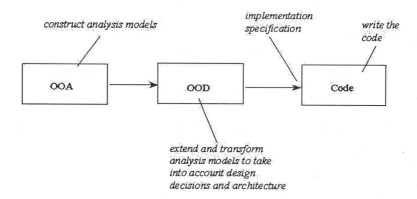

Figure 2.10. An elaborational approach to design.

Object analysis models are created much in the same way as described earlier. Once complete, they are translated into an implementation using a set of rules that provide a mapping between the analysis and the implementation.

In such an approach the modeling activity is based on a strict, rules-based formalism, which creates a specification of the system. The set of rules used for translation is then the "design." The distinction between analysis and design is a clear one, whereby analysis is extremely detailed to the point of complete specification of system behavior.

Figure 2.11 illustrates the development process. For this approach, much of the creation of the set of rules can be done in parallel with the analysis, and can be reused across multiple analyses. This approach is easier to use for nonobject-oriented designs than for elaboration because there is a distinct point at which the analysis is complete, and then a translation can be made for each component in the model to a nonobject-oriented construct. Provided the rules of the translation preserve the semantics of the problem domain, as described by the models, any implementation can be used.

The development process described in section 2.2 supports a translational approach in all phases except the design-and-implementation activities outlined in sections 2.2.6 and 2.2.7, respectively. To follow the translational approach, the diagram of Figure 2.11 must be appropriately substituted into that of Figure 2.3.

The translational approach is heavily promoted by Shlaer and Mellor (1993), whose method (1988, 1990) is the only one to directly support and advocate a fully translational approach to implementation, although other methods now also have flavors of translation as well. Transformation is also mentioned briefly by Martin and Odell (1995) and Jacobson, Christerson, Jonsson, and Overgaard (1992).

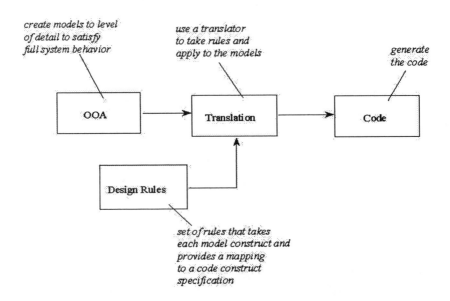

Figure 2.11. A translational approach to design.

2.3.3 Discussion of the Two Approaches

These two approaches to system development are very different in nature. The elaborational approach is an additive approach to system development, whereas the translational approach is a generative one. The difference is important to pragmatists because the design stage is radically different in both approaches. This means that the results of the analysis will be used differently, and will require different levels of rigor during modeling.

The elaborational approach does have the perceived advantages of seamlessness and traceability in that the same modeling constructs and notation are used throughout the design process. The argument for seamlessness would be that the same constructs are used from analysis to design and then to implementation. This argument is flawed, however, as the translational approach allows for a seamless approach to *all modeling* (in fact there are no "seams"at all). The translation takes the rules and applies them to the models to generate code. The models are the valuable artifact here, as the code can be generated by applying the set of rules. For changes to functionality, the models are updated and code regenerated. The seamlessness argument goes away.

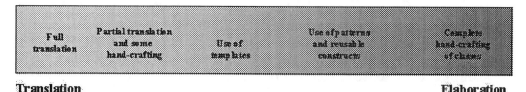

Translation   **Elaboration**

Figure 2.12. A spectrum of approaches for moving from models to code.

The translational approach also allows for a completely traceable process, as the mapping from analysis models to code is rigorously specified in the translation rules. Interestingly, if we compare the two approaches against structured analysis and design (SA/SD) we see that SA/SD is a transformational approach (Daniels, personal communication, June 4, 1996). That is, each stage has a formalism associated with it that one must transform to reach the next. As Daniels points out: "In any approach that is transformational, the transformations can be automated to some extent only if the formalisms are complete at the chosen level of abstraction and if they have precise semantics."

Elaboration and translation can be viewed as two extremes in a spectrum of approaches to managing the transition from analysis to implementation. Shlaer and Mellor reside firmly on the side of translation, whereas methods such as OMT and SOMA (Semantic Object Modeling Approach) are certainly elaborational.

It is certainly possible, and for practical reasons in many cases it is necessary, to have some combination of the two. Figure 2.12 shows some approaches that sit along the spectrum.

Complete handcrafting of classes. This refers to every class within a model being written by hand. This is a manual-intensive process that requires every object, attribute, and relationship of the model to be examined in detail and decisions made as to how that object will be implemented. Decisions around the architecture and object distribution need to have been made already and these are taken into consideration when writing the code. This scenario includes situations in which the generation of code frames is provided by a CASE (computer-aided software engineering) tool.

Use of patterns and reusable constructs. A little further along the spectrum from elaboration is the use of design patterns and reusable constructs that allow a designer to introduce some notion of translation, as patterns in the analysis can be mapped to common design patterns (Gamma et al., 1993) and thus it is possible to reuse abstract classes and common interfaces. The mapping of object models to design constructs has been done by patterns, but large parts of code still need to be written for each analysis construct to ensure it fits into the scheme required by the pattern. There is some room for automation here through substitution, but it is more likely to be through code reuse of pattern constructs.

Use of templates. A largely manual process that is a mid-point between elaboration and translation. Once the modeling has been completed it is possible to move to a specification for implementation using a set of standard conversion templates that map analysis constructs to implementation ones. Odell and Fowler provide some reasonable discussion around this issue in a few articles (1995a, 1995b, 1995c). Templates exist for relationships, generalizations, creating and deleting objects, deriving objects, and so on. As Odell and Fowler (1995c) point out: "design templates both define the interface of the software components and suggest the implementation of those components." There is room for automation in such a scenario through the use of macros and textual substitution; however, the application code still needs to be written by hand to a large extent.

Templates provide a repeatable way of moving from analysis models to implementation, and a relatively new analyst should be able to relate large parts of the code to the models once familiar with the templates.

Partial translation and some handcrafting. Further along the scale toward translation we find the use of a combination of translation and handcrafting. Here templates are taken one step further with large parts of application code being generated by translation engines into standard constructs. These code constructs are optimized, changed, or augmented as necessary to take into account performance, and so on.

Full translation. This is being carried out today through the use of CASE tools that have engines allowing one to take a set of analysis models and translate them into a *fully operational* implementation according to a set of rules (Lato & Parks, 1995).

Which approach is best? There is no one correct answer.

In order to fully consider the two approaches and determine which is "better," one needs to understand the organization in which the approach will be applied and, more important, the implications of using either philosophy.

Choosing a fully translational approach requires a commitment to carrying out a detailed analysis, designing reusable architectures, and investing in the appropriate tools (for execution of analysis models and for translating these models into code). Elaboration approaches means that analysis models are not separated from design models and requires manual reorganization during design.

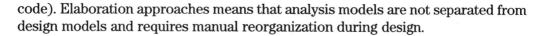 Translational approaches are probably best for creating similar medium-to-large applications where the cost of creating architectures (translation rules) is offset by their repeated (re)use.

A fully elaborational approach is very labor-intensive and best used for smaller, highly optimized applications that require fine tuning at the class cluster, class, and attribute level.

Most organizations employ a technique somewhere along the spectrum, perhaps closer to the elaborational view. One is more likely to find a combination of techniques, depending on the size of applications and maturity of the software process. Some organizations with a strong history of rigor in their process will be able to use templates without too much discomfort. Other organizations, however, that employ more of an ad hoc process, may find the use of templates too restrictive and would favor an approach somewhere between handcrafting of classes and the use of patterns. The approach used is also dependent on the background of the individuals involved who would feel more comfortable writing code than generating it.

Partial translation is attractive because so much functionality can be found in the models and the real question for many people is whether or not 100% translation is achievable, and if so, does it meet performance goals, and so on. As documented in recent publications, by Lato and Parks (1995), for example, full translation is achievable and delivers systems with satisfactory results. As Lato and Parks point out, however: "The two main requirements for automatic code generation are: (1) the code must meet the project constraints, and (2) the code must work without modification."

Perhaps a more pragmatic approach in which the above requirements cannot be met (for whatever reason) is to use standard templates for common analysis constructs and generate code for most of the system through translation. Fine tuning and redistribution of objects, which would be the manual process required after generation, can thus take place at a very late stage in the process to ensure that performance and other system requirements are met.

2.4 Summary

This chapter has provided some of the pieces of "the big picture." It has enumerated a number of ideas that have proven popular within the object community and some of the problems associated with them, a description of the development process, and an introduction to two very different approaches to system development that undoubtedly affect the latter half of that development process.

In looking at the myths and magic surrounding objects we examined the role object methods play and how they can take objects so far but need the addition of practical techniques to develop applications. Therefore, we introduced strategies to help develop applications such as technical and nontechnical practices and techniques that augment methods to make objects work in the real world.

We also looked at how objects model the real world. There is some truth in this statement, but it should not be taken too literally. Objects represent concepts in the real world and as such make the models much more understandable to all concerned, they also bring the software system "closer" to nonsystem professionals.

One of the most popular constructs in object technology today is the use case—a totally nonobject-oriented construct. Although very powerful and appealing, we should be careful with its usage.

A major myth associated with objects is that they provide reusable code. This is simply not true. Objects facilitate reuse; it does not come automatically for free. The principal barriers to reuse are nontechnical—many organizations have learned this the hard way.

Business-object modeling is the latest object technique and as such has suffered from too much hype. A business-object model should be created carefully and incrementally. Grand plans to totally model a business using objects are heading for disaster before they begin.

A reuse-enabled development process was outlined in section section 2.2, based on a number of real-world projects. A key feature is the involvement of reuse throughout the process from the high-level scoping-analysis activity through to the user-acceptance testing. Variants of this development process have been used to support rapid application development as well as a number of longer projects operating with more traditional timescales. The development process is method independent. The development process's constituent stages were detailed, highlighting key activities and work-products. These descriptions should provide the context for future chapters.

Finally, two distinct views to the approach to move from analysis to implementation were provided—the *elaborational view* and the *translational view*.

Elaboration is an approach whereby analysis models are successively added to until they become implementation specifications, whereas the translation approach maps analysis to implementation using a set of design rules. Numerous intermediate approaches were also identified along the spectrum from elaboration to translation. The distinction between the approaches is important to the practicing object-oriented developer, as it affects the strategies one uses for architecture and design, as we shall see later in this text.

References

August, J. (1991). *Joint Application Design: The Group Session Approach to System Design*. Englewood Cliffs, NJ: Prentice-Hall.

Booch, G. (1994). *Object-Oriented Design With Applications (2nd ed.)*. Redwood City, CA: Benjamin Cummings.

Carey, J.M. (1990). Prototyping: Alternative systems development methodology. *Information and Software Technology*, 32, 119–126.

Cook, S., &. Daniels, J. (1994). *Designing Object Systems: Object-Oriented Modeling With Syntropy*. Hempstead, UK: Prentice-Hall, Hemel.

Gaffney, J.E., & Cruickshank, R.D. (1992). A general economics model for software reuse. In *Proceedings of the 14th International Conference on Software Engineering* (327–337). Melbourne, Australia: IEEE Press.

Gamma, E., Helm, R., Johnson, R., & Vlissides, J. (1994). *Design Patterns: Elements of Reusable Object-Oriented Software*. Reading, MA: Addison-Wesley.

Gossain, S. (1990). *Object-Oriented Development and Reuse*. Unpublished doctoral thesis, University of Essex, Essex, UK.

Gossain, S., & Horan, B. (1995, Oct.). User-driven strategies for object-oriented development, *OOPSLA 95* tutorial notes, Austin, TX.

Graham, I. (1995). *Migrating to Object Technology*. Wokingham, UK: Addison-Wesley.

Griss, M. (1993). Software reuse: From library to factory. *IBM Systems Journal*, 32(4).

Griss, M. (1995). Packaging software reuse technologies as kits. *Object Magazine*, 5, 80–81, 89.

Grossman, M. (1994). Implementing C++ libraries. *Object Magazine*, 4(*3*), 55–59.

Hansen, W.J. (1971). User engineering principles for interactive systems. In *AFIPS Conference Proceedings* (Vol. 39, 523–532), Montvale, NJ: AFIPS Press.

Henderson-Sellers, B., & Edwards, J. (1994). *Book Two of Object-Oriented Knowledge: The Working Object*. Sydney, Australia: Prentice-Hall.

Jacobson, I. (1994). Basic use case modeling. *Report on Object Analysis and Design*, 1(*3*), 7–9.

Jacobson I., Christerson, M., Jonsson, P., & Overgaard G. (1992). *Object-Oriented Software Engineering: A Use-Case-Driven Approach*. Reading, MA: Addison-Wesley.

Jacobson, I., Ericsson, M., & Jacobson, A. (1995). *The Object Advantage: Business Process Reengineering With Object Technology*. Reading, MA: Addison-Wesley.

Johnson, R. E. (1992, Oct.). Designing object-oriented frameworks. *OOPSLA'92* tutorial notes, Vancouver, Canada.

Karlsson, E.A. (Ed.) (1995). *Software Reuse: A Holistic Approach*. Chichester, UK: Wiley.

Lato, K., & Parks, T. (1995). Automatic code generation at AT&T. *Object Magazine*, 5(*7*), 71–72, 74–75.

McIlroy, D. (1969). Mass-produced software. In *Software Engineering Concepts and Techniques: Proceedings of the NATO Conferences* (88–98). Petrocelli/Charter.

Martin, J., & Odell, J. (1995). *Object-Oriented Methods: A Foundation*. Englewood Cliffs, NJ: Prentice-Hall.

Meyer, D. (1994). *Reusable Software: The Base Object-Oriented Component Libraries*. Hempstead, UK: Prentice-Hall, Hemel.

Nielsen, J. (1993). *Usability Engineering*. Orlando, FL: Academic Press.

O'Connor, K. (1995). CMS object-oriented domain framework. (Technical Report). Cambridge, MA: Cambridge Technology Partners.

Odell, J., & Fowler, M. (1995a). From analysis to design using templates, Part I. *Report on Object Analysis and Design*, 1(*6*).

Odell, J., & Fowler, M. (1995b). From analysis to design using templates, Part II. *Report on Object Analysis and Design*, 2(*1*). 10–14.

Odell, J., & Fowler, M. (1995c). From analysis to design using templates, Part III. *Report on Object Analysis and Design*, 2(*3*), 7–10.

Rumbaugh, J., Blaha, M., Premerlani, W., Eddy, F., & Lorensen, W. (1991). *Object-Oriented Modeling and Design.* Englewood Cliffs, NJ: Prentice-Hall.

Shlaer, S., &. Mellor, S. (1988). *Object-Oriented Systems Analysis: Modeling the World in Data.* Englewood Cliffs, NJ: Prentice-Hall.

Shlaer, S., & Mellor, S. (1990). *Object Lifecycles: Modeling the World in States.* Englewood Cliffs, NJ: Prentice-Hall.

Shlaer, S., & Mellor, S. (1993). A deeper look . . . at the transition from analysis to design. *Journal of Object-Oriented Programming,* 5(9), 16–21.

Tracz, W. (1995). *Confessions of a Used-Program Salesman: Institutionalizing Software Reuse.* Reading, MA: Addison-Wesley.

CHAPTER 3

MODELING SYSTEM STRUCTURE

A SOUND SET OF object models is the key to successful object development, as they lay the foundation for the forthcoming design. It is therefore imperative that the initial parts of the analysis are based on solid business- and technical-modeling decisions. The object-oriented analyst can be confused by which objects to include in his or her model, how to decide which relationships are important enough to be captured, and how to recognize real-world situations in which aggregation, inheritance, or dynamic classification are appropriate. This means that the developer must be provided with a set of techniques and guidelines with which to attack the analysis process, and a set of useful modeling constructs that form part of the modeling armory.

In this chapter I will describe a broad set of strategies for modeling the structure of a problem domain. This covers system partitioning (an area not many methods address) and all areas related to constructing the static object model—finding objects, modeling relationships, effective subtyping, and modeling rules.

Each object method provides some notation for depicting objects, attributes, and their relationships. The notation used in this chapter is from OMT (Object Modeling Technique) although as you will see I have had to change a few things slightly. Anyone familiar with that notation should understand the changes, however. In many ways the use of this notation is quite accidental, as it is the notation most widely supported by CASE (computer-aided software engineering) tools on the PC (personal computer) platform.

Most object-oriented methods have a formal approach for modeling the static structure of a system. In object methods, objects are at the center of such a model, and these are represented in an object model. It is usually the first model constructed, as it allows one to understand the principal "players" in the domain and their relationships. Much as with understanding a play, one likes to know a little bit about the characters and their relationships before delving into the storyline.

3.1 System Partitioning

The first step in any analysis process, especially for large systems, is to partition the system into more manageable units. Each unit can then be analyzed by separate teams, or at different times in the process, or even just be used to organize the analysis process, providing a focus for each analysis section.

These units should be based on a strategy that is compatible with the principles of the object-oriented paradigm in order to take advantage of the use of objects. For example, a partitioning approach based along functional lines would prove unwise as a single object may be split across functional boundaries. The partitioning strategy must therefore allow the analysts to take full advantage of the object-oriented paradigm.

3.1.1 Partitioning by Subject Matter

A popular method of system partitioning that I feel is the most effective is partitioning by subject matter, or domains. Two object methods have fully taken up this approach: Shlaer and Mellor (1990) and Syntropy from Cook and Daniels (1994). Other methods, such as the new real-time method from Awad, Kuusela, and Ziegler (1996), are now using these concepts also, as they value the benefit it brings.

I have found partitioning by subject matter to be by far the most effective way to partition a large system into some coherent logical units. The reason for this preferred approach, as opposed to clustering, is because the partitioning is done "up front." That is, it is one of the first activities in the systems-analysis process. Note that clustering into subsystems can also be done within domains if the model becomes quite large. The domain approach to system partitioning is also in harmony with object principles because it is based on object types and not object instances, as pointed out by Cook and Daniels (1994). It is also very useful in organizing work across teams and providing a means of focus for those teams.

The formal definition of a domain, as defined by Shlaer and Mellor (1990, p. 133) is: "a separate real, hypothetical or abstract world inhabited by a distinct set of objects that behave according to rules and policies characteristic of the domain."

Examples of perhaps the two most obvious domains are the user-interface domain and the application domain. Most people are familiar with the notion of separating the user interface from the application, and doing so affords the developer some clear advantages, the most obvious being the potential reuse of parts of the interface for future applications. This is only possible because the user interface and application are two very different subject matters with different rules and policies governing their behavior. These are just two of the domains that exist in any final system, however. An object-oriented analysis approach should go one step further and identify *all* the different domains in a system. Separation of these domains at the outset means they can be analyzed in parallel and each has the potential to be reused in subsequent versions of this system and in other systems.

The final system from the end user's point of view is an amalgamation of all the different subject matters in the system. It is the analyst's task to first untangle all these subject matters so that they can be more readily understood, and their interdependencies, which are based on the requirements, more clearly understood.

The Shlaer–Mellor method prescribes the construction of a domain chart at the beginning of a project in order to identify and describe the different domains in the system and their dependencies. An example of a domain chart is shown in Figure 3.1. Even if I am not using the Shlaer–Mellor method, I find it useful to construct a domain chart, as it helps provide a context for the overall system from a logical analysis point of view.

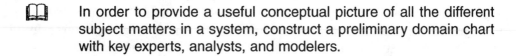 In order to provide a useful conceptual picture of all the different subject matters in a system, construct a preliminary domain chart with key experts, analysts, and modelers.

Domains have client–server relationships with each other. Each domain can be either a client or a server for one or more other domains. The domains are laid out with client domains above server domains. A client and server domain are connected by a *bridge*, which acts as the contract between the two. The bridge is represented by an arrow from the client domain to the server domain. The client domain uses a number of services provided by one or more server domains. The server domain provides services to one or more clients.

In Figure 3.1 the communications domain provides communications services for the application domain that allow it to communicate over a telephone line or some

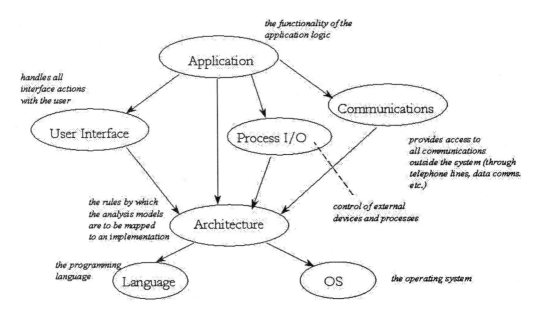

Figure 3.1. A domain chart from Shlaer-Mellor.

other communications media. As far as the application domain is concerned it could be two cans connected by a piece of string, as long as it could provide the services required by the application domain. At the beginning of the analysis process the actual services required by the application are not known, and so the definition of the bridge between the two is just a broad general-purpose statement. As the analysis proceeds, however, the understanding of the application domain increases and the requirements it places on the communications domain become clearer. In this way the contract between the two domains becomes more defined until it is something akin to an interface definition.

Shlaer–Mellor categorize their domains into four categories:

1. *Application domain*—the problem domain as perceived by the end users.

2. *Service domains*—those domains that provide services to the application domain. Typical service domains include inventory handling, alarm handling, performance data collection, hardware interface, user interface, and performance monitoring, among others.

3. *Architecture domain*—this describes the set of rules by which analysis models are transformed into an implementation. The "design" of the system in a translational approach, if you will.

4. *Implementation domains*—this includes programming languages, operating systems, class libraries, and so on.

Interestingly, Cook and Daniels also categorize their domains. They identify three types of domains: concept domains (similar to application domains and some service domains such as accounting and history), interaction domains (similar to some service domains such as user interface [UI] and process input/output [I/O]), and implementation domains (as above).

Shlaer–Mellor base their definition on the application in hand (because service domains can be application domains in other applications, e.g., an accounting domain is an application domain in an accounting application), whereas Cook and Daniels base their definition on general-purpose concepts. The categorization is not that important; what is important is that domains are useful in practice and can lead to more reusable object models. Partitioning by subject matter, or domains, is an appealing concept both intellectually, and practically.

3.1.1.1 Finding Domains

Finding domains is not easy. The most obvious domains are the application domain and the user-interface domain, and these are usually identified first. After these the analysts must try to identify the services an application requires that are not part of the application itself but can be thought of as separate subject matters. Domains can be difficult to identify at the beginning of an analysis, especially as the system is often thought of as the final interaction of these subject matters. So how do we find domains?

One of the most useful techniques is to hold a brainstorming session at the outset of the analysis. These sessions should be arranged with some of the most experienced and diversely interested parties: application domain experts, system engineers, and experienced developers. Each person should be allowed to throw ideas on a whiteboard without evaluation or comments by others, and then after the ideas have slowed down or stopped, the group critically evaluates each contribution. The goal is to try to trim the list down to the "real" domains in order to arrive at a preliminary domain chart.

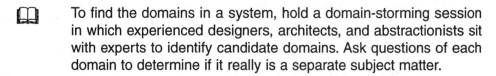 To find the domains in a system, hold a domain-storming session in which experienced designers, architects, and abstractionists sit with experts to identify candidate domains. Ask questions of each domain to determine if it really is a separate subject matter.

A useful way of finding the "real" domains from the impostors is to ask questions about each domain. Questions to ask about each candidate domain include the following:

> *Can this subject matter exist independently of other subject matters?* If this domain's rules and policies can be understood without requiring knowledge of other domains, then it is likely that it is a true domain. For example, an inventory-management system is a true domain because one can reason about inventoried items, off-site storage locations, quantities of items, inventory reorder dates, and so on without having any knowledge about what is being inventoried (which would be application knowledge). The actual inventoried items could be kitchen equipment just as easily as printed circuit boards (PCBs).

> *Can this domain provide a service to other domains?* What services will this domain provide to any possible client? Who are its clients? Try to write a short description of a domain's "mission" in this system. This will serve to identify the services it will provide, and who its clients are. For example, an inventory domain will provide services related to storing, retrieving, reordering, and controlling stock. Difficulty in writing an adequate mission statement may occur because the domain is not really a separate subject matter, but may be part of another domain.

> *Can this domain be taken out of this domain chart and replaced with another domain with a similar mission statement that provides the same services?* If it is possible to take this domain out, say a graphical user interface (GUI), and replace it with another domain, say a character-based interface, and still provide the same services, then it is probably a real domain. In this case, it is possible to replace a GUI with a character-based interface without affecting the contract between the user interface and the application. The application will certainly look different to the user but as far as the application domain is concerned, the services it requires from a user-interface domain (presentation of information) are still being provided.

> *What services does this domain need from other domains in order to be able to perform its tasks?* A service domain, acting as a server to one or more clients, may still be a client in relationship to another domain. Does this domain require services from another domain in order to be able to do its job successfully? If the answer is yes, then this domain will place requirements on another domain. If no, then this may not be a domain unless it is a low level domain. Asking this type of question can be useful in identifying further domains.

Can I conceive of a way in which I may be able to buy an off-the-shelf package that will provide the services required of this domain? Domains are potentially excellent units of reuse, especially as it may be possible to buy packages that provide many or all of the services required of a domain. Using the user interface as an example again, we are all aware of GUI packages or frameworks that can be purchased off the shelf and reused with a multitude of applications.

It is possible to buy packages for other service domains also, such as inventory management, statistical data analysis, and communications. Some thin layer of functionality may be required on top of a purchased domain package in order to make it directly applicable to the system.

More recently we are seeing the emergence of frameworks in specific application domains, such as financial trading and customer-management systems. In fact, many organizations are now constructing their own frameworks with a view to reusing them across applications.

After identifying all the domains, a mission statement for each domain and a description of each bridge should be written. These descriptions, coupled with the domain chart, are essential as they provide the context for understanding the system as a whole, a road map to the various parts of the analysis, and also form the foundation of the analysis process.

Figure 3.2 shows a more specific domain chart. We see that the application domain, Kitchen Design, uses the services of the Inventory domain to manage the inventory and keep control of the locations of various pieces of kitchen furniture. It also uses the Accounting domain to manipulate financial information regarding the kitchen equipment. The User Interface is based on the X Tool kit and so this package is shown as a separate domain. The User Interface domain is still necessary because it needs to provide some functionality on top of the tool kit. The software-architecture domain is the domain that describes the rules and policies of how to implement the system using the services of the C++ language domain and the UNIX operating-system domain. In this case an object-oriented architecture will be employed, as shown on the domain chart. We can see that an object database management system (ODBMS) will be used by the object-oriented architecture to provide persistent storage for the objects.

We observe that some of the domains identified already exist, such as the C++ language and the UNIX operating system. These are the obvious ones of course, but it may be that a corporate Accounting class library will be used that provides all of the functionality required by the Kitchen-Design domain. If so, then the functionality that needs to be addressed with regard to this system is the use of that

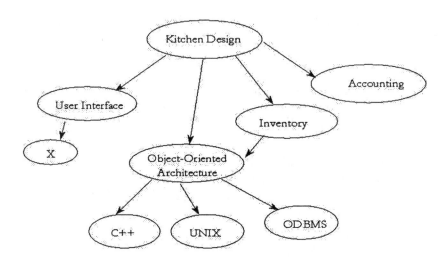

Figure 3.2. A domain chart for a kitchen-design system.

library in this application, that is, the bridge between the Kitchen-Design domain and the Accounting domain. Figure 3.3 indicates existing domains through shading. So, for this system only the User-Interface, Inventory, and Kitchen-Design domains need be modeled.[1] It is worth noting that the Accounting and User-Interface domains do not have a dependency on the Object-Oriented Architecture domain, as they are domains that either already exist (Accounting) or will be implemented using an alternative architecture (User Interface).

3.1.1.2 Working with Domains

If you are using the Shlaer–Mellor method, then the use of the domain chart is an essential activity. If you are not using the method, there is still room for domains in your world. There are essentially two ways to work with domains. Construct a separate object model for each domain (as in Shlaer–Mellor) or model multiple domains on a single-object model.

1. *Constructing Separate Object Models:* Analysis proceeds on a domain-by-domain basis with separate object models being constructed for each

---

[1]The Architecture domain is a "special" domain in the Shlaer–Mellor method and its use will be detailed later in the book (chapter 5).

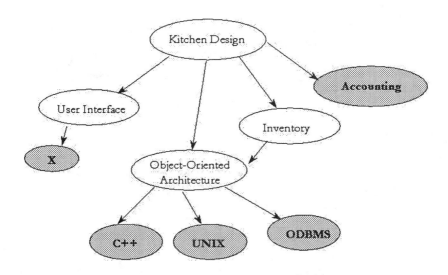

Figure 3.3. Existing and new domains.

domain. This makes it possible to analyze domains concurrently. For example, for the teams working from the domain chart of Figure 3.1, experts on the application domain can analyze the application domain at the same time as the communications experts can solve issues regarding the transmittal of information to other sites.

2. *Modeling Multiple Domains:* Analysis proceeds with all domains being shown on the same object model. It is still possible to analyze domains concurrently, but there is one object model constructed. Relationships between objects across domains are allowed in such a scheme. There are no bridges.

To make these ideas more concrete, let us consider an example. Our two domains shall be an Inventory domain and a Kitchen-Design domain. The Kitchen-Design domain is the application domain, and a client of the Inventory domain. Modeling each domain separately, our two object models will be as in Figures 3.4 and 3.5.[2] We can see that the models can be understood independently of each other.

Let us now look at what happens when a new kitchen cabinet arrives in the warehouse. For this occurrence, a KitchenCabinet object must be created in the Kitchen-

---

[2] The notation used in this and all subsequent diagrams can be found in Appendix A.

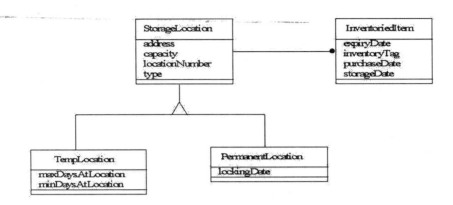

Figure 3.4. A portion of the Inventory domain object model.

Design domain and an InventoriedItem object must be created in the Inventory domain. Both of these objects correspond to some aspect of the real kitchen cabinet being delivered. When is this dependency shown?

In this approach the dependency is formalized by the bridge between the two domains. The application domain places a requirement on the Inventory domain that it must be able to create a new object for the Inventoried item when it arrives. How this is to be done is not a concern early in the analysis process because it is sufficient to say that some indication will be provided. Once all the requirements the application domain places on the inventory domain have been identified, an appropriate design for the bridge may be carried out.

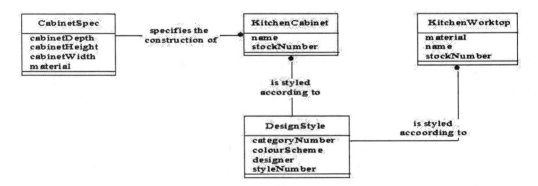

Figure 3.5. A portion of the Kitchen Design object model.

Figure 3.6. Bridging across domains via inheritance.

For example, if the bridge is to be specified through subtyping (i.e., all items needing to be inventoried will derive from InventoriedItem—see Figure 3.6) then the realization of the requirement that a new InventoriedItem needs to be created is automatic.

If the bridge is to be specified by communication (see Figure 3.7) then the dependency is implemented totally through the bridge and only need be shown via events entering and exiting the domain. Of course, if there was an existing Inventory-domain package or framework, then the application programming interface (API) of that package, say, could be used to fulfill that requirement.

There is a third possibility for creating a bridge that is possible using the JAVA programming language. JAVA allows objects to define multiple interfaces, providing an alternative to inheritance. This would mean that InventoriedItem could be defined as an interface of KitchenCabinet. In turn, this would mean that KitchenCabinet could later be used to implement other interfaces as appropriate.

Defining the interface between two domains can be a complex task that requires input from parties working on both domains. Small workshop-like discussions are useful for exploring the requirements one domain places on another, hence driving the definition of the bridge.

> To determine the interface between two domains, hold regular "bridge-definition workshops." These workshops need to be short, focused sessions held at regular intervals during the modeling. There needs to be a "sign-off" about 70% of the way into the modeling activity in which both parties agree to the interface and stick to it.

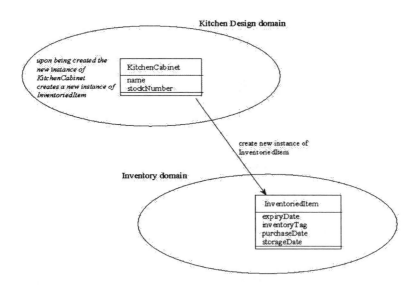

Figure 3.7. Bridging across domains through messaging.

Constructing separate models for each domain can be both time- and effort-consuming. For large systems the effort is certainly worth the investment, however, as it results in domains that are more reusable. The effort is questionable for small systems that may use a fraction of the amount of functionality of another separate domain.

> Construct separate object models for each domain when modeling large systems, as this results in more reusable object-domain models. For smaller systems, build a single-object model that can be geographically segregated into domains.

Constructing a single-object model for multiple domains is worthwhile if the system to be built is small- to medium-sized, but benefits can still be achieved by identifying domains. In such an approach there will be relationships and dependencies between objects across domains (see Figure 3.8). In this approach the dependency can be shown at any time, irrespective of whether the dependency is realized by subtyping, communication between objects, or by some relationship.

The general guideline is to separate information of different domains from one another as long as possible. It will become necessary to integrate them when it is no longer possible to understand the problem without looking at models of both

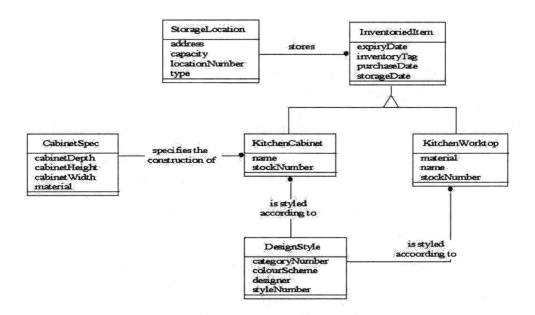

Figure 3.8. A portion of an object model showing more than one domain.

domains. Don't show cross-domain relationships on the same object model until later on in the process.

> Separate information of different domains from one another as long as possible. Don't show cross-domain relationships on the same object model until later on in the process.

Domains provide an excellent means of partitioning a system, but they also partition work across teams. Each team or group within a project can focus on the modeling of their subject matter, and thus remain focused on the issues that pertain to that subject matter. Partitioning also allows teams to work on modeling domains in parallel, providing numerous advantages. Working in parallel can also have its problems, however. Modelers are often working with incomplete information, as the remainder of the information may not yet be available from other domains. This requires good organization, project management, and commitment, and regular cross-domain meetings should be held to identify requirements being placed from one domain to another. The bridge-definition workshops identified earlier are another forum in which such issues come to light.

3.2 Working with Domain Experts

The purpose of analysis is to understand a problem domain. Naturally, a domain expert can be a very useful ally during this process. According to Coad, North, and Mayfield (1994, p. 492), a domain expert is: "a person that (sic) has experience working within a specific area of concern. Ideally, the person is somewhat introspective, too (someone who has spent some time thinking about what he or she does, fitting that work within an overall scope or larger perspective)."

It is important to make the distinction between a domain expert and a user. For example, experts who may assist in understanding retail systems where point-of-sale terminals are the user tools are not usually the people who will eventually operate those terminals. The domain expert and the user can sometimes be the same person, however.

Domain experts can sometimes be instrumental in uncovering requirements that may not be documented elsewhere, and can also provide the insight needed to fully understand the more complex aspects of a domain. In doing so, domain experts are often responsible for identifying key abstractions and relationships of the problem space that can allow an order-of-magnitude improvement in the expression of the domain concepts. Above all, domain experts can validate the object models.

There are a number of ways in which experts can be involved in the modeling process:

> *Interviews:* These can be particularly useful if experts are not directly involved in conducting the analysis. A number of short directed sessions of 1–2 hours' duration are most profitable. The modeler should be well prepared before the interview with a ready set of questions. During the interview it is a useful idea to try to prepare a précis of one's understanding at regular intervals in order to verify that the information is being interpreted correctly. Sketch out typical constructs and issues as you go along and make good notes. Guidelines for conducting interviews exist (McGraw & Harbison-Briggs, 1989), but one should always be aware of the possible sources for error in such a process, such as bias and expert specialization. If possible try to interview a number of domain experts to avoid such problems.

When interviewing experts to elicit requirements, limit sessions to 1–2 hours' duration, ask questions continually, and summarize your understanding to verify information is being interpreted correctly.

Reviewing models: Experts can make excellent reviewers of models, as they will be best able to understand if the models being constructed best describe the problem domain. Just sending the models to an expert to review as if he or she were reading a book will not be sufficient, however. Early on, the expert will need to be walked through the models and every attribute and relationship will need to be explained and justified. This certainly does reinforce the need for rigorous documentation. Later, as he or she becomes more familiar with the notation and the models, the expert will require less of your time.

📖 Provide a basic class in reading object models for your experts. A short class covering notation, how-to-read models, and understanding the issues should be given at the beginning of an expert's involvement in the process.

Participation in the analysis: Full-time participation of experts during the modeling process is the ideal. Expert participation ranges from occasional involvement to full-fledged team membership, however. As with modelers, some experts make better modelers than others, and sometimes experts can be the best modelers of all. When involving experts, seeding each team with an expert can often be the best way to gain maximum leverage out of his or her involvement. In such a situation, however, the experts should be fully trained in the approach being used.

📖 When you have the luxury of experts on your modeling teams, it can be a good idea to seed each team with an expert. Often this can be the most effective use of the expert's time and will provide the maximum benefit to the modeling effort.

As we will see later, there are a number of avenues through which to explore a problem domain. It is often best to use the path that the experts are most comfortable with, rather than forcing them to try to think the same way the analysts do.

📖 If an expert would rather explore dynamics before structure, then this should be facilitated, and if he or she is more comfortable in looking at structure first then this should also be allowed. The analyst's role becomes that of facilitator and driver.

In the above scenario, the analyst's role becomes more of facilitator and driver of the process and the responsibility is to ensure that the analysis is proceeding satisfactorily. Use the techniques that the experts feel most comfortable with and offer suggestions for alternatives rather than forcing a modeling construct down their throats. Also, frequent use of sketches and examples helps considerably. Don't try to rename concepts that experts feel comfortable with unless they fully buy-in to the new name. Incorrect naming of abstractions and ideas can be a prime source of confusion.

> When working with experts don't try to rename concepts they are familiar with, even if they seem to have incorrect names, unless you have a consensus. Remember you're constructing a model of the problem domain and should use the language of that world.

3.3 Finding and Modeling Objects and Attributes

3.3.1 Finding Objects

Numerous methods exist for finding objects, these range from the passive activity of noun identification (Rumbaugh, Blaha, Premerlani, Eddy, & Lorensen, 1991) to the more dynamic use of CRC (class–responsibility–collaborator) cards, as originally outlined by Beck and Cunningham (1989). Brainstorming sessions coupled with abstraction techniques, which are followed by scenario exploration, provide a useful combination of techniques.

3.3.1.1 Object Blitzing

The brainstorming ideas are similar to those used in the identification of domains, and can be the initial activity in a Rapid Application Development (RAD) session. Object blitzing, as suggested by Balcer (1993), is another name given to the group activity of throwing candidate objects onto a whiteboard without any comment from others and then refining the list when the ideas slow down. Shlaer and Mellor (1988) note that there are typically five different types of objects in a system: tangible things, roles, incidents, interactions, and specifications. Thinking about each of these categories of abstractions during the object blitz may help to offer some useful strategies. Using abstraction techniques such as these is a superior method of finding objects.

> Hold a brainstorming session with domain experts and modelers to find objects. Use object categories as a means of getting started and follow up with scenario exploration.

There are some interesting patterns that emerge when identifying objects. Role objects typically have a tangible thing associated with them. For example, the object ClassroomInUse is a role object that may have a Classroom object (tangible thing) associated with it. The characteristics of a classroom when it is in use would be different from a classroom that is empty. Also, the ClassroomInUse object would be participating in relationships other than those that would apply when the classroom is not in use. Similarly ClassroomEmpty may be another object.

Another example of a role object is BookOnLoan in a library system, which will have different attributes to LibraryBook (tangible thing). Later on in the modeling process we will evaluate each of these objects to determine if they warrant being a separate object, or if they can be represented as a state of the tangible (onLoan could be a state of a LibraryBook object), or maybe even by an attribute (onLoan could be an attribute of LibraryBook taking the value TRUE or FALSE).

> When you identify a role object, try to think of a tangible thing that may be acting in that role for a period of time. Or, if you identify a tangible thing, see if there are roles that it fulfills that may warrant being identified as a separate object.

Tangible things sometimes have a specification object associated with them, especially if there are cases in which many objects are created from one design or specification. For example, a Refrigerator object may have a RefrigeratorDesign object from which it derives its specification. Typically, there would be fewer object instances of RefrigeratorDesign than of Refrigerator.

> When you identify a tangible thing, see if there is a specification object that is necessary. To help do this, see if there are attributes that need to be captured that do not change with each instance of the tangible, but more with a set of tangibles.

Workshop participants should evaluate each suggestion to see if it is an object in the domain. Look out for suggestions that are actually attributes of other objects, objects that fall outside the domain being considered, objects that are outside the scope of the domain, objects that are duplicates of other objects, and objects that are vague or irrelevant to the problem being modeled. Elimination from this initial list is not always easy; vigorous discussion is valuable at this stage because it helps to clarify ideas and understanding, and may identify further useful abstractions. Analysis at this stage is a group-centered activity with the emphasis on exposing all information relevant to the domain under study. A major determining factor in deciding on objects is the relevance to the problem at hand, which is ultimately driven by the requirements of the problem.

3.3.1.2 Using Use Cases

In addition to object blitzing, focusing on the behavior of the domain through use cases (Jacobson, Christerson, Jonsson, & Overgaard, 1992) can help in finding objects and in understanding poorly defined domains with especially weak definitions. As identified in the previous chapter, identify the possible use cases that this domain is subject to (based on stimulus from outside the domain or the system) and the required responses (functionality of the domain on receipt of this stimulus).[3] For each event sent to the system within a use case, identify the information associated with it, the functionality to be carried out, possible exceptions, and the response (if any) with any information associated with it. A table can then be drawn up listing each event at a very high level, as shown in Table 3.1. This table shows three use cases for a financial domain. (We shall revisit this table later as it weaves an essential thread through our process.)

Using these use cases to identify events and the categories of objects previously discussed, we can try to visualize some more of the objects in the domain.

> Create a high-level event table derived from the use cases identified at the beginning of the modeling process. Use this table to further identify objects, with the assistance of domain experts.

Using use cases to identify objects is an activity that must be carried out with some care. Use cases are essentially processes through the system and are therefore "functionally oriented." Use cases are an external view of the system from the user's point of view. When describing use cases do so from an external view point and do not indicate any internal steps on how the processing is carried out in order to meet the required functionality.

So, for Table 3.1, the expected-functionality column contains sufficient description for an external view at this early stage. Later, it will be the goal of the modeling activity to define how this functionality will be provided through objects and operations.

I have had experience finding objects from use cases directly and have found an explosion of fine-grained objects that seem to be specific to the use cases.

---

[3]See Chapter 2 where we talked about the "Big Picture."

Table 3.1 HIGH-LEVEL EVENTS

Scenario	Input Information	Expected Functionality	Output Information
Value portfolio	Portfolio number	Calculates value of selected portfolio	Value of portfolio
Add new customer	Customer name, address, code, amount	Create new customer object instance and assign a new customer number	New customer number
Deposit amount	Customer number, amount	Deposit cash sum into customer's account	Confirmation

These objects were too fine grained to be helpful across use cases and often led to a series of "functional" objects that were questionable at best.[4] Aside from the other caveats aimed at use cases (see Chapter 2), potentially the most important caveat concerns finding objects through use cases. Berard (1995, p. 7) states the issues around use cases most succinctly:

> It is perfectly proper and appropriate to use use cases to describe an external (user-oriented) view of the system. However, avoid the temptation to use this functional view of the system as a basis for the creation of an object-oriented architecture for that same system. As many of my clients will tell you, objects and functions do not map to each other on a one-to-one basis, and the architecture of an object-oriented system is significantly different from the architecture of a functionally decomposed system.

As we shall see in the next chapter, a list of the use cases can be used as a first-pass relationship between objects and each interaction. Later, Table 3.1 will be extended to include information about the objects participating in each scenario. It is important to note that this initial relationship is only a first pass and is subject

---

[4]"Functional" objects, such as those used to encapsulate algorithms (Gossain, 1990), are quite common in object systems and provide many advantages. However, they are usually identified later in the process, after much modeling. Their creation from the outset can be a little premature. It is this that is of concern when identifying objects through use cases.

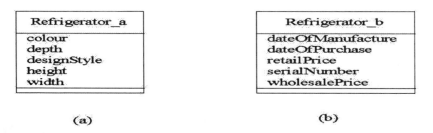

Figure 3.9. Two ways of modeling a refrigerator.

to change later on as we begin to understand the domain better. At this point we do not know much about each object and have not assigned any roles and responsibilities, so interaction can be described at a high level if only to gain an understanding of the domain functionality. We shall return to these use cases later on.

3.3.2 How to Find and Model Attributes

Objects in a domain have their characteristics represented as attributes. An attribute should be a representation of some characteristic of the concept from which the object is abstracted, and should have some semantic value. In finding the attributes of an object we should ask questions about the object. What information is required concerning that object? What characteristics of that object need to be remembered over time? What data is important when considering that object in the context of the application? We should not just blindly list all possible attributes of an object, however, but should qualify them based on the problem under consideration.

For example, let us suppose we are interested in kitchen equipment. We might have an object Refrigerator whose potential attributes might be: dateOfManufacture, dateOfPurchase, cubicCapacity, serialNumber, color, height, width, depth, and retailPrice, among others. Deciding which attributes are relevant depends on the problem domain. If it is kitchen design, then we are most likely to be interested in the refrigerator shown in Figure 3.9(a) with its color, height, width, depth, and designStyle, so that we can match and fit it with other pieces of kitchen equipment. If our interest is solely in the sale of kitchen equipment, however, then the retailPrice, wholesalePrice, dateOfPurchase, dateOfManufacture, and serialNumber are more likely to be of interest, as one can see in Figure 3.9(b).

All attributes in Figure 3.9 are certainly valid attributes of a refrigerator and we can think of many more, but the abstraction we choose for a refrigerator depends on its usage within the domain. It may be that we have more than one object we are modeling here: RefrigeratorSpecification, RefrigeratorDesign, and Refrigerator, perhaps. The importance of the perspective you are taking during modeling cannot be understated.

> When deciding which attributes are important, consider the perspective you have of the object. Ask yourself: "What information pertaining to that object is important in the context of the system?" If in doubt, add the attribute to the object; it can always be removed later if it remains unused.

Although it may seem a somewhat trivial and minor issue, the placement of attributes is extremely important because it provides an understanding of the object within the context of the problem. The existence of an attribute in an object means that its value may vary from one object instance to the next., Does an attribute belong with one object or with another? One useful way of deciding where an attribute belongs is to take the object out of the model and consider it in isolation. If it still seems to make sense then it is likely it belongs to the object. If not, consider placing it elsewhere.

> In determining whether an attribute belongs to an object or not, take that object out of the model and consider it in isolation. If all the attributes still seem to make sense, then it is likely they belong there. If not, consider placing those out-of-place attributes elsewhere.

Another way of deciding is to consider if the attribute can vary from one object instance to the next. For example, for an object JumboAircraft, wingspan may be suggested as an attribute (see Figure 3.10(a)). Unlike the other characteristics of a jumbo aircraft, however, such as weight and the number of passengers, the wingspan of a jumbo aircraft does not vary from one object instance of JumboAircraft to the next. It would be better to create a specification object called JumboAirCraftDesign and have a model similar to that of Figure 3.10(b). Here we have modeled the fact that from one object instance of design to the next we can have different wingspans, but from one object instance of an aircraft (of the same design) to the next, the value of the attribute wingspan will be the same.

The naming of attributes is also very important and should not be underestimated. The names of attributes (and objects) will live throughout the lifetime of the system and will be interpreted by numerous people, some of whom will not have been part of the model. Therefore, it is important that care should be taken in naming attributes such that they convey the meaning of the attribute as understood by domain experts.

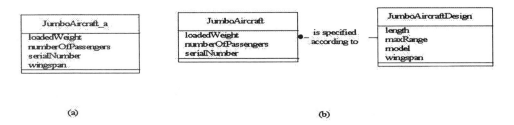

(a)   (b)

Figure 3.10. **Modeling specification objects and tangible things.**

Verify attribute names with domain experts. Use names that they are comfortable with, and that convey the meaning of the characteristic as understood by domain experts.

3.4 Modeling Relationships

3.4.1 Capturing Relationships

Using the objects found earlier, we now attempt to identify relationships between the objects that will be shown on the object model. These relationships should capture some valuable information about the relationships between objects in the problem domain, and should describe the static rules and policies of the problem domain. The relationships here are not the same as the interactions between object instances used later on to capture dynamics.

Relationships are said to have cardinality (which can be 1 to 1, 1 to many, or many to many) and optionality (unconditional where relationships always hold, and conditional where there are cases in which object instances are not participating in the relationship). The analyst should evaluate each relationship on the basis of cardinality ("How many object instances of this object can there be involved in the relationship at any one time?") and on optionality ("Are there ever cases where object instances may not be participating in this relationship?").

When assessing cardinality only look at the relationship at a moment in time, whereas when assessing optionality, examine the relationship over the whole period covered by the analysis.

The lifetimes and existence of objects and relationships are also determined from the optionality and cardinality of relationships. This is an important consequence of

Figure 3.11. Relationship between Company and Person.

relationships that many modelers do not realize until late in the development process, and as a result this often requires going back and changing the models.

Consider the model shown in Figure 3.11. The relationship between Company and Person is one to one-or-more (1:1,M). This implies that every Person object instance will have a company by which they are employed. It also means that a Person can only work for one Company and that a Person object instance cannot exist without being employed by a company. Therefore a Person cannot be unemployed. Another implication of this mandatory relationship is that a Company must have at least one or more Persons whom it employs. That is, a Company cannot exist without having a relationship to at least one employee.

There are also implications about deleting object instances here. If I delete a Person object then the relationship with the Company object must also be deleted. If I have deleted the last Person object, then the instance of Company object must also be deleted, because the relationship as represented in no longer holds: The Company object no longer has at least one object instance of Person related to it.

If the aforementioned implications are correct for the domain being modeled, then the above relationship has been modeled correctly. However, if it is not then the cardinality and optionality must be examined in closer detail. It is important to consider such implications for every relationship in the model. So for a relationship between object A and object B, typical questions to ask include the following:

> If I create an object A, must it have an associated B object? If not, under what conditions is the relationship with B created? (and vice versa)

> If I delete an object A, what happens to the associated B object? If it is the last object that I have deleted, what are the consequences for the other object?

For each relationship in the object model, consider the implications of the cardinality and optionality with respect to creating and deleting instances, by asking questions of the model.

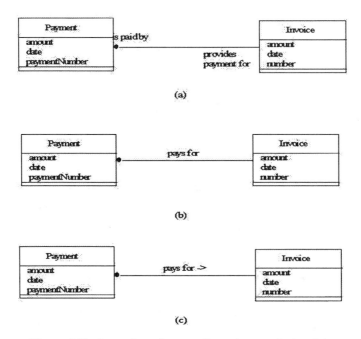

Figure 3.12. A number of ways of naming a relationship.

In asking such questions analysts are raising issues that may not have been addressed. Asking questions of experts, sifting through requirements specifications, clarifying vague requirements, exposing information to understand a problem domain: These are the essentials of any analysis activity.

Relationships are annotated with a brief statement on the diagram. In Shlaer–Mellor OOA (object-oriented analysis), this statement is written from the perspective of each of the participating objects. This is different from other methods that merely annotate each relationship with a single description, such as OMT.

I have found it useful to describe the relationship from both perspectives (Figure 3.12(a)). It may initially seem unnecessarily time-consuming but it does ensure that the analyst considers the relationship from both perspectives, rather than just describing it from one direction with the possibility of ignoring it from the other direction. In many cases a description from each perspective provides a better understanding of the relationship than that provided by a single description (Figure 3.12(b)) and may even lead to the discovery of more than one relationship between the same objects because the analyst must think more deeply about the nature of the relationship being abstracted. This is especially important in domains that are either obscure or unfamiliar to the analyst.

An alternative approach is to use directed descriptions (Figure 3.12(c)), but using this technique one can miss important relationships that need to be captured in the model. It is a matter of personal preference which you use, but whichever you choose the key is to decide on a policy, be consistent in its use, and to make sure each relationship is named in some way.[5]

📖   Label relationships from the perspective of each participating object. This will aid in domain understanding and also may assist in identifying further relationships. This also leads to a more comprehensible model for all concerned, current and future. Remember the model will live long after the modelers have finished modeling.

The object model represents the information that our system must maintain over the lifetime of the system, and so must contain all the data necessary to carry out the required functionality. The collection of models is a representation of the knowledge of a domain, and so the models should provide as true an understanding of that domain as possible. The naming of relationships, objects, and attributes is therefore very important. Care should be taken when choosing names, paying particular attention to their use in the everyday language of the domain experts.[6]

When naming relationships, use words that provide a deeper semantic meaning than phrases such as "is connected to" (as in Figure 3.13(a)) or the ubiquitous "is related to." *Why* is the Monitor "connected to" the ProcessorBox? Asking ourselves this question will ensure that we think about the nature of the relationship rather than just writing it down as a matter of course, and will allow us to provide more insight into the problem domain for those who will use our models later. Figure 3.13(b) provides a more suitable representation.

📖   Name relationships with phrases that provide the semantic context for the relationship. Don't just use the first phrase that comes to mind.

The novice analyst may try to involve an object in all possible relationships that she or he can think of. One of the most common questions asked is: How do I know which relationships are important and need to be represented and which do not? The analyst should examine each relationship between objects in isolation to see

---

[5] One of the most common sources of error in any analysis activity is due to errors caused by omission. Ensuring that every construct in every model is labeled will mean that there is no room for such errors.

[6] This was already mentioned in the previous section.

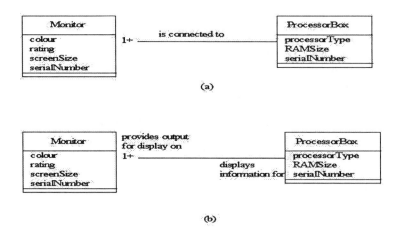

Figure 3.13. Choosing names for relationships.

if they are still important (just as with attributes). Each relationship should also add some meaning to the model as it codifies the current understanding of the problem domain.

📖   Examine each relationship in isolation to determine whether that relationship is really needed in the model. Ask yourself: What value does this relationship bring to the understanding of the domain?

In exploring relationships, analysts should ask questions of the model that may arise during run time: "If I receive the event X with some data Y, do I have sufficient data to carry out the functionality required?" In answering this question the analyst must look at the objects and relationships to see if sufficient data exists in the model and if it can be retrieved by traversing the relationships. If it does not exist or cannot be retrieved, then some concepts are missing: either objects, attributes, and/or relationships.

📖   Test the objects and relationships by ensuring that common questions (typical data queries for example) asked of the model can be satisfied given the initial information, the objects, and the relationships. Use domain experts to provide you with typical examples.

3.4.2 Subtyping

Aside from the relationships described previously, there is a special relationship, called subtyping, which allows the analyst to capture commonalities across objects (through a supertype) while still capturing their differences (through subtypes). Subtyping is a powerful and expressive construct that can unfortunately be overused by the enthusiastic modeler who has just discovered its usefulness.

3.4.2.1 When to Subtype?

The subtype–supertype structure is used to capture the IS-A relationship between two objects. That is, the subtype IS-A supertype. Within this context there are two reasons for creating a subtype–supertype structure:

- to explicitly capture the differences and commonalities across different objects through their attributes; and
- to explicitly capture differences and commonalities in behavior.

The latter reason is dealt with specifically in chapter 4, when we examine modeling object behavior. As we shall see, however, behavior can often require us to revisit the structure model and reorganize our subtype–supertype structures on the basis of behavior.

In looking at the former reason, all of the attributes in the supertype should apply to all subtypes and have the same semantics. This would seem to be a straightforward enough guideline but it is amazing the number of times it is not followed, such that it can affect the integrity of the solution, and limits its reusability.

For example, the structure of Figure 3.14 would be an inappropriate use of subtyping because a Helicopter does not have a propeller, and hence the attribute of propellerLength would not be appropriate. One could argue that the Helicopter has a rotor blade and so the value of propellerLength could represent the length of the rotor blade. Although this may work, it would change the semantics of propellerLength from one subtype to the next, and would not truly represent the problem domain accurately. An alternative structure would need to be found.

Aside from the data-inheritance issues, there are also the behavioral issues whereby a Helicopter can have different behavior than a PropBasedAircraft.

Subtyping can also be appropriate when some subset of object instances may be involved in relationships that other subtypes are not. Although the WallLamp does not have any significant additional attributes to those of the supertype, Lamp,

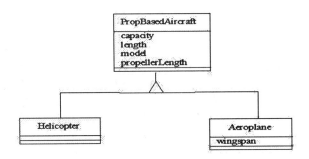

Figure 3.14. Incorrect subtyping or attribute placement.

the model does show that WallLamps are obtained from a supplier, whereas FloorLamps are made in the Factory (see Figure 3.15).

The primary goal of modeling is to provide an understanding of the problem domain; the model should reflect the problem under study. Therefore analysis subtyping is for representations of IS-A constructs, and not for utilizing inheritance to the maximum effect.

I have found that a commonly recurring question is: Do I create a new subtype for keeping track of one attribute or do I create one object and then have the

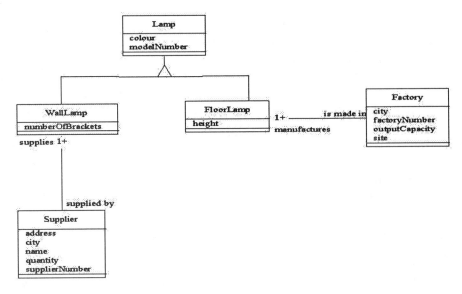

Figure 3.15. Subtyping example.

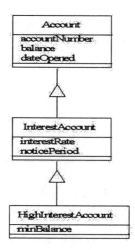

Figure 3.16. Subtype—supertype structure.

attribute be meaningless for all instances where it doesn't apply? For example, which structure is better—Figure 3.16 or Figure 3.17?

The answer is, it depends. The difference is that Figure 3.17 requires an extra attribute to distinguish between the type of interest-bearing account—high or regular. For a high-interest-rate account a minimum balance is required, hence the additional attribute. For those InterestAccount object instances in Figure 3.17, which are regular-interest bearing accounts, the minBalance would be set to zero. I would contend that the former model is the more expressive of the two and that despite the single attribute difference, the extra object is certainly worth it. In the

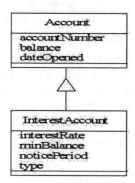

Figure 3.17. Alternative subtype—supertype structure.

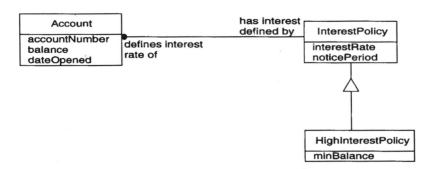

Figure 3.18. Interest-policy objects allow for changing interest rates.

above example there were also some behavioral differences, so that strengthened the need for an extra object. This is not always the case, however.

Given the above structures, what if an account owner wishes to change theaccount from a regular account to a high-interest one? As an alternative to the above, let us create a new object called InterestPolicy, which captures the different interest-rate policies that can be used in a bank. This object has a relationship with Account that is used for all types of accounts. Thus an account holder can now move from an Account with one interest policy to another (see Figure 3.18).

Analysis is not the time to try and build the world's greatest class hierarchy. This may sound like an obvious statement but it is amazing how complex some models can become if inheritance, that most powerful and dangerous of object-oriented features, is used without careful consideration to each new subtype. The desire to allow for change, especially unforeseen change, is perhaps one of the greatest advantages of constructing a class hierarchy, but, as many experienced designers have found out, it is almost impossible to predict how a class hierarchy will be used, and thus evolve. Abstract objects can certainly be created, but only for cases in which there is more than one subtype.

Abstract objects are very useful when capturing common behavior, as we shall see in chapter 4. As an example of an abstract object, consider the structure of Figure 3.19. It shows an abstract object, Publication, with two subtypes, Magazine and Newspaper. They may have further subtypes. This structure comes from a model for a business involved in distribution of newspapers and magazines. This model seems reasonable after discussion with domain experts and how they view their business.

In order to make the model more reusable, we might then create an abstract DistributionObject, as shown in Figure 3.20. This object now allows for the

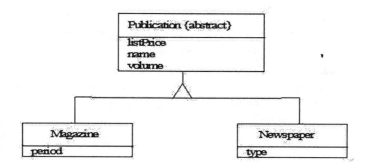

Figure 3.19. Abstract object Publication with subtypes.

model to support the distribution of other objects also, not just newspapers and magazines. As of the time of creating this structure, however, there were no other identified targets for distribution. The domain experts did not see any future in distributing other items. It therefore seems rather unnecessary to create the abstract object DistributionObject when nothing else needs to be distributed other than Publications.

> As a guideline, try to create abstract objects when there is more than one subtype. An abstract object with only one subtype should always be justified, as it may be a solution looking for a problem.

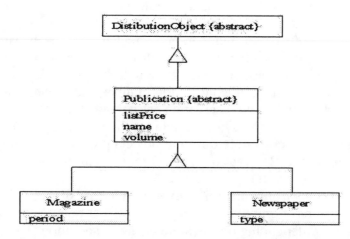

Figure 3.20. Abstract object DistributionObject with subtypes.

One should only model the problem domain as one sees it, and not as one antic- ipates it will look like. Although the goal for creating abstract objects—to make a model that is both amenable to change and extensible—is a valiant one, it is pos- sible to go too far. Before creating abstract objects, one should investigate the types of changes that the model may undergo in the future. What aspects are most likely to change? What aspects are most likely to remain the same? The business- domain experts can be involved in these discussions, as they will have a good understanding of the future of the problem domain being modeled. Trying to model change before it happens is like trying to predict the future.

> Don't create extra objects in the model, in order to anticipate change, unless instances of them exist in the problem domain.

3.4.2.2 Migrating Subtypes

A very powerful modeling construct that is underused is the notion of represent- ing states of an object as objects in themselves. Shlaer–Mellor call these migrating subtypes. D'Souza (1992) calls them states-as-classes. Martin and Odell (1994) call the phenomenon dynamic classification.

Consider a reservation for a hotel. It can go through a number of states—initial booking, confirmed booking, canceled booking—when the guest arrives it becomes an actual stay and when the guest leaves it is a completed stay. It is quite possible to represent these using states in a state model for the Reservation object. In fact this is quite an appealing model, as it naturally models the problem domain.

There are a number of different pieces of information the system will be record- ing, however, depending on the state of the objects. For example, a confirmed reservation has a confirmation number, and an agent who dealt with the confir- mation and a credit-card number used to confirm the reservation. Once the guest arrives that information is no longer useful. Similarly, a canceled reservation has other information of interest: a cancellation number and a date that it was can- celled, for example. A fully paid reservation has a relationship with a Payment that needs to record details of the payment made for the room. All this different infor- mation would normally constitute different objects if it weren't that they were all part of the same object: Reservation. Therefore, one can make them subtypes of Reservation (see Figure 3.21).

You can see that each subtype of Reservation is a state of that object. The alter- native would be to have one Reservation object with a number of attributes that would only be valid depending on the state of the Reservation. The relationships between Reservation and Payment and OccupiedRoom would then be conditional

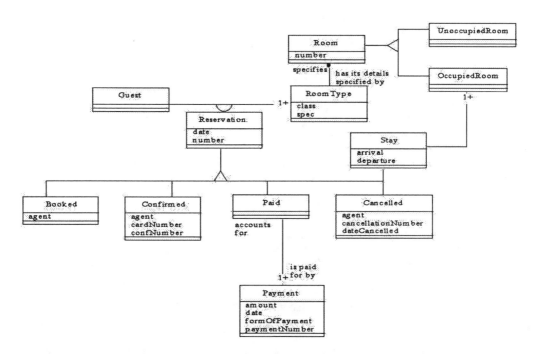

Figure 3.21. Use of migrating subtypes.

based on the state. The figure also shows the use of migrating subtypes for the Room object.[7]

The guideline for determining whether or not to use migrating subtypes is as follows:

> If an object has three or more states, each with at least one additional attribute or with at least one having a different relationship, use migrating subtypes on the object model instead of a using a state model.

3.4.3 Associative Objects or Relationships As Objects

The associative object is a powerful modeling construct, which when used correctly, can capture problem domain knowledge more expressively than some of its alternatives. An associative object represents an object that only exists when

_____

[7]The implementation of migrating subtypes is a topic covered in a later chapter.

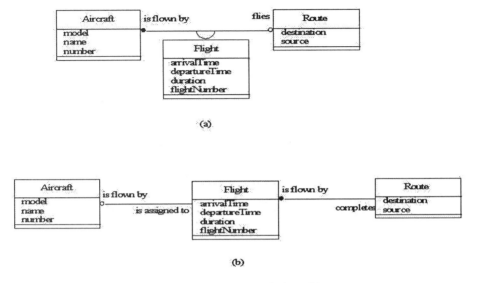

Figure 3.22. Use of associative objects.

instances of two other objects are involved in a relationship. When the two object instances are no longer involved in that relationship then the concept is no longer meaningful. Figure 3.22(a) shows an object Flight that has meaning only when an instance of the relationship between Aircraft and Route exists. Contrast this with the modeling construct of Figure 3.22(b). Both are "correct"and describe the problem domain adequately, but the construct of Figure 3.22(a) is more expressive. It tells us that there will be one object instance of Flight for every relationship between Aircraft and Route. It also tells us that the concept of Flight only makes sense when an Aircraft flies a Route. Figure 3.22(b) does not capture that information.

When do we use associative objects? The question to ask ourselves is: Does an instance of the associative object C only exist when there is an instance of object A and object B involved in a relationship? If so, an associative object may be appropriate.

> Use an associative object when it is instantiated as a result of two other objects participating in a relationship. As a further test, see if the object's attributes are really capturing attributes of the relationship.

An associative object is also useful if the relationship itself has some interesting dynamic properties. Rather than capturing these dynamics through the life cycles of the participating objects, the relationship dynamics can be expressed through the life cycle of the associative object. In some cases there may be more than one instance of the associative object for each relationship.

3.5 Modeling Rules

The static model can also be used to effectively model business rules. A rule can be modeled in a number of different ways: as a relationship in an object information model, as part of the action logic of a state in an object's state model, as the series of steps being executed by a number of objects in a series of object interactions, or in a number of other ways.

We offer the following loose definition for a rule, as stated by Odell (1993a):"A rule is the codification of an organization's policy or condition that must be satisfied in order for the organization to function." Rules are therefore essential to the requirements of a problem. A rule can be modeled in a number of different ways. Simple rules, for example, may be captured as follows:

- They may create a relationship on the object model, for example, a "Landlord leases an apartment to a Tenant" is a rule that can be modeled by a relationship between Landlord and Tenant.

- They may follow a state model of an object, for example, "the tank must be emptied before it is filled" can be modeled through the state model of a tank.

Not all rules can be adequately captured in this way, however. Some are combinations of simpler rules that span objects, relationships, and processes, and others are reflected as constraints on objects and relationships. Rules are often identified in the latter part of analysis, after the objects have already been identified and the relationships formalized. It is therefore usually not possible to incorporate these rules into an existing model merely by simply adding an object or a relationship. Changing the model may also result in the exclusion of some rules. Some other ways to think about rules are required.

In this section we shall look at a few other techniques in modeling rules that afford the object developer some advantages both during analysis and design. We will also describe how to model rules that place constraints across objects and relationships, followed by an examination of how best to capture rules that affect attribute values of an object.

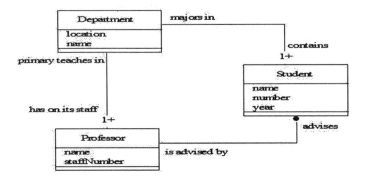

Figure 3.23. Relationship between Student, Department, and Professor.

3.5.1 Rules for Objects and Relationships

To illustrate the type of rule that affects objects and their relationships, consider the object model extract of Figure 3.23. The model represents a possible example of a university or college where students major in a particular subject and must choose a professor as their adviser. It also shows that each professor must belong to one department.

3.5.1.1 Simple Rules

In this triangle of relationships, however, there is a rule that must be adhered to:

> A student must be advised by a professor from the same department in
> which he or she is majoring.

For example, if a student is majoring in Physics, then that student's adviser must be a Professor in the Physics department.

This rule is a key element of our understanding of the domain and should be captured in our analysis. Figure 3.23, as it stands, does not indicate this rule in any way and there are apparently no obvious ways in which to model this constraint. We can of course always add some natural-language description to our model and capture the constraint this way (see Figure 3.24; Odell, 1993b). As the model and the number of rules grow, however, the adding of natural descriptions will soon make the model cluttered and unreadable. Such a scheme for describing rules is limiting.

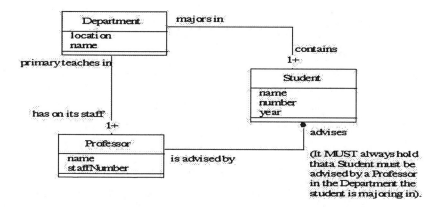

Figure 3.24. Natural-language capture of rules.

An alternative representation is to indicate that the relationship between Department and Student is constrained (see Figure 3.25). In Shlaer–Mellor each relationship is given an identifier, typically *Rn*, where n is a unique number, and this is indicated in the relationship. This is useful, as it can be annotated to show a constraint relationship. In the absence of such an indication within OMT, say, we have found it useful to indicate this on the relationship line. The line is marked as constrained (with <constrained>). This constraint can be documented in the description of the relationship and stored as part of the data dictionary.[8]

For example:

> **Relationship:** Student is advised by Professor; Professor advises Student (1:M).
>
> **Description:** Each student must be advised by one professor. The student may choose which professor he or she wishes to have as his/her adviser. This relationship is constrained, however.
>
> **Rule:** The college policy is such that a student can only be advised by a professor from the department in which the student is majoring.

    Simple rules that pertain to one attribute or one relationship can be captured through some diagrammatic annotation with a suitable description in the data dictionary.

---

[8]An object model is not complete unless textual descriptions of objects, attributes, and relationships have been documented.

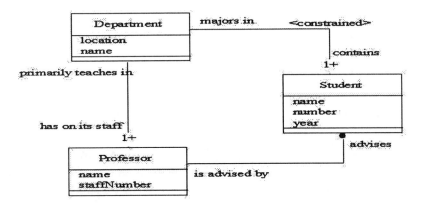

Figure 3.25. **Constrained relationship annotated with constrained.**

This annotation of the object model shows that there is a constraint, but it does not indicate how this constraint is met. Ensuring that the rule is adhered to would be part of the analysis of dynamic behavior. If state models are being used to represent the dynamic behavior of objects, then the rule execution can be codified into the state model of one of the objects participating in the relationship. As a student selects a Professor, it would make sense to do this in the partial state model of the Student object, as shown in Figure 3.26.

We can see from the state model that the logic associated with the rule is in state 2 of Student. The trigger for the firing of this rule is either of the events S2: SelectAdviser or S4: ChangeAdviser.

3.5.1.2 Complex Rules

Let us now consider a more complex rule or set of rules. The rules to be modeled are now:

> *A student must be advised by a professor from the same department in which the student is majoring.*
>
> *No professor can be adviser to more than five students.*
>
> *No professor can be adviser to the same student for more than 1 year.*

Now our rules are more complex, and they also apply to more than just one instance of the relationship. There is also an issue of contention here: How do we cope with the situation in which more than five students wish to be advised by the

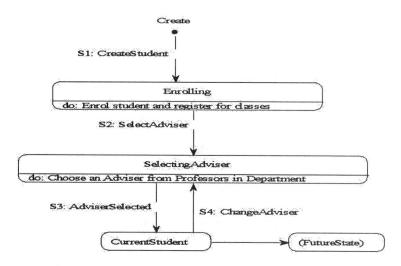

Figure 3.26. State model for selecting an adviser.

same professor? It is no longer possible to have the Student object responsible for managing his or her own choice of adviser, and so the firing of rules must be abstracted elsewhere.

To deal with this situation we could encapsulate these rules within the Professor object. There is contention among Professor objects, however, as they are one of the objects that must be assigned. It is unlikely that any Professor object instance will have sufficient information to be able to adequately assign across all Professor object instances. An alternative is the Department object. The Department object shall encapsulate the policy and decision making logic responsible for ensuring that the above rules for the assignment of students to advisers are met in that particular department. The Department's role in this situation is very similar to the Assigner concept described by Shlaer and Mellor (1990), in which an Assigner object is responsible for handling contention issues in the problem domain.

The rules that the object Department captures can form part of the description of the object and the object may even abstract attributes, such as maxNumStudents and maxAdvisingPeriod, which may be used in enforcing the rules. Our object model only changes by the addition of some attributes to Department.

Let us now suppose that the rules for assigning students to advisers are the same across all departments. Now, the rules should be fired by another object, say a University object. University will be responsible for assigning students to advisers and will contain any attributes necessary for this task. Our object model now becomes that shown in Figure 3.27.

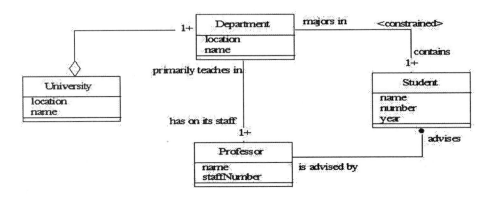

Figure 3.27. Addition of University object to perform some assignments.

Abstracting the rules into an object in this way means that any changes to the rules will be localized to one object. So if next year the rule is that a professor can have at most 10 advisees, this change can easily be incorporated into the model. Fowler (1994) has also recognized the importance of incorporating rules as objects in an analysis.

> Complex rules can be abstracted into an object such that they can be localized. The object that is a natural fit for the rules may already exist. If not, you may need to create one.

The above strategy then begs the question: Is all the data now being placed into individual objects and all the "work" being done by the object executing the rules? This is a possibility that must be addressed by the modelers. There is a balance between centralization and distribution of execution, which must be considered during the modeling process.

3.5.2 Rules for Attributes

Let us now consider the situation in which we have rules that are not defined across objects and relationships, but that seem to be more centered around attributes of the same object.

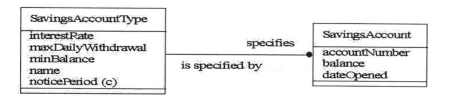

Figure 3.28. Rules varying with instances.

3.5.2.1 One Rule Across All Instances

For example, consider Figure 3.28. This object-information-model extract from a bank shows one SavingsAccountType specifying the policies for many different instances of SavingsAccount. Each object instance of SavingsAccount reflects an actual account opened by an account holder (e.g., Account number 123456, opened by John Smith, etc.), whereas each instance of SavingsAccountType reflects the type of savings account it conforms to (e.g., high interest, easy access, etc.)

The rule we wish to capture here is the dependency between the interestRate of the account type and the noticePeriod (the length of notice an account holder must give before making a withdrawal from the account so as not to lose interest). The rule is:

> If interestRate <= 5% then noticePeriod = 30 days.
>
> If interestRate > 5% and =< 10% then noticePeriod = 60 days.
>
> If interestRate > 10% then noticePeriod = 90 days.

Thus we have a dependency between attributes of SavingsAccountType based on this rule. The value of noticePeriod is constrained by interestRate. One can show this constraint by marking the attribute noticePeriod with a "c" on the object-information model, and by going into more detail in the textual attribute description. The trigger for the execution of this rule is any change in value of interestRate. Therefore, we also need to augment the description of interestRate to indicate that it is a trigger for the firing of the rule. The example descriptions accompanying the object model may be as follows:

> **interestRate:** The rate at which interest is accrued on the type of account. Usually calculated monthly. Note that this attribute is a trigger for Rule 2.

Domain of this attribute: This is a percentage figure.

noticePeriod: The period of notice required to be given by the account holder before making a withdrawal to ensure that no interest is lost. Note that this attribute is constrained by Rule 2.

Domain of this attribute: This is a whole number of days.

> Where one rule applies across multiple instances but is dependent on an attribute of a specification object, capture that rule by annotating the attribute in question.

3.5.2.2 Rules Varying by Instance

The previous rule applies across all instances of AccountType. The situation may be a little more complex, however, such as when the rule can vary from one instance of AccountType to another.

For example, the "Plus" account type may have the following rule:

If interestRate <= 5% then noticePeriod = 0 days.

If interestRate > 5% then noticePeriod = 30 days.

The "Easy Access" account type may have the following rule:

If interestRate is >= 0% then noticePeriod = 0 days.

We can see that the rule is dependent on the name of the account, and varies from one instance to the next. Having the same rule across all instances of SavingsAccountType will not be possible in this situation. Therefore, we shall abstract the rule into a separate object as shown in Figure 3.29.

Each InterestRateTier object will represent a different interestRate and noticePeriod policy. So, if the "Plus"account type has its rule defined as above, and the "Easy Access" and "Instant Access" account types have the same rule, then we shall have three instances of AccountType, and only two instances of InterestRate-Tier. This is because the same instance of the rule can be involved in multiple relationships with account types. As we can see, the object InterestRateTier is treated in the same way as any other object on the object-information model.

As before, the description of SavingsAccountType will indicate which rule the attribute noticePeriod is constrained by, and the attribute interestRate is triggering. The execution of the rule may be handled by the instances of InterestRate-

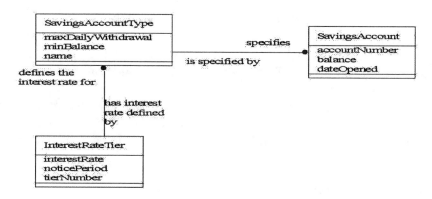

Figure 3.29. Definition of InterestRateTier to capture rules.

Tier. Figure 3.30 shows a possible object-interaction diagram showing how a SavingsAccountType object checks to ensure its rules are met.

The advantages afforded by encapsulating rules as objects is again the localization of change caused by any modifications to an organization's policies. Each InterestRateTier object will be a different rule. So, if the "Plus" account type has its rule defined as above, and the "Easy Access" and "Instant Access" account types have the same rule, then we shall have three instances of AccountType, but only two instances of InterestRateTier. The object InterestRateTier is treated in the same way as any other object in the object-information model.

Complex rules that vary from instance to instance can be captured within an object. Look for rules that vary from one instance of a specification object to another.

Looking ahead to design and implementation, one possible implementation would be to have each rule as a separate instance of a class, in C++ say, with the rule execution being implemented by a member function: fireRule. An attempt to change

Figure 3.30. Ensuring rules are met.

the value of a triggering attribute in a SavingsAccountType object would invoke fireRule of the InterestRateTier object associated with it, passing it any necessary data (e.g., a handle to itself maybe). The InterestRateTier object can then process the rule using the data it received. This InterestRateTier object can execute the same rule for multiple account types.

Following such a scheme segregates the logic of the rule execution from the account type on which it is operating. As an organization's policy changes more frequently than its account types, modifications to the rules can be easily incorporated.

3.6   Testing the Object Model

Our object model reflects our understanding of a problem domain, which is ultimately driven by the requirements. All through the building of this model (and subsequent models) we should be testing our model against the problem domain. To do this we should ask questions of the model, and see if the model reflects the rules and policies of our domain. The questions to be asked can be drawn from typical queries the system will be subject to and also from discussion with domain experts. Consider the object model of Figure 3.31, which describes the documentation control for specifying products.

Using the model it should be possible to test it against the problem domain. What are the answers to the following questions?

What is the minimum number of specification documents needed for a product? The object information model shows that a product must have at least one specification.

How many people contribute to writing a section of a specification? Any number. The model shows that a section is authored by one or more people.

Is it "permitted" to have a product specified by only one user-interface specification, and not have any other types of specifications? Yes. According to the model a product must be specified by one or more specifications. It does not place any constraints on which combination of types of specifications are used.

Given that I have the name of an author, can I find out all the sections of all the specification documents he/she has been involved in writing? Yes. At the moment the model shows that an author can contribute to multiple sections of a specification. So to find out which sections an author has contributed to we can search through the set of instances of SectionVersion. This will tell us which sections an author has written and for which specifications.

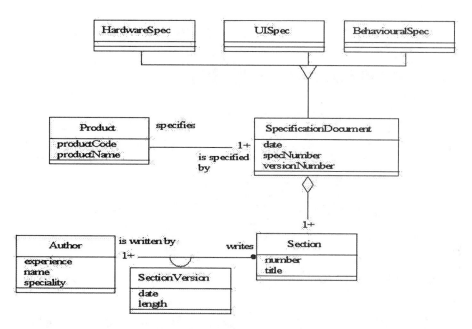

Figure 3.31. Documentation control for product specifications.

In this way, by asking questions of the model we can test our object model, making changes where it does not reflect the rules and policies of the domain.

In order to test your static object model to see if the objects, attributes, and relationships are representative of the problem domain, ask questions of it and see if the answers correctly reflect the rules and policies of the problem domain.

3.7 Evolution of the Object Model

The object model is complete once it contains all the data necessary for meeting the requirements and it provides a satisfactory model of the domain. As we discussed in chapter 1, however, the overall process is iterative, such that it is difficult to say when to pause while working on the object model and when to continue with the dynamic models and vice versa. As we shall see in the next chapter, working on the dynamics more often than not helps in understanding the structure of the problem domain.

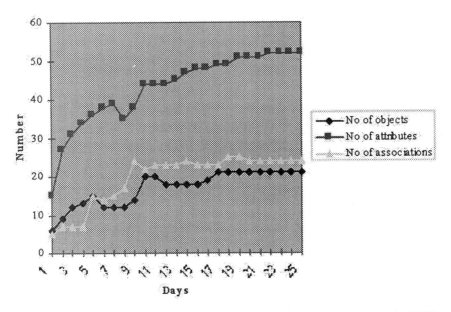

Figure 3.32. Evolution of an object model over time (a small project in 1995).

The above comments notwithstanding, there are some statements we can make about progress with some degree of certainty. In the early parts of modeling, the object model is subject to continual change and revision as the modelers understand the problem domain. The number of changes required daily or weekly will decrease as the problem domain becomes better understood, however. This is a sign of the increasing stability of the model.

Figures 3.32 and 3.33 show the number of changes made to object models over the design period on a couple of projects. Figure 3.32 shows data from a small project from 1995, whereas Figure 3.33 shows data from a much larger project over a longer period of time back in 1994.

We can see from both graphs that the initial parts of the project show an upward trend in objects and attributes and then relationships as the more obvious candidates are identified. All curves eventually level off as the number of changes decreases and the model becomes more stable. The modeling of dynamics is not shown on these graphs.

It is interesting to note that Figure 3.32 shows data from one project and this means that the project's individual characteristics are visible. We can see that during the third week (days 10–15) there is a consolidation and the number of objects, attributes, and relationships drop. This was because of a merging of what had pre-

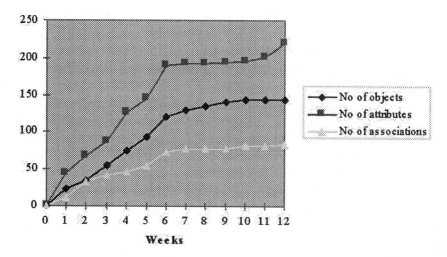

Figure 3.33. Evolution of three object models over time (large project in 1994).

viously been separate objects, and this is followed by an increase in objects because of the creation of abstract objects as the domain became better understood. Similar changes occurred in the individual domains of the project in, but these changes seem to be masked because of the effect of the other models (each model went through the same stages at different times).

These graphs capture common evolution paths across projects. Although the scale may change from one project to another, the shape of the graph should be very similar.

3.8 Summary

In this chapter I have tried to provide some insights into the processes and techniques behind analyzing and modeling system structure. One of the most powerful ways of partitioning a system is by domains. We looked at this method and found that there are two ways in which it is possible to work with domains—either by constructing a separate object model for each domain or by constructing a single model showing multiple domains.

We also examined how to find domains through domain-storming and examining whether domains are "real" or not through a series of qualifier questions. Domain experts play a crucial role in any object-modeling activity, and we examined the ways in which experts can be involved in the process: through interviews, reviews of models, or most preferably through active participation in constructing models.

In finding objects and attributes, object blitzing was introduced as a means of throwing out candidate objects, and looking for different categories of objects is also a useful process. Some of the concerns about employing use cases for finding objects were raised, especially as they have the potential to lead to more functional objects somewhat prematurely. Different ways of modeling attributes and deciding on whether or not to include attributes in object definition were also presented.

In modeling relationships we examined how to label relationships, when to subtype, and we also looked at the different forms of subtyping available to the modeler. Some strategies for assisting in the use of subtyping were provided.

We have also shown that business rules can be modeled in an object-oriented analysis in a number of ways. The decision of how best to represent the rule—as a constraint on a relationship or attribute, or to abstract it as an object—varies from case to case. However, we offered some basic guidance:

- Simple rules are best expressed as constraints to attributes and can be checked easily at design time.

- Rules that affect multiple attributes in one object can be contained within that object.

- More complex rules and those varying from instance to instance can be abstracted as an object outright.

We also provided some data on how an object model evolves over time on small and large projects and discussed the common patterns across systems.

References

Awad, M., Kuusela, J., & Ziegler, J. (1996). *Object-Oriented Technology for Real-Time Systems*. Englewood Cliffs, NJ: Prentice-Hall.

Balcer, M. (1993). How to conduct an object blitz. *Objects and Projects*, 1(*1*).

Beck, K., & Cunningham, W. (1989). A laboratory for teaching object-oriented thinking. In *Proceedings of ACM Conference on Object-Oriented Programming: Systems, Languages and Applications 1989*. New Orleans: ACM Press.

Berard, E. (1995). Be careful with use cases. *The Object Agency* white paper.

Booch, G. (1994). *Object-Oriented Design With Applications, Second Edition.* Redwood City, CA: Benjamin Cummings.

Coad, P., & Yourdon, E. (1990). *Object-Oriented Analysis.* Englewood Cliffs, NJ: Prentice-Hall.

Coad, P., North, D., & Mayfield, M. (1994). *Object Models—Strategies, Patterns and Applications.* Englewood Cliffs, NJ: Prentice-Hall.

Cook, S., & Daniels, J. (1994). *Designing Object Systems: Object-Oriented Modeling With Syntropy.* Hempstead, UK: Prentice-Hall, Hemel.

Coleman, D., Arnold, P., Bodoff, S., Dollin, C., Gilchrist, H., Hayes, F., & Jeremaes, P. (1993). *Object-Oriented Development: The Fusion Method.* Englewood Cliffs, NJ: Prentice-Hall.

D'Souza, D. (1992). Desmond's paper on states as classes. *Journal of Object-Oriented Programming, 5(5),* x.

Firesmith, D. (1995). Use cases: The pros and cons. *Report on Object Analysis and Design, 2(2),* 2–6.

Fowler M. (1994, May). Lessons in OO analysis and design from three commercial projects. In *Proceedings of Object Development Experiences, UNICOM Seminars,* London, UK.

Gossain, S. (1990). *Object-Oriented Development and Reuse.* Doctoral thesis, University of Essex, Essex, UK.

Gossain, S. (1994, May 17–18). Practical techniques for object-oriented analysis. In *Proceedings of Object Development Experiences, UNICOM Seminars,* London, UK.

Jacobson I., Christerson, M., Jonsson, P., & Overgaard, G. (1992). *Object-Oriented Software Engineering: A Use-Case-Driven Approach.* Reading, MA: Addison-Wesley.

Martin, J., & Odell, J. (1994). *Object-Oriented Methods: A Foundation.* Englewood Cliffs, NJ: Prentice-Hall.

McGraw, K. L., &. Harbison-Briggs, K. (1989). *Knowledge Acquisition: Principles and Guidelines.* Englewood Cliffs, NJ: Prentice-Hall.

Odell, J. (1993a). Specifying requirements using rules. *Journal of Object-Oriented Programming, 6(2),* 20–24.

Odell, J.(1993b). Using business rules with diagrams. *Journal of Object-Oriented Programming, 6(4),* 10–17.

Rumbaugh, J., Blaha, M., Premerlani, W., Eddy, F., & Lorensen, W. (1991). *Object-Oriented Modeling and Design.* Englewood Cliffs, NJ: Prentice-Hall.

Shlaer, S., & Mellor, S. J. (1988). *Object-Oriented Systems Analysis: Modeling the World in Data.* Englewood Cliffs, NJ: Prentice-Hall.

Shlaer, S., & Mellor, S. J. (1990). *Object Lifecycles: Modeling the World in States.* Englewood Cliffs, NJ: Prentice-Hall.

Shlaer, S., & Mellor, S. (1993a). The Shlaer–Mellor method. *Project Technology Technical Report.*

Shlaer, S., & Mellor, S. (1993b). A deeper look . . . at the transition from analysis to design. *Journal of Object-Oriented Programming*, 5(*9*),16–21.

Shlaer, S., & Mellor, S. (1994). A deeper look . . . at testing and integration, part 1. *Journal of Object-Oriented Programming*, 5(*9*), 8–14.

CHAPTER 4

MODELING SYSTEM BEHAVIOR

I N ADDITION TO MODELING the structure of a domain, its behavioral properties must also be modeled. In doing so, modelers need to understand the stimuli that a system is subject to and the behavior expected of the system in response to those events. Using techniques from a number of different methods, the practicalities of identifying and modeling system behavior are presented in this chapter.

Too often, analysts are content with modeling communication between objects as simple point-to-point messaging, typically in a synchronous fashion. The importance of differentiating between asynchronous and synchronous messaging at the early stages of analysis is presented, as is the need for a richer set of communication mechanisms to model system behavior: broadcast, publish–subscribe, and request–reply.

Analysts are often confused about the use of state models: their appropriateness, deciding which objects need state models, or in fact whether state models are even suitable are issues of concern. A discussion of the trade-offs regarding when and what type of state models to use is also included in this chapter.

It is often necessary to iterate back to the structure model during and after the behavior modeling, but it is not always apparent when, or under what circumstances this should be done. Usually there is some uncertainty about the level of changes needed and how to determine which changes are necessary and appropriate. These issues are addressed in this chapter.

4.1 System Behavior

In chapter 2 we examined the overall process of object-oriented development. Looking at Figure 2.7, we can see that the rapid object modeling activity indicates that both the modeling of system structure and system behavior are possible after the initial system partitioning. It was explained that deciding which area to pursue—structure or behavior—depends on a number of factors:

- *The experience of the team:* Although this factor is by no means the ideal way in deciding how to proceed, it can be a contributing factor. All things being equal, the level of comfort of the team in either exploring structure first or examining behavior should be taken into consideration.

- *The method being used:* Some methods propose looking at one aspect before the other. For example, Rubin and Goldberg's (1992) object behavior analysis (OBA) proposes the examination of system behavior prior to object identification, as does Objectory (Jacobson, Christerson, Jonsson, & Overgaard, 1992), whereas OMT and Shlaer and Mellor propose modeling system structure first.

- *The comfort of the experts:* As mentioned in the previous chapter, some experts prefer to think about system behavior and functionality as opposed to the main objects of the domain. Begin with behavior if this is the case, and abstract objects from the definition of use cases and scenarios as you proceed. Construct an object model in the background, and present it to the experts for feedback.

The above factors notwithstanding, modeling is an iterative and nonlinear activity and often requires iterating between modeling structure and modeling behavior. Often, changes in one may require reconsideration of the other.

In modeling system behavior the ultimate goal is to arrive at a specification of the objects of the system and how they interact to provide the required functionality. In doing so, there are a number of techniques that can be utilized:

- Prototypes can be used to provide a means of exploring system behavior and deciding how objects should interact. Small prototypes can be developed within relatively short time frames to test ideas and assess suitability of certain constructs. For example, Smalltalk can be used in rapid time frames to explore how the user will work with the system and also how the objects will interact to provide the functionality. Smalltalk interfaces can take time to develop, but the speed with which "model" behavior can be developed is not in question.

- Object-interaction diagrams, as described by Jacobson et al. (1992), describe a series of message sequences that provides the system behavior required in response to a system event.

- An object-communication model (OCM) is a summary of all the communication between objects in a subsystem or domain. This comes from Shlaer and Mellor (1990), and is used to provide a summary view of communication between objects in a domain and thus indicates dependencies between objects.

- An object-instance diagram is a snapshot in time of object instances, their attributes and values, and the relationships those instances are participating in at that time. These diagrams are especially useful in validating correctness of the structure model and also in ensuring that an object's behavior is correct over a period of time. The use of these is described in chapter 8.

- State models are used in many methods to specify the behavior of an object over time. State models have their roots in finite-state automata theory, and are especially useful in real-time and embedded systems, although they are also very effective in modeling the state changes of objects within business systems.

The above is not an exhaustive list of work-products created during system behavior modeling, as there are a number of intermediate work-products, such as scenario tables and event schemas, which are also created. The above list provides a set of more formal work-products, however.

Before getting into the detail of the strategies it is perhaps worth describing the interrelationships between the work-products used in modeling behavior.

For large systems there will be a number of business processes that need to be used as inputs to the behavior-modeling process. Figure 4.1 shows how the model of one of the future business processes requires a number of system interactions to support it. These system interactions can be described in a high-level scenario table showing the inputs, the expected system behavior, and the outputs. The same system interactions may be present across business processes. Typically, we find that a portion of the business-process flow can be used to provide input to defining the use cases for the system. These use cases are then utilized to provide focus on the system interaction needed to support the use case.

Each use case is described in detail and is used to create scenarios that are used for modeling system behavior. Each scenario is modeled by one or more object-

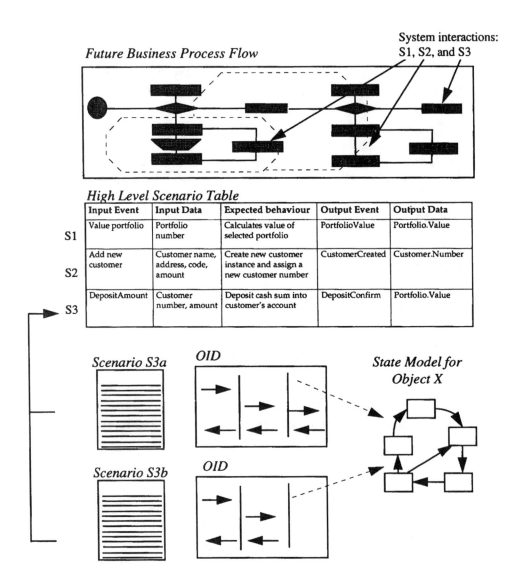

Figure 4.1. The relationships between major work-products when modeling behavior.

interaction diagrams depending on its complexity. Figure 4.1 shows two possible object-interaction diagrams for scenario S3. Each object-interaction diagram shows a different aspect of system behavior catering to differences in data, error conditions, and so on; object-interaction diagrams are then used to create state models for objects, where appropriate, which in turn may provide feedback to the object-interaction diagrams and the object-structure model.

4.2 Working with Scenarios

As mentioned in the previous section, business-process models are an ideal way of identifying system behavior through the events that the system must respond to. Activities within a process that require system interaction are identified, and from these it is possible to create a high-level scenario table to describe the interaction with the system. This table can be constructed with the help of domain experts and users, as described in chapter 3. An example of a scenario table is shown in Table 4.1.

> Use future business-process models to identify system usage and create use cases. From these use cases one can define a number of scenarios to model using object-interaction diagrams.

The table is then used to drill down into the expected system behavior to model how the objects interact to provide the system functionality. The table can be used throughout the modeling process, and more detail can be added as the modeling proceeds. For example, the exact input data for an event may be unclear during the early stages of analysis, but later, as the details are fleshed out, this informa-

Table 4.1 THREE ENTRIES IN A HIGH-LEVEL SCENARIO TABLE

Input Event	Input Data	Expected System Behavior	Output Event	Output Data
ValuePortfolio	Client name, Portfolio	Calculate value of client portfolio	PortfolioValue	Value of portfolio
OpenAccount	Client details, initial amount	Opens a new account for a client	AccountCreated	Number of new account
CloseAccount	Account number	Closes an account for a client	AccountClosed	Amount to be paid out

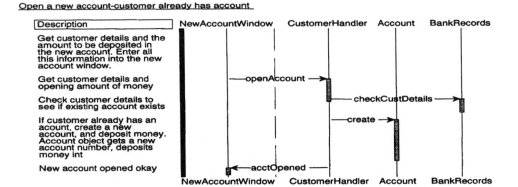

Figure 4.2. Object-interaction diagram for the opening-a-new-account scenario.

tion can be added to the table, so that it forms a detailed description of the domain's interaction with the outside world.

Each row in the table should be used to provide different expected system behavior. Where the same input event with the same data may result in different expected system behavior, perhaps on the system being in different states, then a new line should be created for the different behavior.

Looking at the second row in Table 4.1, we can see that the entry in the third column, expected system behavior, is to open a new account for a client. The input data are the details of the client and the initial amount to be deposited. The system processing for opening a new account can be written in textual form and then used as a basis for modeling the system behavior for that functionality. An object-interaction diagram can then be created for this scenario (opening an account) as presented in Figure 4.2.

A number of object-interaction diagrams can be created for each scenario, taking into account error conditions, different data, and so on. So for the scenario described in Figure 4.2, there can be several more object-interaction diagrams created: one for the situation in which the customer does not have an adequate credit rating and is refused a new account, and one for the customer who does not have an account already and whose credit rating is successfully checked. There may be other scenarios depending on the case in hand.

The business-process analysis may not provide all the instances for system behavior. It is therefore important to also be able to identify system events and their behavior through other means. Through working with users and domain experts it is possible to find other events—asking questions of users and experts such as when instances are created, understanding when instances are deleted or changed, taking users through tasks, identifying how they interact with the system—these activities will help to identify other events. As before, a high-level scenario table can be created, and each scenario subsequently modeled through object interactions.

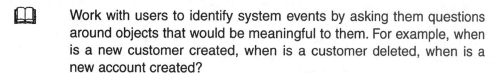 Work with users to identify system events by asking them questions around objects that would be meaningful to them. For example, when is a new customer created, when is a customer deleted, when is a new account created?

As we mentioned in chapter 2, there are a number of issues surrounding the use of use cases and scenarios.

4.3 Object-Interaction Modeling

Object interaction is typically initiated by some stimulus from an external source, such as a user-initiated event (e.g., mouse click, key press), or a temporal event (e.g., polling, time-out), or perhaps an event generated due to some system state or hardware change (e.g., communication failure, alarm). The collection of interactions across all objects provides the system's behavior. Because these interactions are fundamental to the execution of the system, the design of object interactions is a very important part of object-oriented development.

Most object-oriented methods have some way of representing interactions. Typically, the sequence of messages sent between objects on receipt of some event is captured diagrammatically. Each incoming event typically leads to a sequence of messages sent between objects. The diagrams used by some of the various methods are as follows:

- Booch (1994) and Syntropy (Cook & Daniels 1994) use mechanisms.
- Jacobson uses interaction diagrams.
- Rumbaugh (1991) uses event traces.
- Shlaer-Mellor (1990) use a thread-of-control chart.

In each of the above strategies an object can be considered an autonomous agent that sends and receives messages performing some item of work on receipt of a message. An object has some notion of responsibility that drives its behavior within the system. This viewpoint is representative of that held by users of nearly all object-oriented methods. Therefore, although exact details may differ from one method to another, the above types of diagrams are roughly equivalent in their purpose, and their ability to capture object interaction.

In most object-modeling approaches, interobject communication is considered to be a synchronous send-and-receive mechanism; that is, an object A sends a message to an object B, waits for a result while B does some task on receipt of the message, and once B has completed its task the result is returned back to A, and A continues its tasks. While B is performing its task, it may utilize other objects in doing so, and would communicate with them using a similar communication protocol, as with object A.

The above communication paradigm is a result of the object communication typically found in object-oriented programming languages such as C++ and Smalltalk. In those environments, a synchronous form of communication (as described above) is the norm. In modeling problem domains, however, such a form of communication carried through to the object modeling can limit our thinking and our approach to problem solving, resulting in models that are less than optimal and perhaps preclude us from certain design options.

Many problem domains have tasks that can be conducted in parallel. For example, when calculating the complete value of a financial portfolio, it should be possible to calculate the price of each item in the portfolio independently. Using synchronous send-and-receive mechanisms for object communication would mean that the pricing of each item in the portfolio would have to be calculated sequentially. Synchronous communication will therefore limit our modeling as we would lose the possible parallelism in mapping the real world to a set of models. The modeling of system behavior should not be limited to synchronous communication. Asynchronous communication should also be considered.

Very few methods recognize the importance of distinguishing between synchronous and asynchronous communication, and therefore do not propose that this distinction be considered during modeling. It is my experience, however, that the distinction between asynchronous and synchronous communication is a very important one in object-oriented modeling. It needs to be addressed very thoroughly if we are to build systems that accurately reflect the problem domain and also have acceptable performance characteristics.

4.3.1 Synchronous Communication

A communication between two objects whereby the object sending the message, A, relinquishes control to the object receiving the message, B, until object B relin-

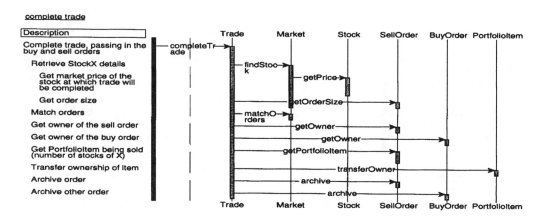

Figure 4.3. An example of synchronous communication.

quishes that control; this is an example of a synchronous communication in implementation and would be a member-function invocation in C++.

An example of object interaction using synchronous communication is shown in Figure 4.3. In this scenario the user wishes to complete a trade on some financial instruments. We can see that the interaction across the object is sequential and that there is a certain order in which things are done. The final price cannot be computed until the current market price for that stock has been determined. Only then can the broker's commission and the tax on the trade be calculated (not shown in the figure). The interaction between the objects is synchronous because control is passed from one object to another as each message is sent. There is a prescribed sequence in which the operations will always be carried out.

4.3.2 Asynchronous Communication

A communication between two objects whereby an object A sends a message to object B, object A continues its processing while object B, on receipt of this message, also begins processing, is an example of asynchronous communication. Asynchronous communication in an implementation environment may be some form of interprocess communication.

Figure 4.4 documents the interaction among objects when a user selects a stock item about which she or he wishes to obtain some more detailed information (e.g., company profile, recent trading history, etc.). This query could be rather extensive, and accuracy and volume of information is more important than the speed of the

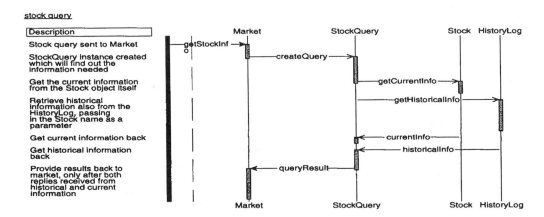

Figure 4.4. An example of asynchronous communication.

query, especially as it may require access to multiple third-party data warehouses. While the query is being executed, the user expects to be able to carry out other trades and dealings if desired, and then be informed of the query result once the information is available.

In the scenario detailed in Figure 4.4, the firing of the query requires a sequence of interactions that are not dependent on the resulting interactions being carried out in a particular order. So, the results of getCurrentInfo and getHistoryInfo from the objects Stock and HistoryLog, respectively may return in any order. There may even be other messages sent by the StockQuery object to other objects to retrieve data in executing the query. The interaction between objects here is asynchronous.

We can see from Figures 4.3 and 4.4 that we have used different notation to distinguish between synchronous and asynchronous communication. The difference is required because we find that a scenario often contains both forms of communication. In Figure 4.4, the asynchronous messages are denoted by a thinner arrowhead, and the synchronous ones by a filled-in arrowhead. So we have decided that the createQuery message and all subsequent messages will be *asynchronous*, whereas the messages to the Market object will be *synchronous*.

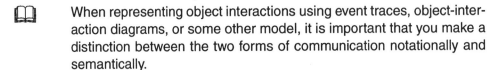 When representing object interactions using event traces, object-interaction diagrams, or some other model, it is important that you make a distinction between the two forms of communication notationally and semantically.

4.3.3 Modeling Interactions

The distinction between synchronous and asynchronous communication is important for a number of reasons:

1. The distinction fundamentally affects the way in which the group of cooperating objects interact in providing the required functionality. This is important because we are aiming to provide an accurate picture of how our objects will communicate based on the constraints of our problem domain. If there are no ordering constraints in the problem domain, then there is no need to introduce any into the models.[1]

2. The distinction can assist us in understanding how the design may best be mapped into a suitable architecture. The set of interactions will have to be mapped to a physical architecture at some point. Capturing the communication differences will help in determining which is the best architecture for our problem.

3. Asynchronous and synchronous communication may be implemented differently, if need be, for architectural reasons.

We need to consider the type of communication between objects up front during the design of object interactions and not try to retro-fit them after the design has been completed and the objects must be distributed across the physical environment. When designing object interactions, responsibilities have to have been assigned to objects and a control style for the application has to have been determined, as we described earlier (Wirfs-Brock, 1994). Once this has been decided, even loosely, the interaction between the objects should be addressed. Typically this is done on a case-by-case basis in which each scenario is designed giving consideration to responsibilities of objects and the control structure of the application.

Each message between objects in each scenario should be examined to see whether asynchronous or synchronous communication would be most suitable. To do this the following questions should be asked for each scenario:

> *Does the sequence of tasks need to be carried out in a defined order?* If so, then a series of synchronous messages between the objects would be the best technique to use. The specified sequence of tasks can thus be guaranteed to be preserved.

---

[1] If ordering is introduced into the models for some reason, then the rationale for doing so *must* be captured in the documentation for that particular scenario.

Are there tasks that can be performed concurrently? If there are, then asynchronous messages may best be used to initiate these separate tasks. These tasks may of course be performed using synchronous communication among other objects themselves if necessary.

4.3.4 Some Considerations

For each scenario being modeled consider the following:

1. *The semantics of the interaction*—what is the intention behind the scenario, what are the inputs and outputs?

2. *The roles and responsibilities of the objects involved*—consider what each object knows, and what each object must know from other objects.

3. *What behavior needs to be processed serially?*—look at the steps without the objects and identify what needs to be done and in what order.

4. *What behavior can potentially be carried out in parallel?*—when assigning behavior, consider taking advantage of the natural concurrency of the problem.

📖   When modeling interactions, do not just consider synchronous communication between objects, but also give consideration to the natural parallelism in the steps needed to perform a task. Model using asynchronous communication where necessary.

There are a number of important observations that are worth noting when designing object interactions.

- Addressing the issues of communication must be done right at the outset of designing the object interaction, that is, when you first look at a scenario in detail.

- It is important to note that even though the interaction may be designed as being asynchronous, it does not need to be implemented that way if the architecture does not require it. A set of asynchronous messages and resulting interactions can be implemented *serially* as a set of synchronous invocations in a particular order. If the ordering was not important when considering the scenario during design, then the order is not important at implementation time.

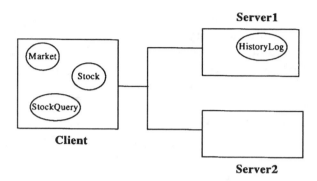

Figure 4.5. Possible object-distribution architecture.

- Because synchronous and asynchronous messages can be found in the same scenario, it may be that when it comes to implementation some of these asynchronous messages may be *implemented* asynchronously, whereas others in the same scenario may be implemented synchronously. The outcome depends on the architecture used, for example, where the objects lie in a distributed environment.

4.3.5 A Brief Discussion on Moving to Implementation

From the above discussion it is clear that there is more than one way to implement a scenario. We shall touch briefly on moving to implementation here, as it helps to understand the value of considering asynchronous and synchronous communication during modeling. We shall return to implementation issues in a later chapter.

When moving from design to implementation there are numerous issues that need to be addressed that depend on the deployment environment to be used. I shall be addressing these issues in a later chapter, but for the purposes of this discussion let us look at two possible implementations of the scenario described in Figure 4.4.

The most straightforward is to place all objects inside one process of the operating system. If we had designed the interaction such that all objects communicated synchronously, all messages could be implemented, in C++ say, as simple member-function invocations.

An alternative implementation is to distribute the objects as shown in Figure 4.5. If we had designed the interaction to be synchronous, we would still have the same sequence of messages except that the performance would be affected by the extra overhead in network traffic communicating between client and server. The user would also have to wait for the query to complete before she or he could continue.

Using the object-interaction diagram of Figure 4.4, however, we can still place the HistoryLog on a remote server, and also may have other servers located elsewhere for other searches. The query can be executed concurrently while the user can continue with his or work.

We can see from this rather simple example that the mixture of asynchronous and synchronous communication is a more flexible way of designing object interactions because it can more readily be mapped to a variety of architectures.

The natural concurrency of the application has been used to the fullest effect. Concurrency should not be forced into a scenario if it does not exist. The asynchronous communication was not forced in the example shown in Figure 4.5, but was a natural choice for the current scenario.

4.4   Assigning Roles, Responsibilities, and Organizing Flow of Control

In designing object interactions when distributing behavior across the objects, each is assigned some responsibilities in performing the tasks required, and in doing this will define roles for each object. Deciding on the responsibilities for each object can be difficult.

Using scenario exploration as part of a JAD (joint application design) workshop is an extremely rapid way of arriving at a first cut of responsibilities. Interactive group activities such as CRC (class–responsibility–collaborator) card sessions or workshops in which participants can work together on flip-charts or a whiteboard with a designated scribe and moderator, can be used to arrive at this initial set of responsibilities.

In previous JAD sessions where scenarios were identified and documented in a high-level scenario table (see Table 4.1), responsibilities were addressed at a high level, but now they need to be documented in considerably more detail. Whereas previously we may only have been interested in scenarios from an external perspective (input event, expected system behavior, domain response), we are now interested in each scenario from an internal perspective, that is, we wish to model how the expected system behavior will be provided by the objects.

For each scenario we need to determine which objects are involved in providing the expected functionality, assign roles and responsibilities to each object, and identify the data accessed in each scenario. For each scenario it is necessary to do the following:

1. Identify the input event. An input event, such as a keyboard entry, may be a solicited event based on a previous scenario, or it may be an unsolicited one, such as an alarm notification. In either case it is useful to treat the arrival of each event as a separate scenario.

2. Identify any input data arriving with the event.

3. Assign an object to deal with the initial event.

4. Form a thread of communication among objects involved, giving each object a responsibility in providing the functionality expected of this scenario and any output event. Each of these objects will do some processing in order to meet its responsibility.

5. Identify the information each object uses to perform its task in this scenario. If some information is required and it does not exist in the present model, then attribute(s) may need to be added to some object(s) to allow for this. Note that each object only has access to its own attributes, the data of instances to which it has relationships (albeit indirectly), and the data it received through communication with other objects.

For item 4 above, the difficulty can be in trying to create a thread of communication among objects. To help in getting started, we have used CRC workshops quite successfully. These small cards provide a very powerful means of bringing people together to arrive at a common understanding of the problem area so they can arrive at a common solution (Beck & Cunningham, 1989).

In such workshops it is important to have approximately six to eight people from different backgrounds. Typically, for information systems, we have found a good mix to be two to three users, two domain experts, one business person, one facilitator, and one scribe. For real-time and embedded systems there is typically a greater focus on domain expertise, as there is often no human user.

The goal is to go through a number of different scenarios and assign roles and responsibilities for each object in the scenario, and also to identify communication across objects. A useful technique is for the scribe to create object-interaction diagrams as the scenarios are being "acted" out by the participants. This will help in documenting more accurately the results of the session. Wilkinson (1995) provides some useful ideas behind extending the use of CRC cards.

> A CRC workshop requires a mix of people. Sessions with six to eight people work best. An example is two to three users, two domain experts, one business person, one facilitator, and one scribe. Keep sessions to 2–3 hours with a target number of scenarios to go through.

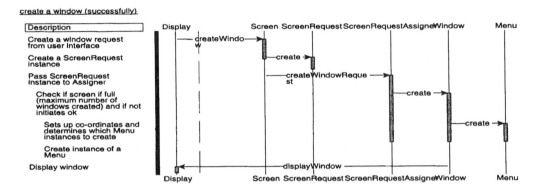

Figure 4.6. Object-interaction diagram for creating a window successfully.

CRC cards are not always the best form of exploring system behavior. I have run CRC workshops in which the participants did not like the process or the concepts at all, and were much happier working on a whiteboard in more detail and creating object-interaction diagrams. For very complex systems, it is easy to get lost in a CRC session, as the number of cards and objects participating can become overwhelming. It is important therefore to be able to reject their usage if it is not proving valuable and move on to a different technique for exploring behavior, such as creating object-interaction diagrams on a whiteboard as described. The use of stereotypes as described by Wirfs-Brock (1994) is a very useful technique for trying to categorize objects as you go through defining their responsibilities in the system.

📖   When the use of CRC cards seems too simple, and not detailed enough, for the the scenarios being explored, use a whiteboard to work with the participants to create detailed object interaction diagrams. These will not be correct the first time around, but will begin to delve into the detail that CRC cards can miss.

Figures 4.6 and 4.7 show two possible object-interaction diagrams for a simple user-interface domain. The rules and policies of this domain are such that windows may not overlap because valuable information may be missed, and so there is an object responsible for determining whether or not windows may be created or opened, and if so, where they must be situated. This object is a ScreenRequestAssigner. This object then issues the create/open commands to the windows. The two scenarios show successful opening and closing of windows. Failed attempts at opening and closing windows will be documented in alternative scenarios.

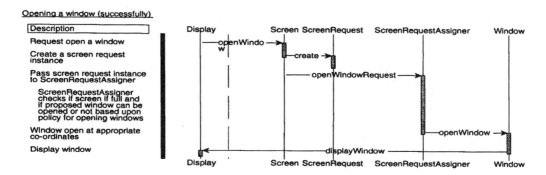

Figure 4.7. Object-interaction diagram for opening a window successfully.

Only the message names are shown on the object-interaction diagram here, the data dictionary of the CASE (computer-aided system engineering) tool being used will provide details of the message data for each message in the domain. In fact, the amount of information shown in the description column for each scenario is a matter of preference and modelers should use whatever they feel comfortable with. It is advisable, however, to go down to enough level of detail so that the behavior of each object on receipt of a message is clear enough to be able to be written into pseudo-code without any further explanation. Once again, this is a place where conventions and standards should be adopted and adhered to.

> When creating object-interaction diagrams, go into enough detail such that each task an object performs on receipt of a message can be written in pseudo-code. Doing so means that the level of detail is adequate for implementation and also ensures that the behavior required is understood sufficiently to not be open to interpretation.

Across all scenarios:

- Ensure that roles and responsibilities of objects are consistent. Layering objects can be used to good effect here. Those objects that have greater "knowledge" of the intentions of the domain are placed on the left-hand side of the object-interaction diagram (e.g., ScreenRequestAssigner), and those with restricted knowledge are placed nearer the right (e.g., Menu). In the scenarios of Figures 4.6 and 4.7, we observe that the Screen object is a high-level object that receives all initial requests. In contrast, the responsibilities of Window and Menu are simply to open, close, and display their contents.

📖   Use object-interaction diagrams to provide a graphic indication of the "knowledge" an object has through its positioning on the diagram.

- Add attributes to objects where necessary. In addressing the functionality of each scenario it may become apparent that some objects do not have sufficient information to complete the task at hand. Add attributes where necessary, making sure that the guidelines on placement of attributes are followed.
- Add objects if necessary. It may turn out that additional objects are required, and if so they should be added to the structure model as appropriate.

Also, it pays to localize policy information in certain objects when appropriate. One example is the localization of domain policy regarding some practice in one object. If this knowledge is embedded in a single object (across all its states or perhaps in a single state), then the effect of any changes in policy will only affect this object. All other objects will remain unaffected as their interface to the object concerned can remain unchanged. A fine example of this is the use of Assigner objects in Shlaer and Mellor OOA (object-oriented analysis; 1990) to deal with issues of contention. In its simplest form the Assigner state model localizes policy for dealing with contention into one of its states. In the previous object-interaction diagrams, ScreenRequestAssigner localizes the policy of deciding whether or not windows can be opened and created.

📖   Hold object-interaction diagram checkpoints and reviews regularly. Go through each object-interaction diagram, explore responsibilities of objects, cross-reference and update documentation to record them. Ensure that they are consistent across objects. Use of stereotypes can help in categorizing them.

The collection of object-interaction diagrams will provide the basis for a preliminary draft of the OCM (Shlaer & Mellor, 1990) summarizing all the communication between the objects. An event list should be produced describing each event, the data carried with it, the sender, and the receiver.

Once a preliminary version of the OCM has been created, work can begin on the state models of the individual objects. When creating state models start with those objects that have the most limited responsibility, as these will be easier to do. The events received by each object as drawn on the OCM will provide a description of the interface to the object, the collection of tasks that the object must perform will provide the rough behavior of that object. These can then be used in creating the state model. After work has started on the state models, there will probably be

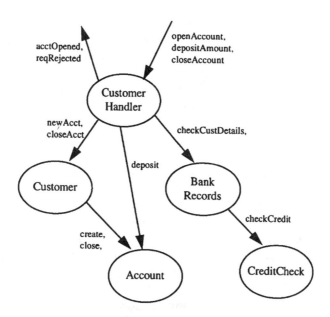

Figure 4.8. An object-communication model.

changes required on the OCM and the object-interaction diagrams as new insights are gained, and as more detail is required to describe the required functionality. The OCM and object-interaction diagrams should be updated as the state models are created, and should reflect the current status of the models. State models are addressed in more detail in section 4.6.

The number of object-interaction diagrams in a small domain can get large very quickly, and for larger domains the number of object-interaction diagrams will easily increase beyond the 100–200 range. The sheer number of object-interaction diagrams can mean that the big picture of communication across objects can sometimes be missed. This big picture is important as it provides a way of ensuring there is consistency across the object-interaction diagrams, in the roles and responsibilities and communication paths. The OCM is a very useful tool for examining the communication across a number of objects independent of the particular scenarios.[2] This is useful as it allows the modelers to identify anomalies and "odd" communication paths between objects. For example, the OCM of Figure 4.8 shows one

---

[2] The OCM is also a very useful tool during design and when partitioning the objects across a distributed architecture, as we shall see in later chapters.

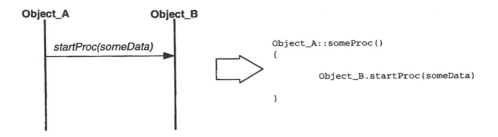

Figure 4.9. Mapping from an object-interaction diagram to some code.

message between CustomerHandler and Account. This communication could be inconsistent with the responsibilities of CustomerHandler if its responsibility is to handle all customer issues outside this domain. Therefore the scenario(s) in which this message is sent should be reexamined to see if it needs to be remodeled.

Use the OCM to identify communication between objects that is inconsistent with the larger picture. Do this on a regular basis, say every week during the modeling of behavior.

4.5   Messaging Mechanisms

Objects send messages to each other to communicate and initiate some activity. In simple object-oriented programming languages this communication is mapped to a single method invocation. Figure 4.9 shows this mapping to a single C++ member-function invocation. This point-to-point communication, which is either synchronous or asynchronous, is perfectly suitable for some applications. For many of today's complex, distributed applications, however, a richer set of messaging mechanisms is needed.

These mechanisms are: broadcast, publish/subscribe, and request/reply. These will be described, with examples of when to use them in practice. In my experience, a combination of these forms of messaging mechanisms is needed to provide a flexible, configurable object solution.

4.5.1 Broadcast

This type of messaging is used when an object sends a message to all other objects without directing the message at any objects. In fact whether the message is received or not is of no concern to the sender. It has performed its responsibility by sending the broadcast message. This message is a like a radio signal being broadcast in a certain region, and anyone interested in the music can tune-in if he or she wishes.

In a modeling setting, this mechanism is useful when an object wishes to inform others of some information that would be of wide interest, such as a hardware state change, or some pending system failure, or some price change in the market index.

Broadcasts need not be systemwide. For example, an object in the alarm domain (a service domain in Shlaer & Mellor's categorization) would wish to inform all the client domains about an alarm. A broadcast message to all objects outside the domain is necessary. The broadcast region in this case is all objects outside the domain.

An object such as a CompanyStock, however, whose price may fall below some threshold may wish to broadcast a pending crash in its price to those objects in the same domain. The broadcast region here is then all objects in the same domain.

> Broadcast messages need not be system wide. The notion of broadcast regions can be very useful if an object needs to broadcast messages only to a limited set of objects, perhaps those in the same subsystem or perhaps in all other domains other than that in which the sender resides.

Broadcast communication is essentially asynchronous, as the sender continues processing, if necessary, after the message has been sent. There is no form of synchronous broadcast. Figure 4.10 shows a broadcast message being sent by the object CompanyStock when its price reaches a certain threshold. The message priceChange sends the new price of the stock as data. There is no method support for broadcast messages so a symbol had to be developed: The arrow with the circle indicates a broadcast message.

There are a number of issues that surround the use of broadcast messages. They should be used very rarely, as they can potentially result in a vast number of messages being sent to other objects every time a broadcast message is sent.

There are no implementation infrastructures that automatically provide a broadcast facility. Therefore they need to be mapped manually or by the architec-

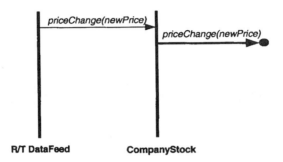

Figure 4.10. Broadcast messaging.

ture being used. If mapped directly to an implementation, such as one broadcast being implemented as a message to every instance within the broadcast area, this can potentially lead to performance problems. Broadcast messages should be used for very important messages only, such as potential system failure problems, alarms, and so on.

> Use broadcast messaging very rarely in your design. Broadcasts are excellent for modeling the handling of system failures, major events, and alarm conditions.

4.5.2 Publish — Subscribe

This messaging mechanism can be considered a specialized form of broadcast. A sender sends a number of messages to receivers who have registered an interest in receiving the message. For example, a CompanyStock object representing some company stock may publish its price at the end of every day, or perhaps every time it changes. Requesters may subscribe to this service if they are interested in receiving such information. The sending object accepts subscribe messages and then publishes results to subscribers.

The sender (publisher) need not know the identities of the requesters (subscribers) as it is merely fulfilling its responsibility by fulfilling the subscriptions. Uses of the subscription form of communication are similar to those of broadcast, but need not be used for such severe situations. Here the limit on the number of messages sent is dependent on the number of subscriptions.

An example is shown in Figure 4.11, where two separate portfolios subscribe to price changes in the CompanyStock object, which publishes the price change when it receives the price change information from the R/T DataFeed object.

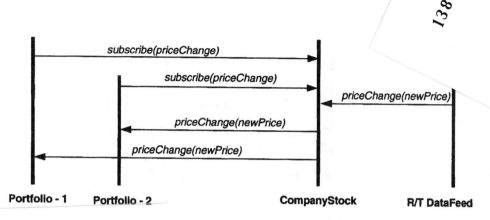

Figure 4.11. Publish—subscribe messaging.

The figure shows a subscribe message sent for each piece of information required. This may not necessarily be the case, as there are a number of different types of subscription. Therefore, using the financial example again, an object could subscribe to: the price of a specific stock crossing some threshold, all price changes in some stock, all price changes in all stocks in a particular market sector, or to a stock reaching a particular price. The exact nature of the publish–subscribe protocol really depends on the nature of the problem domain and the information needed.

 Consider using publish–subscribe messaging mechanism when a number of different objects are interested in receiving some pieces of information from another object asynchronously.

The model–view–controller pattern used so successfully in Smalltalk implementations (Goldberg & Robson, 1983) uses publish–subscribe between the model and the view. Views subscribe to changes in models, and once a model changes in some way it publishes those changes to the list of subscribing views that it maintains. The Teknekron Information Bus uses this mechanism to great effect in providing financial information to interested parties.

The advantage of publish–subscribe over broadcast is that if mapped directly to an implementation mechanism it potentially improves performance because it can limit the number of messages being sent. If the subscription becomes high, however, one should consider broadcast messages instead.

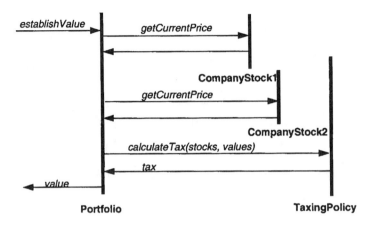

Figure 4.12. Request—reply messaging mechanism.

4.5.3 Request — Reply

The request–reply form of messaging is the one that will be the most familiar to readers. An object requests some information from another by sending a message and receives a reply. It can of course be directly mapped to a member-function invocation in a programming language. Figure 4.12 shows the Portfolio object requesting and receiving information from three other objects: CompanyStock1, CompanyStock2, and TaxingPolicy.

In the modeling of this mechanism, however, we can add a couple of additional features that provide for a richer form of communication. It is possible to have one request with numerous replies, as opposed to a single reply. This would require asynchronous communication. It is also possible to have one request serviced by no reply, again requiring asynchronous communication or some time-out in the absence of a reply with some synchronous communication.

> Consider expanding conventional request–reply messaging mechanism to allow for requests with numerous replies and requests with asynchronous replies. Doing so will ensure that the most flexible solution will be possible.

4.6   Modeling the Internal Behavior of Objects

Object interactions describe the behavior across objects. Objects may also undergo internal behavioral changes over time. State modeling is a valuable means of describing the internal behavior of objects, and is probably the most popular mechanism for doing so, within object-oriented methods.

State models have their roots in finite-state automata and have been exceptionally useful in real-time and embedded systems. They are also especially useful in capturing the life cycles of business concepts in nonreal-time systems, however. Objects such as Account, Trade, Transaction, and Sale can have their life histories captured through the use of state models just as effectively.

State models are not necessary for every object in the domain, and some methodologies today do not recognize the need for state models in business systems. The issues are not whether or not they are appropriate, but how one knows when they are useful techniques to use that can model some aspect of the domain usefully.

> If you have just started using object technology, use simple state models for your objects. For example, Moore state machines. As you become more experienced you can begin to use more advanced features, such as nested states, and actions on multiple parts of the model (transitions, entry, exit, etc.)

Some object methods use single-level state models, such as the Moore state models described earlier, whereas others use hierarchical state models, primarily derived from Harel's (1987) work on statecharts. There are arguments both for and against each type of state model, my personal preference is for the single-level state model. Although the hierarchical state models can be more expressive, I have found that a state model of this form for a single object can be decomposed into a few separate single-level state models for a few objects. This can be done without losing any expression from the original form, and in many cases the hierarchical state model has unnecessarily combined a number of concepts together, thus losing some of the representation of the problem domain.

The exact type of state model you use is not as important as agreeing on a set of conventions, rules, and guidelines to follow. I have seen a number of serious problems occur later in the development life cycle resulting from misinterpretations of state models during reviews because of the complexity of some of the models. In such cases the notation and semantics of the models were not clearly defined across the teams and as a result there was much confusion.

> Whichever form of state model you choose for your modeling process, a key issue is to agree on the semantics of the constructs so that there is no room for ambiguity or vagueness in the models. Consistency and completeness are the keys to successful modeling.

When we build state models for individual objects, we usually have some of the events it will receive and send already defined from the set of object-interactions diagrams, and these may have been collated on a preliminary OCM. From the collection of object-interaction diagrams we have a list of descriptions of the object's expected behavior based on its role and responsibilities. From these it is possible to create the state model. Typically a state-transition diagram is created first, as it provides a visual and comprehensible version of the object's state model. This if followed by use of the more formal (and less readable) state-transition table to construct the definitive state model for that object.

We can start with received events and show the transition to expected states and the behavior in each of those states based on our descriptions from the object-communication scenarios. We need to describe the action associated with that state in detail and ensure that all of the necessary data required is available. It is important to be aware of the data available to an instance when it is in a particular state. If data is required from another object then we have two possibilities: send an event to the other instance and request the data that will arrive by a received event, or use a synchronous access to the attribute of the other object.[3] In each case this object must have some means of identifying the other instance: Usually this is possible because it is involved in a relationship with the other object, or because it received the handle through event data of the received event. Deciding which to use depends on the needs of the problem domain (see Figure 4.13).

One way in which the analyst can construct the state diagram is to focus on each event and identify the state it will transition to on receipt of that event. In this way a collection of transition-state pairs are constructed (there may be more than one transition-state pair per event). Once all known events have been accounted for, the transition-state pairs can be linked together based on the typical sequence of states the object would go through.

State-model construction is an iterative process, as it may be necessary to cre-

---

[3] Although the synchronous access is "direct" during analysis, it does not violate encapsulation because there is a number of different ways that it can be implemented. A member function invocation in C++ or a message in Smalltalk are two possibilities. Addressing implementation issues such as these is not a concern at analysis time. The distinction between synchronous data access and asynchronous event sending is, however.

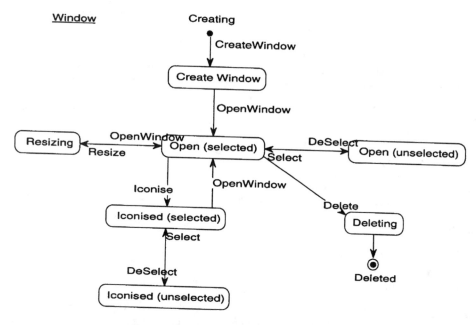

Figure 4.13. A state model for Window.

ate a few more states and subject the instance to more events. As the state model is constructed modelers should check the following:

- Have all states been defined?
- Can the object exit from all nonfinal states?
- Have we considered the possibility of receiving all events in each state?

Once the analysts feel that the state-transition diagrams have reached some degree of stability, the next step is to create a state-transition table for each object. The state-transition table provides a formal definition of the state model for the object, and requires one to consider each event being received in each state. Shlaer and Mellor (1990) recommend three possible entries in any cell of the table: the number of the next state, "can't happen" and "event ignored" (see Table 4.2). It is important that the logic of the diagram is not copied directly onto the table, as this may duplicate any errors on the diagram. One must assess the contents of each cell for the table, ensuring that it has been adequately considered rather than assuming the diagram is correct. Also, a diagram may often seem to be complete, but it is often the case that not until the table is constructed does it become apparent

Table 4.2 STATE-TRANSITIONS

	Create Window	Open Window	Resize	Select	Deselect	Delete	Iconize
1. Create Window	can't happen	2	can't happen	can't happen	can't happen	can't happen	can't happen
2. Open (selected)	can't happen	can't happen	4	ignore	3	6	5
3. Open (unselected)	can't happen	can't happen	can't happen	2	can't happen	can't happen	can't happen
4. Resizing	can't happen	2	can't happen	can't happen	can't happen	can't happen	can't happen
5. Iconized (selected)	can't happen	2	can't happen	can't happen	7	6	can't happen
6. Deleting	can't happen	can't happen	can't happen	can't happen	can't happen	can't happen	can't happen
7. Iconized (unselected)	can't happen	can't happen	can't happen	5	can't happen	can't happen	can't happen

that the model is, in fact, incomplete. Considering every event in each state and then attempting to fill in the table also means that any unclear or vague policies can be questioned and clarified.

Create a state-transition table for every object with a state model. Doing so will ensure that all possible events have been considered for all possible states, and thus reduces the possibility of error.

Until now the modeling has been interested in expected behavior, but later in the modeling process as the majority of scenarios have been modeled, the models must deal with unexpected behavior (i.e., what happens when an event is received in a state where the table entry should be a "can't happen" ?!). In doing so each "can't-happen" entry must be reexamined and changed to either an event ignored or a transition to another state. Error-handling states may need to be created to deal with unexpected behavior, and these will need to be added to the table as necessary. This process continues until we are sure that this object can satisfactorily deal with the receipt of any event in any state. Only then can we say that the state model is complete.

4.7 Iterating Back to the Static-Object Model

As the modeling of system behavior proceeds, it is inevitable that there will be changes required to the static-object model if it was created earlier, or there will be ideas for assisting in the creation of the object structure model. There are a number of types of changes that can be possible when iterating back to the static-object model. Some of the more minor ones include rearranging relationships and subtype–supertype structures in the light of clearer understanding.

Some of the more major changes include the following:

- adding a new higher level object
- adding new attributes
- adding abstract objects
- removing items

4.7.1 Adding New Higher Level Objects

Modeling behavior through object-interaction diagrams may provide further insight into the classification of objects and identify some commonalities that were not apparent earlier in the modeling activity, when considering structure alone. Often we find that two unlikely objects can share a common supertype that only becomes evident after some behavior modeling.

Consider the two subtype–supertype structures of Figures 4.14 and 4.15. The diagrams show portions of a structure model that were created for a bank's Accounts and Mortgage structures. After modeling the behavior of the various instances it became apparent that there was some common behavior that tied Account together with Mortgage. Although they had different operation names because they were being modeled by different people, and were in different business processes, it was identified that the checkSales operation of Account was very similar to the viewSuccess operation of Mortgage. It also soon emerged from discussion with domain experts that the behavior of examineHistory for Account and checkHistory for Mortgage were also very similar.

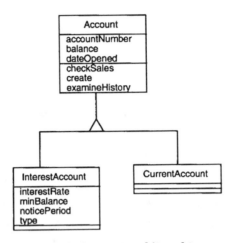

Figure 4.14. Account and its subtypes.

As a result of these semantic commonalities and after further investigation, it was decided that a new object, Product, would be required that captured the common behavior across Account and Mortgage structures. This object also had two attributes: productCode and productName, which were applicable to all bank products, including accounts and mortgages.

It is important to note that in Figure 4.16 adding Product was valuable in capturing behavior across the two types of structures because it addressed further requirements of the domain, namely, analyzing and examining bank products. It is exceptionally important to ensure that the addition of a new object is not purely a short-cut for capturing common behavior but is also semantically correct, and therefore, justified.

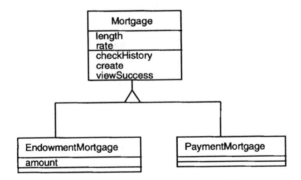

Figure 4.15. Mortgage and its subtypes.

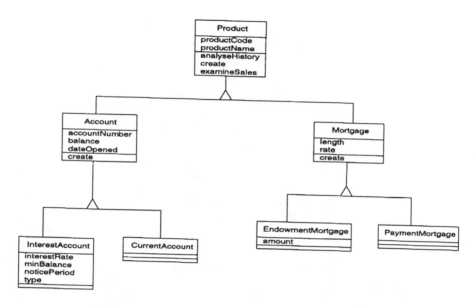

Figure 4.16. Revised structure with a new supertype.

During the object-interaction-diagram reviews, examine the semantics across objects to see if there are potential commonalities across objects that can be taken advantage of through the use of new higher level objects.

4.7.2 Adding New Attributes

This rather simple change is one of the most common and arises from a lack of information on the part of an object when performing some task. When an object receives a message it has direct access to its own attributes and the data passed with the message. It can also request data from the objects with which it has relationships and any objects whose references were passed in with the message. If this information is insufficient to perform the task at hand, then the missing information must be obtained. This can be done by adding attributes to the object in question, or to other objects, and ensuring that the information is made available to the object that needs it.

4.7.3 Adding Abstract Objects

One of the most powerful means of expression in an object-structure model is through the use of abstract objects to capture a high-level understanding of the problem domain. Many experienced modelers say that in order to understand a domain best, they first look at the high-level abstract objects before diving into the detail of the concrete objects on a model.

As with adding new high-level objects after modeling system behavior, abstract objects are the result of insights into the problem domain that become possible only after gaining a deeper understanding of that domain. Abstract objects do not participate in object-interaction diagrams because instances of them are never created, but their subtypes do participate in them. It is difficult to arrive at a strategy for finding abstract objects because abstract objects are not found, but rather created.

A useful practice is to take a step back from the work that is going on in the project and try to understand at a higher level some of the concepts that are participating in the scenarios and are present in the domain. Look for common behavior, common structure, or some combination of the two that brings concepts together. It is my experience that sometimes these objects can be found early in the process. Abstract objects provide a high-level understanding of the domain and this can be used as a means to find them early on.

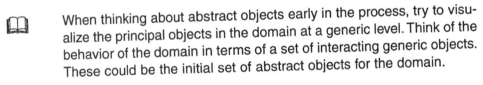 When thinking about abstract objects early in the process, try to visualize the principal objects in the domain at a generic level. Think of the behavior of the domain in terms of a set of interacting generic objects. These could be the initial set of abstract objects for the domain.

4.7.4 Removing Items

Items can also be removed from an object-structure model. Attributes that remain unused should be removed from the model. Objects that seem useful in structure modeling but then remain unused should also be removed.

4.8 Model Validation and Verification

Object models may be tested both statically and dynamically for the purpose of verifying the modeling. Static checking can be achieved by reviewing models to ensure their semantic correctness by asking questions of the model during the building of the object-structure model. This was discussed in some detail in the previous chapter. Some CASE tools today will check the models against the rules of construction corresponding to the method.

It is dynamic checking, however, which confirms that the models exhibit the desired behavior. Given that the functionality of the system is provided by a number of interacting objects, an environment that allows simulation of these instances can provide considerable assistance in verifying the modeling, there are now CASE tools that support this dynamic simulation.

The object-interaction diagrams developed earlier can be used to provide the source for test cases for the analysis verification.[4] A systematic, exhaustive simulation of the models based on the scenarios will ensure that the analysis models provide the correct functionality, and will also provide an excellent means of tracing the requirements through to the analysis models.[5]

The steps for "executing" scenarios in order to ensure that they are modeled correctly are as follows:

1. Identify the input event and the initial conditions. Initial conditions are described by a high-level statement of the state of the domain.
2. Identify the objects involved and their expected states.[6]
3. Identify the attributes that will influence the outcome of the scenario (determinant attributes), and assign a value to each determinant attribute based on the expected state of the object and the initial conditions.
4. Document the expected outcome of the scenario.
5. Execute the scenario.
6. Check the values of each determinant attribute and the state of each object that participated.

    Define test cases from the scenarios identified in the early parts of analysis. Use the high-level-scenario table to step through each

---

[4] The scenarios can also provide excellent sources for test cases for the code after the implementation has been completed.

[5] They will also provide an excellent means of traceability from requirements to the analysis models to the code.

[6] It will be necessary to have several simulations of the same input event, but with different initial conditions. Each should be treated as a separate scenario.

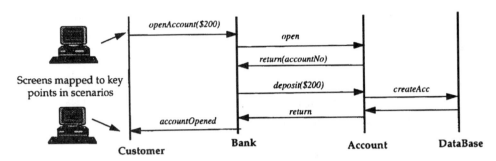

Figure 4.17. Mapping the screens to the scenarios.

object-interaction diagram to ensure correct behavior. Also, prescribe sample test data for the test cases based on the different scenarios.

Following the above guidelines for each scenario means that an analysis can be exhaustively tested using either CASE tools or manually through the use of thread-of-control charts. Using CASE tools that support simulation, the scenarios can be profiled (based on expected values for processing and data access) and modified if necessary to allow improved expected performance.

One useful technique in gaining an understanding of the big picture behind the behavior of the system is to map screen designs to the interactions that objects will perform in response to the events generated by the user interface. As mentioned in chapter 2, the process of screen design can generate sample screens, and working with users will identify information and events being sent by the user interface to the system. These events, which trigger object-interaction diagrams, can be used to tie together screens with the object-interaction diagrams.

As Figure 4.17 shows, a screen flow can be mapped to inputs and outputs from object-interaction diagrams. This can be repeated for multiple flows and object-interaction diagrams to provide a picture of how the system will be used and also how the objects interact to provide the required functionality. Although this is not a rigorous means of verifying the models by any means, it does serve to strengthen understanding of the domain through a graphic depiction of the models and their interaction.

In gaining the big picture of the models and presenting the results to those not directly involved in the models, tie the user-interface windows to the object-interaction diagrams. Pictures of the windows corresponding to object-interaction diagrams can then be presented graphically to all concerned.

4.9 Summary

In this chapter some strategies for modeling system behavior have been presented. These strategies have allowed us to examine the relationships among the different models. The models most commonly used in describing system behavior are a high-level scenario table, object-interaction diagrams, and state models. Prototypes and object instance diagrams can also be used.

Scenarios from use cases are a major thread that runs throughout the modeling of both structure and behavior. The future business-process models, if applicable in the system context, can be used to identify use cases and scenarios. If not appropriate, events can be identified from instance creation, deletion, and so on.

In this chapter the importance of giving due consideration to the type of communication between objects when designing object interactions has been emphasized—namely, synchronous and asynchronous communication. This consideration clearly affords the designer some advantages:

- Giving consideration to each communication for each scenario means that each scenario is analyzed in considerable detail. This means the analyst/designer is more likely to understand the fundamental issues of the problem.

- The natural concurrency of the application can be exploited to the fullest by giving careful consideration to the type of communication used.

- Maximum flexibility in implementation is also provided as asynchronous messages can easily be serialized into a string of synchronous communication. It is much more difficult to map synchronous messages to an asynchronous communication at implementation.

- These communications do not preclude certain types of architecture.

We also examined the usefulness of different messaging mechanisms:

- *Broadcast communication*, which is useful for low-usage, high-priority messages.

- *Publish–subscribe*, in which a number of different objects are interested in receiving some pieces of information from another object or set of objects.

- *Request–reply*, which is the most familiar form to many. This can be expanded to include asynchronous communication and one or many replies.

We also explored some of the instances in which it is appropriate to iterate back to the structure model, which include adding new attributes and objects and removing items from the structure model.

References

Booch, G. (1994). *Object-Oriented Design With Applications (2nd ed.)*. Redwood City, CA: Benjamin-Cummings.

Coleman, D., Arnold, P., Bodoff, S., Dollin, C., Gilchrist, H., Hayes, F., & Jeremaes, P. (1993). *Object-Oriented Development: The Fusion Method*. Englewood Cliffs, NJ: Prentice-Hall.

Cook, S., & Daniels, J. (1994). *Designing Object Systems: Object-Oriented Modeling With Syntropy*. Hempstead, UK: Prentice-Hall, Hemel.

Goldberg, A., & Robson, D. (1983). *Smalltalk-80: The Language and Its Implementation*. Reading, MA: Addison-Wesley.

Harel, D. (1987). Statecharts: A visual formalism for complex systems. *Science of Computer Programming*, 8, 231–274.

Jacobson, I., Christerson, M., Jonsson, P., & Overgaard G. (1992). *Object-Oriented Software Engineering: A Use-Case-Driven Approach*. Reading, MA: Addison-Wesley.

Rubin, K., & Goldberg, A. (1992). Object behavior analysis. *Communications of the ACM*, 35(*9*), 48–62.

Rumbaugh, J., Blaha, M., Premerlani, W., Eddy, F., & Lorensen, W. (1991). *Object-Oriented Modeling and Design*. Englewood Cliffs, NJ: Prentice-Hall.

Shlaer, S., & Mellor, S. J. (1990). *Object Lifecycles: Modeling the World in States*. Englewood Cliffs, NJ: Prentice-Hall.

Wilkinson, N. (1995). *Using CRC Cards: An Informal Approach to Object-Oriented Development*. New York: SIGS Books.

Wirfs-Brock, R. (1994). Characterizing your application's control style. *Report on Object Analysis and Design*, 1(*3*), 47–49, 51.

CHAPTER 5

ARCHITECTURE

T HE IMPORTANCE OF system architecture is becoming increasingly more apparent as today's systems become more complex and more distributed. Objects have undoubtedly made a large contribution to the growth in architectural awareness within the software community.

This chapter examines the increasingly important role played by the architect on a system-development team. The success of an object-based system can often be dependent on constructing a sound architecture that provides the right balance of vision with pragmatism. This is a task led by the architect.

This chapter also presents the notion of service-based architectures: This is a means of structuring enterprise solutions that are aimed at crossing application boundaries such that business solutions are constructed using reusable services rather than stove-pipe applications. The cornerstone of the service-based architecture is the service object. It is presented along with some strategies around creating reusable services.

A four-layer architecture that uses the principles of service-based architectures is also presented. This extension of existing three- and four-tier architecture models is especially useful for business applications but variants of it can be used for real-time applications.

5.1 Architectural Awareness

Objects allow us to describe, discuss, and reason about software systems in a way that previous paradigms never have. This is not to say that architecture was not an issue until objects became more widespread, but the increasing attention being given to objects has been in line with the increasing awareness of architecture as an important aspect of system construction. It is the unique packaging of data and behavior into objects that allows us to discuss the architectural issues surrounding system construction. The notion of encapsulation, which is central to the essence of objects also helps; thinking of subsystems and systems as objects allows us to apply such object concepts to larger grain concepts also.

Although it is true that objects are the building blocks of a system, merely following an object-oriented analysis-and-design method does not guarantee a "good" architecture.[1] There are numerous issues, both technical and organizational, that must be addressed in producing a system architecture.

Anderson (1995, p. 25) points out that architectures are the "structuring paradigms, styles and patterns that describe, or make up, our software systems." This fairly broad definition applies to any type of system and encompasses a number of different approaches to describing system architecture, from static structural descriptions of software topology to more dynamic descriptions of module interaction.

There are a number of different types and levels of architecture. One can consider architecture at the low level of two instances interacting, or at a high level of subsystem or system interaction across application spaces. At this higher level one can also consider subsystems and systems as interacting objects (i.e., black boxes). Thus we make the distinction between microarchitectures (typically at the class/object level) and macroarchitecture (at the class cluster or subsystem level).

An object-oriented architecture typically expresses its structural properties through class hierarchies and relationships usually found within class clusters (Booch, 1996; Gossain, 1990a). The dynamic aspect of an object architecture emerges from the series of object interactions used to provide system functionality.

An architecture is not necessarily confined to one application space but can span applications, business solutions, and can now even cover the enterprise. There are numerous efforts being undertaken in organizations to bring together

---

[1] Booch (1996) has recently been stating the importance of addressing architecture during the design process, such that he seems to have incorporated such processes into his method framework.

disparate systems under a single architectural vision in order to provide a uniform structure and technical vision across the business.

5.2 The Architect

An increasingly unique and important role emerging within organizations is that of the software or system architect. This role used to be consumed as part of the development team and, with functional design, was a fairly incongruous concept. Now, as architectural awareness increases, it is recognized as a separate role that drives the development process at a number of different levels. Organizations now assign this role to experienced designers who are adept at balancing sometimes idealized system concepts with real-world practical constraints. The architect's value is in capturing, representing, and communicating these concepts to others in the organization.

5.2.1 The Role of the Architect

Booch (1996) has recognized the importance of the architect in an object-development team such that he has outlined the following responsibilities:

- define the software architecture
- maintain the architectural integrity of the software
- assess technical risks relative to software design
- consult with various design, implementation, integration and quality-assurance teams
- assist marketing regarding future product definition

The need for liaison with marketing as defined above is naturally only applicable to product-development organizations, but the other points are certainly core responsibilities of an architect. I would also add the following two responsibilities:

- Promote the sharing of common architectural constructs and frameworks across projects within an organization.
- Identify and nurture future software architects.

My experience leads me to believe that an architect has to have a unique set of skills in performing these activities. They are as follows:

- An architect needs to be able to balance the practical experience and ideas of system building with a vision. Architecting a system to be a pure implementation of an architectural vision is unlikely to be practical, and hence has less chance of succeeding. The architect is responsible for describing a system with a sound architecture that provides the right blend of vision and pragmatism. Managing this balance, and understanding the trade-offs that need to be made is a skilled task.

- Good listening and communicating skills are essential prerequisites for an architect. An architect is responsible for creating and getting in place a vision of the structure of the software and must therefore be able to understand the needs of the system as expressed by other team members. The architect must also be able to express to the team how the architecture will support those needs and at the same time provide possibilities for extension and growth. The architect also needs to be able to communicate the system architecture to a diverse set of audiences, such as business executives, managers, developers, marketing, and so on. Such communication must cater to the needs of each audience by describing the architecture in a language they understand.

- Probably the key requirement for an architect is experience in designing and implementing systems, preferably of a diverse nature. MIS (Management Information Systems) system architects could learn a lot from real-time system architects and vice versa. The breadth of experience of an architect is nearly as crucial as the depth.

- As well as being experienced in design and implementation, an architect must be well versed in systems he or she had no experience in constructing. Well-structured object-oriented systems, and systems generally, have common recurring patterns that emerge. These patterns, be they structural and/or dynamic, lead to an understanding and characterization of a specific architecture, such that the same principles can be reused in a totally different system.

- An architect is unlikely to be responsible for designing the microarchitectures of a system, but he/she must be able to understand and allow for the use of such structures within the larger framework of the system. This can be enhanced by abstracting microarchitecture principles to provide structure to the larger system.

- Depending on the organizational culture and the size of projects implemented, an architect may be involved in more than one project. This provides opportunities for sharing concepts, designs, and code across projects and the architect must have visibility within the organization and across projects to be able to recognize commonality.

- An architecture must be implemented. The team looks to the architect for providing direction on how to map the architectural vision to a practical implementation. This requires a deep understanding of programming languages, implementation support structures (such as ORBs [object request broker], DCE [distributed computing environment], etc.), and integration tools. Again, experience in system building is essential.

- An ability to approach problems in a considered and thoughtful manner is also necessary. This is probably the most difficult to assess because it seems to rely on some skills that can be difficult to capture in isolation. An architect needs to have a general problem-solving capability. For example, does she or he make a reasonable survey of the problem domain before jumping? Does she/he consider breadth as well as depth? Does she/he apply an identifiable methodology to isolating an issue? O'Connor (Feb. 24, 1995, personal communication) has pointed out that observing behavior while going through a problem-solving exercise is often enlightening as to their readiness for architectural issues.

We can see from the above list that an architect must be almost superhuman! Although the above list presents a diverse set of skills, they are essential in that they allow the architect to be well-placed in an organization so as to provide the maximum benefit of object orientation. Not many organizations have people who can meet the above criteria. Those that do, must value them.

5.2.2 Architects in the Organization

From the large number of companies that have embarked on object-oriented initiatives, many claim to have "hit the wall" because they are not reaping the much-touted enterprise-wide benefits from objects for which they had hoped. Some of the problems they are facing are a proliferation of objects without any real control of their use, incompatible systems that need to interact, no long-term direction for system evolution, no real reuse of architectural concepts across projects, lack of synergy between the business and the software objects, and poor performance due to lack of thought in partitioning in an object-oriented client–server system.

Aside from the possibility that their expectations may have been too high in the short term, one of the principal reasons they are disappointed is that these organizations have been too heavily focused on objects at the lowest level. Often this has manifested itself as a focus on the programming-level constructs of classes as opposed to the larger grain notion of class clusters and subsystems, which provide for a more leveraged exploitation of objects. An architect, or group of architects in the organization would have been ideally placed to identify some of the potential opportunities available from making the transition to objects. Fortunately, those organizations that adopted object orientation early on are now beginning to realize the value of architects and are growing people into those roles and/or hiring them from wherever they can.

The limiting factor in the growth of many organizations' ability to successfully adopt object orientation for the long term is more directly applicable to the lack of experienced software architects than to the technological failings of the paradigm. Object systems place an emphasis on architecture more so than any other structuring paradigm. Therefore, object-oriented architects are more significant than one would initially expect.

5.3   Architecture Design

The process by which architects design architectures and establish the broader framework in which a system is created is often seen as a process of "magic." I have seen organizations where the architect claims to have woken up in the middle of the night and had a "Eureka" experience in which the architecture came to her in a flash. Unfortunately, such chance occurrences cannot be relied on. A more methodical approach to architecture design is preferable.

Figure 5.1 illustrates a process of architecture design that has been abstracted from a number of projects in numerous domains. The square boxes represent stages of the process, the ovals represent inputs, and the boxes with shadows represent work products.

In chapter 2 we described the overall development process and some of the major activities associated with it. The term "Architectural Design" was used (in Figure 2.9) as a means of describing the process by which the architecture is designed. Figure 5.2 shows the relationship between the architecture-design process and the broader development process outlined in chapter 2,[2] by placing the diagrams side by side such that time increases as we read down the diagram. The arrows between the two diagrams indicate information flow from one process to the other.

---

[2]Note that this figure only shows part of the development process.

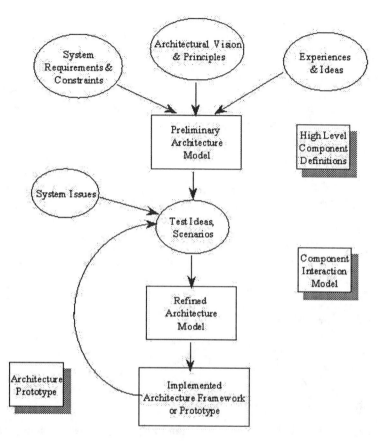

Figure 5.1. Architectural-design process.

Looking at Figure 5.1, we can see that the preliminary architecture model is created early on in the development process. This preliminary architecture is an initial high-level model that will undergo testing and refinement as the requirements become clear. It may have even been replaced totally by the time the object modeling is completed. We also observe that the User-Interface-Design process provides scenarios and examples as input to the testing of the architecture model to ensure that it can support the functionality required.

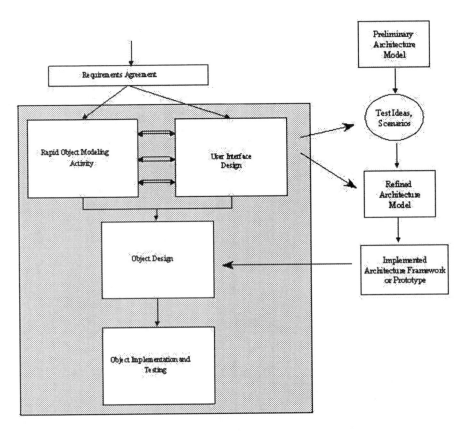

Figure 5.2 Architectural design in relation to the larger development process.

5.3.1 Preliminary Architecture Model

Perhaps the most difficult aspect of architecture design is reaching the first stage—the preliminary architecture model. This initial model is usually a high-level sketch of some of the major architecture pieces and their interaction or responsibilities. There are three primary inputs into the process of creating the preliminary model:

- *Architectural vision and principles.* One of the major inputs to the archi-tecture design process is probably the most difficult to describe. Central to an architecture is a vision. As described earlier, the architect needs to be a visionary who is able to communicate this vision to his/her colleagues. This vision must then be translated to a pragmatic framework for the system at hand, while adhering to the principles of the architecture.

Architectural principles are those basic ideas and guidelines that are used as a basis for reasoning about the architecture. They are usually high-level statements that provide guidance for the architects. We are not addressing abstract principles centered around concepts such as cohesion, coupling, reusability, but principles that are more directly focused on the business at hand. Examples of principles could be as follows:

> *All corporate services will be available for all applications on an equal basis.*
>
> *Location of services will be transparent to all clients.*
>
> *All services will be available for use 24 hours a day, 7 days a week.*

Such principles are usually created as part of high-level architecture blueprints, but are not necessarily present in all organizations.

System requirements and constraints. These are real-world constraints and requirements that the architecture creators must take into account. Examples of such constraints could be: all functionality must be located in one physical server, customer data must be replicated across all sites in real time, performance requirements of the system, other business units must have equal access to part of the systems functionality, and so on. Any existing systems and networks must also be taken into consideration here.

Experience and ideas. This refers to experience and ideas from the whole team and not just the architect. It is the architect's responsibility to synthesize the ideas from the team members into a coherent whole, however.

Creating an architecture model is not one person's lone task. It is best conducted by a team of senior designers who are led by the architect. The architect should drive the process and encourage support of a vision, but should also allow the creativity of her/his colleagues to be expressed and used to provide input to the final result.

    📖   Establish an architecture team to create the architecture for the system. The team should be led by the architect and consist of senior designers, as well as a few junior designers. The size of the team depends on the project, but it becomes difficult to maintain a unified vision with a team of greater than six.

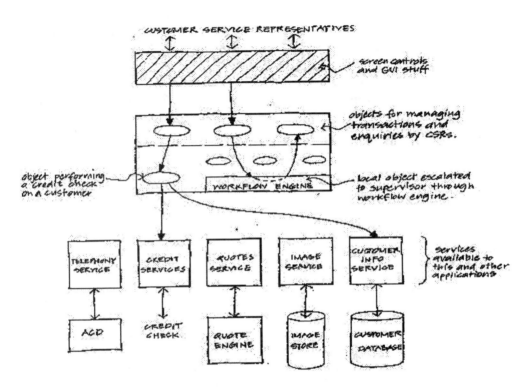

Figure 5.3. Preliminary high-level architecture of system.

Once the early system requirements are known, it is worthwhile bringing the architecture team together to conduct a short workshop during which the system's preliminary architecture is sketched out. An example of such a sketch for a product quotes and transaction system is shown in Figure 5.3.

We can see that it is an annotated box diagram with some notion of separation of concerns between layers of functionality. This architecture is based on the use of services to support this and other applications and a workflow engine, which provides the means for escalating customer calls to supervisors.

Some of the inputs to the above architecture were as follows:

- *Architectural vision and principles:* The vision here is to have services available for multiple applications transparently, hence increasing reusability and substitution of services without the clients necessarily being aware. The principles of 3-tier client–server systems apply here, with distinct separation of the various layers.

- *System requirements and constraints:* Some of the requirements that must be met by this system are: calls must be escalated to a supervisor immediately (this includes the actual call, the information pertaining to the customer, and the context of the call), quotes must be provided for both single customers at a time and for multiple customers (hence the isolation of the quotes engine), the images store already exists and so must be interfaced to, and so on.

- *Experience and ideas:* The contribution of the experience and ideas of the team is more intangible. At this high level, however, their experience has been used to validate the above preliminary architecture model as feasible and that it is able to provide the required functionality. The direct impact of the ideas and experience of the designers will become more evident as the preliminary model becomes refined and more detailed.

5.3.2 Testing and Refining the Preliminary Model

After the initial architecture has been created by the architecture team, it needs to be refined and taken to the next level of detail by the team. The experience and ideas of the team now become more of a factor, as do the system requirements and constraints.

Figure 5.4 shows a sketch of a refined version of the preliminary architecture from Figure 5.3. We can see that the earlier conceptual architecture has been mapped to a physical environment. It may be considered too early to make such a mapping from conceptual to physical, but there are always some things that are "given" when constructing systems that must work in the real world. An example in this case is the Image Server; it can be either one physical machine or multiple machines, but as there is already an Image Server in use for other applications it can be said with some degree of certainty that the image service will sit on such a machine. Later observations during design of the details of the service-and-performance requirements, however, may change this and require that the service be located on a separate machine.

The figure also shows that the other services have also been distributed to machines, based on constraints imposed by existing systems or merely to put a stake in the ground at this early stage. It is important to note that decisions at this stage are by no means binding and can be changed quite easily. Reference back to

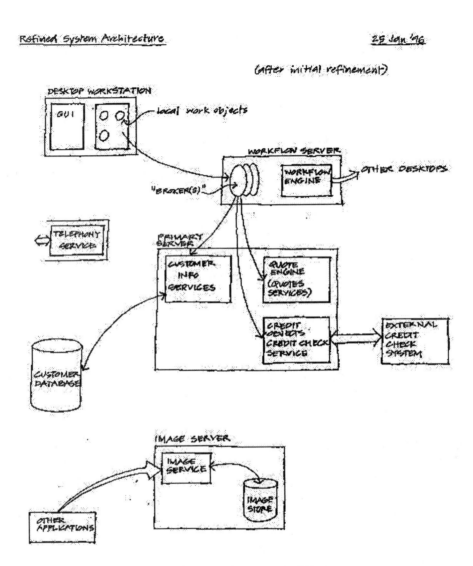

Figure 5.4. Refined system architecture.

Figure 5.2 shows us that the refinement occurs in parallel with the object modeling and is likely to be affected by that activity.

In order to validate the appropriateness of the initial model, it should be tested to ensure that it can support the required functionality. As shown, the testing of the initial model is influenced by scenarios being used as part of user design. For heav-

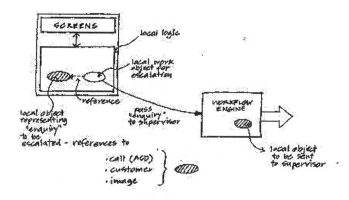

1 Escalating a call

SCREENS

local logic

local work object for escalation

reference

local object representing "enquiry" to be escalated — references to

pass "enquiry" to supervisor

WORKFLOW ENGINE

local object to be sent to supervisor

• call (ACD)
• customer
• image

Figure 5.5. High-level scenario to escalate a call.

ily distributed systems, the most complex transactions should be used to ensure that the architecture can support such work.

At this early stage these scenarios are high-level single-sentence descriptions of the functionality used to diagrammatically show how the architectural vision will support the desired work. Figures 5.5 and 5.6 show two such scenarios that have been sketched out during the user-design processes.

The first scenario is for escalating a call from the customer-service representative to a supervisor. This scenario emanates from the user-design sessions, where many of the requirements were derived. As the sketch shows, at this early stage this scenario is in concept form. This brief sketch would typically be completed during a group workshop of the architecture team. Once the concepts have been agreed on, and the detail of the functionality necessary has been agreed on by the users, this scenario can be taken to the next level of detail by an individual. There is no need to go into detail as a group unless it is a particularly complex and challenging scenario that may require input from a number of different people.

The architecture team, as a group, should identify scenarios to test the architecture. Sketch out the architectural support for each scenario, and then assign the scenarios to individuals in the team to add more detail that describes how the components interact. Scenarios should also include "pseudo-code" that describes the sequence of steps in the process, which are used to validate the architecture.

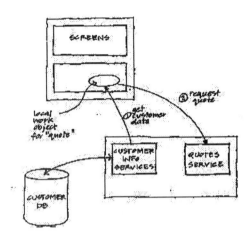

Figure 5.6. High-level scenario to produce a quote.

The second scenario diagram shows the high-level concepts supporting a scenario for producing a quote for a customer on the telephone. We can see that the diagram shows two "message flows" between large grain components that have yet to be defined. As before, the brief-concept diagram is produced during a group workshop and subsequently detailed in an individual session. Much of the detailed work in this area can only be performed late in the modeling process, as it will depend on the inputs from the object-modeling activity, as shown in Figure 5.2. The purpose of the scenarios at this stage is to illustrate architectural support for system functionality, and not to provide a rigorous check on the details.

The architect should participate in the object-modeling activity to understand the requirements of the architecture from a behavioral viewpoint and the architect should also participate, where possible, in the user sessions to understand user requirements more thoroughly, especially when related to the architecture's role in meeting those requirements (e.g., performance expectations).

5.3.3 Specifying the Architecture

In specifying architectures we have found two types of models to be particularly useful.

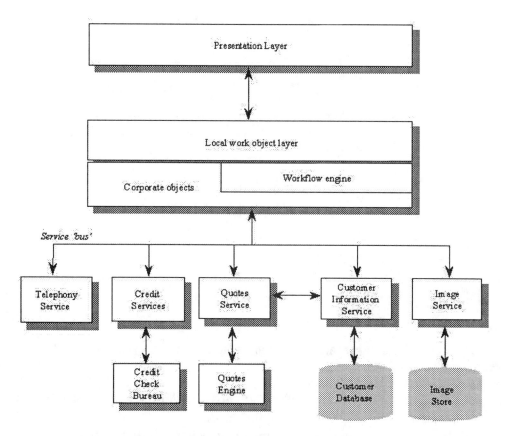

Figure 5.7. Logical software architecture.

1. *High-Level Models.* These are high-level models derived from the preliminary architecture sketches once they have been validated by the architecture team through the use of scenarios. The purpose of these models is to provide a high-level description of the logical architecture and a mapping of that architecture to the physical environment. The high-level models created from the earlier sketches are shown in Figures 5.7 and 5.8. (The second model type, component-interaction models, follows Figure 5.8.)

We can see from Figure 5.7 that it has changed a little from the high-level sketch of Figure 5.3. The notion of a "service bus" has been added. This provides publish-and-subscribe facilities for objects that wish to subscribe to a service. This bus has been reused in large part from another project,

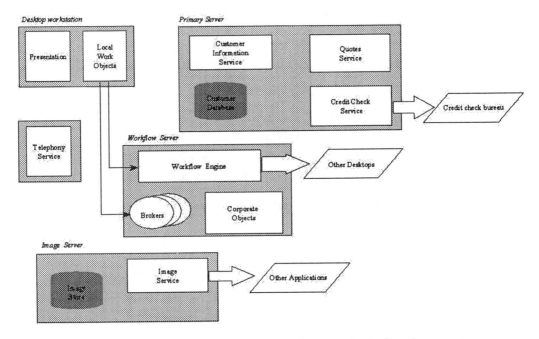

Figure 5.8. Logical architecture mapped onto a physical environment.

where it was found to be exceptionally useful. It also decouples the client from the service being requested.

The position of the workflow engine has changed slightly in order to show that local work objects interact with the workflow engine in order to route calls and information to other customer-service representatives, particularly supervisors. This engine is not another service and as such is not accessible from the service bus.

Figure 5.8 shows the high-level components mapped to a more physical environment with "physical" servers now being shown on the diagram. The addition of "brokers" provides the implementation of the service-bus concept from the logical architecture. This broker may have multiple or single instances, but its responsibility is to direct the flow of requests to the services and ensure transparency of service location to clients.

The inclusion of a broker is an example of the refinement to the architecture that goes on in parallel with detailed object modeling and detailed design (covered in chapter 6).

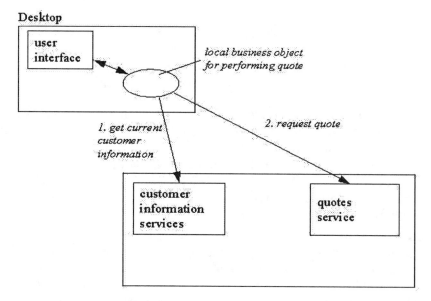

Figure 5.9. An example of a component-interaction model.

The constraints of the deployment environment have dictated that the image server (which already exists) will house the image service. The primary server here houses the quotes service, customer-information service, and the credit-check access.

2. *Component-Interaction Models.* These models provide the definitions of how the various components distributed across the environment will communicate. As before this is a logical view where the protocol between components will be specified. The model outlines the responsibilities of each component and the contracts it has with other components it interacts with. An example is shown in Figure 5.9.

The diagram shows a very high-level component-interaction model that is based on lower level object interactions. It shows a work object (in the local-work-object layer of Figure 5.7) that requests customer information and then requests a quote from the quote service. There will be lower level specification for messages from the object-interaction diagrams. This interaction model can be taken down to the next level of detail, which is one level above that of object interactions.

5.3.4 Creating an Architecture Prototype

Aside from the paper specifications of an architecture there are a number of situations in which an architecture prototype can be very useful. These are as follows:

- *Demonstrating a proof of concept.* Many of the newer technologies can be provided with a means of demonstrating how they will perform in a given architecture. For example, moving from a two-tier client–server solution to a three-tier one places greater emphasis on the choice of middleware. An architectural prototype can be used to explore different approaches to such connectivity as in an object request broker versus a message-oriented middleware product, for example.

- *Gaining support for a solution.* Seeing is believing, and constructing an architectural prototype and exhibiting it to all the stakeholders in a particular business application is a useful means of demonstrating how a proposed architecture can support the business. Such demonstrations can also help in gaining support for a particular solution. This is slightly different than the previous use, which was more for testing a new technology, or exploring technical alternatives.

- *Identifying bottlenecks.* A prototype can be very useful in examining and identifying areas of concern when experimenting with a new architecture. By creating a prototype that uses some of the most transaction-intensive scenarios, it is possible to gain insight into potential bottlenecks and performance issues surrounding a particular architecture. Transactions can be profiled and an overall picture of the potential performance can be created.

5.3.5 Creating an Architecture Framework

The usefulness of frameworks as a means of providing a skeleton application is unquestioned. Frameworks, originating in the area of user interfaces (Schmucker, 1986), have moved on to support application-specific concepts in diverse areas such as very large-scale integration (VLSI)-routing algorithms (Gossain, 1990b), real-time psychophysiology (Foote, 1988), and operating systems (Madany, Campbell, Russo, & Leyens, 1989).

Their usefulness can also be extended to architecture, whereby a set of classes can provide the structure and mechanisms needed to support the architecture. An architecture framework would therefore provide classes for connectivity between components, access to persistent objects, logging and managing contexts, and so

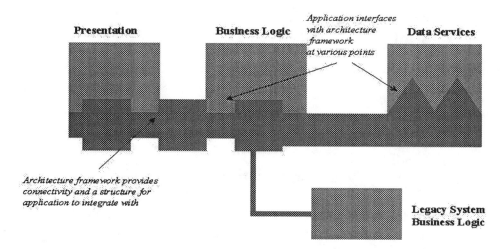

Figure 5.10. An architecture framework.

on. Applications sharing similar architectures can then reuse such a framework and build on it as needed, much in the same way as an application framework.

A simple architecture framework in a three-tier client–server system, for example, could provide the connectivity between the presentation and the business logic and allow queries to the data-services layer to be passed straight through while directing queries to a legacy system through some protocol-conversion classes.

An example of how the architecture framework fits in with a three-tier architecture is shown in Figure 5.10. There are a number of integration points provided with which the application integrates. The framework handles all the generic access to a legacy system and also the connectivity between the tiers. Application-specific logic is then integrated with this to provide the exact connectivity needed.

The architecture framework can be seen as an extension of the architecture prototype into a more formal set of classes that are actually used and extended in the final application. It should be pointed out that creating an architecture framework is similar to creating any other type of framework: it cannot be wholly created from scratch, as the majority of useful components should be abstracted from working applications. As Wirfs-Brock and Johnson (1990, p. 119) point out: "Good frameworks are usually the result of many design iterations and a lot of hard work."

If you wish to create an architecture framework, create the core abstractions first. Then examine other applications with similar architectures to create the reusable and extensible abstractions that will comprise this framework.

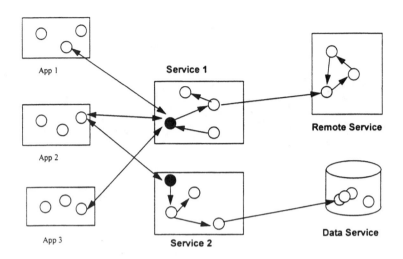

Figure 5.11. Applications using the principles of service-based architecture.

5.4   Service-Based Architecture

Based on numerous applications developed in a variety of domains, one of the most useful application architectures is one that is based around the notion of services; that is, the constructing of system solutions through the use of reusable services. This macroarchitecture emphasizes services provided by objects as units of reuse and some of the units of partition.

Objects are a powerful means of identifying and leveraging reusable, shared services that cross application boundaries. Using the principles of *service-based architectures*, we can compose application units of business-logic functionality accessing reusable enterprise services. In this way it is possible to build *open* applications in shorter time frames. Applications built in this way can provide access to information and data sources that would previously have been locked within closed applications, had they not been abstracted into services available for other applications. Figure 5.11 illustrates a number of applications that use services provided as part of a service-based architecture.

Applications 1, 2 and 3 are using Services 1 and 2. Each service has an object that embodies that service for its clients. These "service objects" are identified in the above figure by shading. Services themselves can, of course, utilize other services as shown above.

5.4.1 What Is a Service Object?

A service object provides an interface to a set of functions that are collectively grouped into a reusable shared service that is available to a number of applications. Examples include the following:

- ImageService, for storing and retrieving graphical images
- PricingService, for calculating the price of a set of complex financial instruments
- ObjectStorageService, for providing the storage and retrieval of objects in some repository
- MarketDataService, for providing simple access to real-time market data

The access to these reusable services is provided in a logical and controlled manner such that the requesters of that service are oblivious to where that service is being provided from, or how that service is being provided.

There are two types of service objects:

1. *Access-based services:* This type of service object provides access to some external data that is requested by the client. It typically returns an instance of an object, which is then manipulated by the client. An example includes an ImageService.

2. *Operation-based services:* This type of service object provides some operation that acts on instances of objects within the business model. These objects are typically used so one can benefit from reusable operations that work across multiple instances. An example includes a PricingService.

The distinction between types of service objects is important, as we shall see later. A service object provides, manages, and tracks a service to requesters, based on a "contract" of services.

Figure 5.12 shows a ServiceObject interacting with two Requesters through a "contract." This contract, defined by the communication protocol between Requesters and ServiceObjects, specifies how Requesters must use the services provided. We can see that the ServiceObject is merely the "front-end" to these services, the actual functionality for the service is provided by a set of cooperating objects. It is similar to the Facade pattern (Gamma, Helm, Johnson, & Vlissides, 1994) in structure, but conceptually it offers much more. It is a logical grouping of objects that perform a set of coherent functions and thus is more akin to a subsystem.

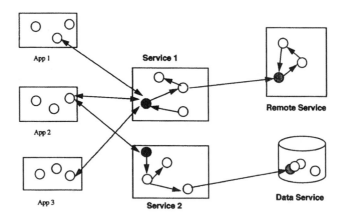

Figure 5.12. Service object.

This group of objects provides a convenient unit of functionality that can be used when partitioning a logical application onto a physical environment (e.g., a client–server configuration). A ServiceObject can exist locally within the same process space as the Requester, in another process on the same machine, or on a totally different machine. It is also possible to have multiple instances of a ServiceObject supporting one Requester or one ServiceObject instance for each Requester.

5.4.2 Reasons for Using Service Objects

As an example let us look at a PricingService object that can be used to implement a pricing service for a financial portfolio. See the object interaction diagram of Figure 5.13. This service is solely responsible for computing the value of a set of financial instruments and returning the result to the requester.

In Figure 5.13, we see that PricingService is requested to compute the value of a set of instruments (InstrumentList). It then divides the work among a number of instances of Pricer,[3] each of which calculates the value of an instrument. For especially large lists, it is of course possible for PricingService to break the list of instruments into smaller lists and use other instances of PricingService to calculate the values. A recursive process, if you will.

---

[3] Observant readers may recognize the Pricer object as the use of the Strategy pattern (Gamma, Helm, Johnson, & Vlissides, 1994), useful in objectifying algorithms.

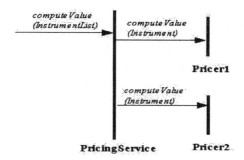

Figure 5.13. PricingService.

Using the PricingService object as an example, let us examine some key reasons for using service objects:

- Rules and policies behind the object providing the service are encapsulated. Any changes to the pricing algorithm can be localized within the group of objects providing the service. This allows for flexibility when a change in business rules is desired, and also means changes are localized to the objects providing the service. Whether the actual calculation is executed by the PricingService or by a Pricer object is transparent to requesters. A requester merely interacts with the service object.

- Service objects can be instantiated in an application as needed, and deleted once used. This affords the designer some advantages in memory usage and in being able to dynamically configure processing distribution by creating and deleting instances as required. Thus, for the PricingService, as the day's closing figures need to be computed, multiple instances of PricingService can be in existence, whereas at other times there may only be a few instances in use.

- A service object can be located on a remote server to take advantage of computing power. A PricingService can therefore be computing prices for a remote client and also be computing prices for a local client. A service object need not be located necessarily in the same process space as its requesters.

- Services can be shared across objects and applications in an enterprise. Access to a set of common shared services in an enterprise means that resources and information previously locked within applications can now be accessed from numerous sources. Applications built on top of shared services also mean that application development time potentially can be reduced through reuse. Thus any new application requiring complex financial instruments to be priced can use the PricingService.

- A service object can track the status of requests, or manage long-running contracts between requesters and providers. This allows for complex interactions to be more easily managed through the use of service objects and also provides a means for the state of complex requests and contracts to be maintained in the event of some system failure.

5.4.3 Designing Service Objects

Service objects are not easy to design. The design is a process of abstraction whereby one examines object interactions to arrive at a more abstract set of interactions that can be grouped together in providing some common functionality. A new object may need to be created to provide the services collectively. It is a similar process to analyzing a selection of instances and identifying the class the instances belong to through abstraction.

Far-sighted analysts can begin to abstract service objects after discussion with domain experts by listening to the language they use and understanding how they view the functionality of the problem domain. An experienced system architect will look for service objects when attempting to model the system at a higher level, such as class clusters or subsystems. Again, an understanding of the enterprise business and its information system (IS) function is useful here. An architect is ideally positioned to do this.

For a more methodical process of identifying service objects, I would recommend analyzing a set of object-interaction diagrams (Gossain 1995) to characterize similar functionality utilized by different clients. Typical examples include looking for similar messages sent to the same object from multiple sources, or looking for similar messages with slight variations sent to a number of different objects, but requesting similar, or related, functionality.

To find services, examine object-interaction diagrams to characterize similar functionality used by different clients. To judge their applicability to other applications, hold a group discussion with representatives from other applications and business units to present the service and its potential interface. Allow participants to present requirements, which should then be evaluated. Be very careful when broadening the applicability of a service, as this will affect your project schedule.

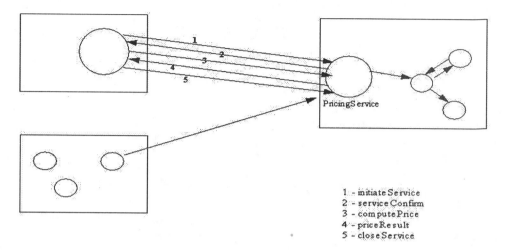

Figure 5.14. Access to service objects.

As briefly mentioned above, it may be necessary to create a new object that will act as the service object. Service objects are a "front-end" to the cooperation of other objects and are therefore similar to a subsystem. The access to the services can then be designed (see Figure 5.14), and this may require minor changes to existing object interactions.

Figure 5.14 shows the sequence of messages from a requester to a PricingService instance. The communication contract spans five messages: three from the client requester and two from the server. In this example, the second requester cannot utilize the services of the instance of PricingService until the first requester has sent the closeService message, and the PricingService has terminated the contract.

A simple data-retrieval server, for example, will not need such a sequence of messages in defining its contract. A one-time message: getData(DataIdentifier, DataType*) say, may be sufficient. It still may be necessary for requesters to register and deregister with that service object, however.

The exact protocol scheme used is a design decision and will vary according to the type of service being used. Designing the contract between requester and the service object is an important aspect of the design, however, as it will affect the performance of the system and also ultimately influence the potential reusability of the service.

Figure 5.15 shows an object-structure model defining a generic class ServiceObject with some member functions defining the initiation -and-registration aspects of the protocol, and two derived services providing their own services.

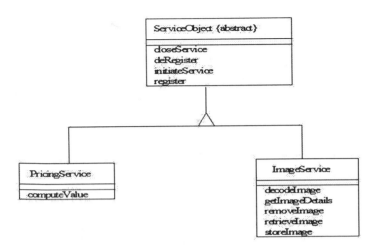

Figure 5.15. Abstract ServiceObject and two derived service objects.

We can see from the above figure that ServiceObject provides the facilities to initiate and close a service, as well as those needed to register and deregister with a service. This is done through its member functions. The two subtypes, PricingService and ImageService, will provide their own services through their member functions and inherit the generic properties of ServiceObject. They may of course also extend the initiation-and-registration protocol if necessary, in order to satisfy their own requirements. For example, the ImageService may require extra security checks to ensure that its clients have the adequate authority to use its services.

5.4.4 Challenges

There are some very serious challenges in designing a service-based architecture, as one can see from the following list:

- *Making services reusable.* A service that can be used in one application may be of benefit in other applications, especially if the service is generic enough. Herein lies one of the real challenges in creating a service-based architecture: being able to extend the service so that it can be useful outside the current application. Domain experts can provide considerable help here, especially if they are familiar with other parts of the business.

- *Managing a contract between parties.* When designing a service the contract between requester and service object must be considered:
  - is it a one-off message that constitutes the overall contract?
  - is it a series of messages that must be communicated in a certain order to form a well-defined protocol?
  - is there key information needed by the service object that must be provided?
  - what is the lifetime of a contract—one message, a series of messages, infinite time?
- *Security.* The authority of a requester to use a service may need to be verified by the service object prior to providing the service.
- *Storing state information about service usage.* It is possible to record service-usage information, requester characteristics, and other such statistics about the service for later use. This can be useful later in order to improve service provision and use of services across applications.
- *Handling failure and loss of services.* If a service object fails for some reason during a contract, how is this to be handled? Possibilities include: standby service objects, rollback to original state, no service until the object returns, and so on. Exception handling must be a high-priority task during design.
- *Allowing access to business objects by services.* As Daniels (1996) points out, one of the criticisms of a service-based approach is that it in some implementations it can require the database to manage the distribution and hence require multiple copies of the same "business-model" object. This can be in direct conflict with managing distribution via an object request broker, in which only one instance need be created, with the ORB managing all references. This implementation issue is the result of poor design. The operation-based service objects typically require access to business-model objects and this can be managed via the ORB.

5.4.5 Relationship with Domains

In chapter 3 the notion of domains was presented as a means of partitioning the system into manageable pieces of work along the lines of subject matter. It is interesting to note the relationship between domains and the architectural components we have been discussing.

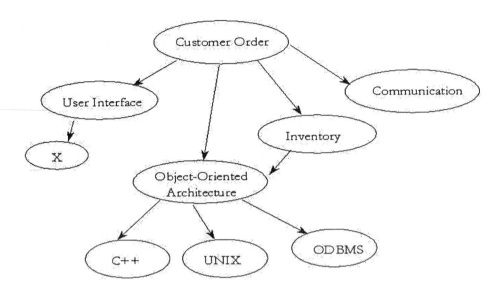

Figure 5.16. A domain chart.

Consider the domain chart of Figure 5.16, which is for a customer-order system. The operation-based services are to be found within the Customer Order domain. An order-pricing service, for example, would consist of objects that belong to that domain. Access-based domains are not likely to be found from analyzing the interactions of the Customer Order domain, but are more likely to be found from other domains and from interactions between domains. Service domains (in the Shlaer & Mellor sense) do not map to services except on rare occasions.

If the bridge between domains is managed through communication from one domain to another, then a service object can be used to manage the contract between the requester and the service. For example, the bridge between the CustomerOrder domain and the Communication domain could be message based. If so, then the Communication domain could be partitioned as an access-based service providing communication services. Use of other techniques, however, such as inheritance for Inventory (see chapter 3), would preclude such an option for the Inventory domain.

> In order to determine access-based domains from a domain chart late in the process, examine the domain chart and identify those bridges that are communication based. These may be candidates for access-based services.

Application domains can be split into subsystems through clustering of objects (grouping of related objects), but the architectural groupings at both the macro and micro levels are based on a large variety of criteria.

5.5 Four-Layer Architecture

As in the previous section where I introduced the idea of building service-based architectures in order to leverage the reusability of services within the enterprise, this section outlines a four-layer architecture for building business systems. It is very similar to the four-layer architecture described by Frost (1996), which is now being accepted as the way to architect object systems in the business world. The addition here is the integration of the service-based architecture with the four-layer model.

5.5.1 Three-Tier Architecture

The three-tier client–server model is now well known and well described (Berson, 1992), and is shown in Figure 5.17. Its principal components are as follows:

- **Presentation:** This tier receives user input and presents information to the user through various media, such as terminals, telephone, and so on.
- **Business Logic:** The business rules are executed in this tier. It deals with the manipulation of data and turns it into information.
- **Data Services:** Provides direct and indirect access to data from local and remote sources.

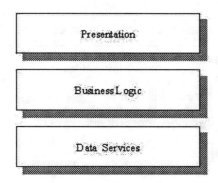

Figure 5.17. Three-tier client-server architecture.

5.5.2 From Three Tiers to Four with Service-Layer Integration

Frost (1996), among others, has proposed the partitioning of the business-logic layer into two layers, thereby creating a four-tier architecture. The business logic functionality would then be split into the following:

1. *Local-business-objects layer:* These objects handle the business requirements of the project being developed. They are fully fledged objects that are equal citizens but are less persistent. They will exist during a session with some users, or during a transaction.

2. *Corporate-business-objects layer:* These objects contain information and behavior important to the whole organization.

The distinction between local and corporate objects is very useful because it allows us to isolate local objects that are relevant to the business unit from the corporate objects, which are of use across business units.

Taking the four-layer architecture as our input we can also add other types of services to our model, as shown in Figure 5.18. These services provided by service

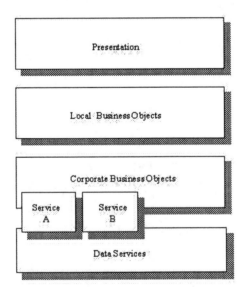

Figure 5.18. Four-layer model integrated with service-based architecture.

objects supply functionality that is useful to the corporation (initiated by CBOs [corporate-business objects]) and useful to the current transaction (initiated by LBOs [local-business objects]). They are therefore shown as overlapping with the CBO layer.

The LBOs and CBOs are first-class objects. That is, they have attributes and operations that perform tasks expected of those business objects. Therefore a CBO such as an Account could have attributes such as accountNumber, dateOpened, and balance, and could perform operations expected of such aCBO, such as openAccount, closeAccount, deposit, withdraw, and so on. The inclusion of services in our model (of Figure 5.18) to perform tasks does not remove the need for CBO or LBO functionality.

> During modeling sessions, try to make the distinction between local-business objects and corporate-business objects. This latter group will be meaningful across business areas and will be relevant to other applications.

In an earlier section we made the distinction between access-based and operation-based services. Typically we see that operation-based services have a much tighter link with CBOs and in many cases are provided by CBOs themselves. An access-based service (such as DataService) may provide access to CBOs but is less likely to be provided by a CBO itself.

5.5.3 An Example of the Use of the Four-Layer Architecture

In order to better understand how the different layers interact in a system, an example would be helpful.

Figure 5.19 shows a four-layer architecture with some interaction between items in each layer. The presentation layer is merely the presentation and is responsible for displaying information to the user. The LBO layer contains information that is specific to the task at hand (e.g., temporary objects, objects representing short-term tasks, objects with short life histories). These LBO objects are very transaction oriented, such as customer order, deposit for an account, and so on. The CBO layer is the layer containing long-term objects that are of interest across users, across units, and represent some of the core concepts of the business. In a bank this could be the types of accounts supported, the customers, and so on.

Consider a customer-order system where orders of stock items are taken over the telephone. A partial object model for this business is shown in Figure 5.20. We

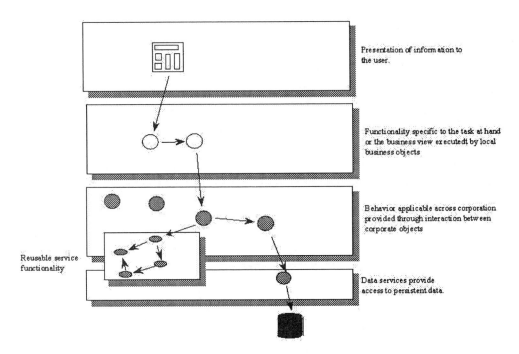

Presentation of information to
the user.

Functionality specific to the task at hand
or the business view executed by local
business objects

Behavior applicable across corporation
provided through interaction between
corporate objects

Reusable service
functionality

Data services provide
access to persistent data.

Figure 5.19. Distribution of functionality across the four layers.

can see here that the local-object model has a view on the corporate-object model. The LBOs shown are Order and OrderItem, whereas the CBOs shown are Customer and its subtypes, Account and StockItem.[4]

Figure 5.21 shows a four-layer architecture with some representative local and corporate objects in a scenario.

Here we see the creation of an LBO—Order A100, which has references to a number of other LBOs—Item B119, Item B129, and Item A127. Each of these are LBOs because they are specific to the functionality of the current transaction and not considered as a corporate resource. The Order object and each of the Item objects have references to CBOs, however, such as Customer and StockItem.

As the order details are entered by the user, an instance of Order (with reference A100, and a reference to the Customer object) is created. As line items are

---

[4]It is possible, using CASE tools, to differentiate between CBOs and LBOs when shown on the same diagram, although this has not been done in Figure 5.20. Some CASE tools place an extra boundary around CBOs, for example.

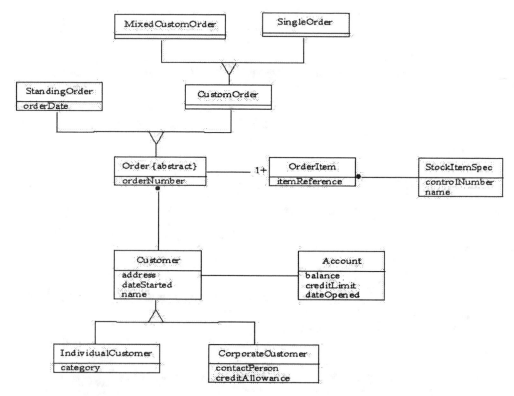

Figure 5.20. Partial high-level object model for customer-order domain.

added to the Order, each Item instance created is responsible for maintaining a reference to the corresponding StockItem being ordered. This reference to the StockItem is used to check the current price of that item including any special offers available. These prices are requested by the Item instance from the StockItem instance. Once the order has been fully entered by the user it is priced.

The pricing of an order is not a simple calculation of the sum of all of the line items as there are a number of various other factors that must to be taken into consideration. Each order has a unique discount code that needs to be calculated and applied based on the customer's credit history, his or her account status, the discount rate he or she is entitled to, the value of previous orders, what type of customer he or she is, and so on. Therefore the pricing is executed by a service object and its collaborators, which capture the pricing algorithm and its associated business rules.

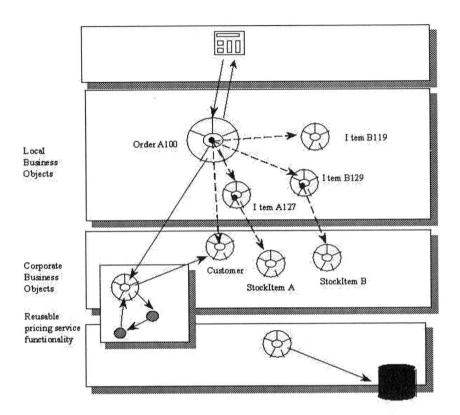

Figure 5.21. Order creation and pricing in a four-layer architecture.

In earlier models of this domain, order pricing was carried out by the order object itself. The different types of orders necessitated numerous subtypes, however (e.g., StandingOrder, CustomOrder, MixedCustomOrder, SingleOrder), and the pricing policy became distributed across numerous objects. Because pricing was such a key activity that was subject to regular change, the PricingService object was created to manage this activity and the logic was removed from the behavior of the Order object subhierarchy.

> Service objects may not become apparent until later on in the modeling process. Examine object interactions to identify service objects later on. If there is logic that is subject to regular change and can be abstracted away from the objects on which it operates, it may be a candidate for a service object.

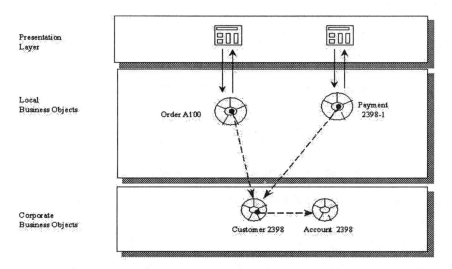

Figure 5.22. Multiple interactions with a single CBO.

5.5.4 Managing Multiple References to CBOs

It is important to point out that there may be many LBOs with references to a single CBO. At the same time as an order is being entered for a customer, it may be possible that another user, say in the Accounts department, is checking the payment history of the same customer and is also interacting with the same instance of the Customer object (see Figure 5.22).

The references between LBOs and CBOs are important, and potentially can become problematic when references to LBOs are passed around a system. Consider the case of an LBO, ObjectX, which contains a reference to two CBOs (see Figure 5.23). If the customer-service representative using the system wishes to escalate the call to a supervisor (as in the scenario of Figure 5.5), then the ObjectX must be passed to the supervisor who will be on another machine. In that case what happens to ObjectX? It must be passed to the supervisor along with the references.

This must be dealt with very carefully as it is tempting to create copies of the two CBOs and pass those instead. Doing so would, however, cause potential problems with integrity and identity, especially if those objects were then passed messages to perform tasks. It is quite easy to envisage more than one instance of the same object in such cases if not handled correctly!

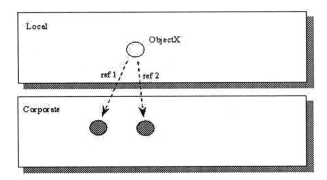

Figure 5.23. Local-business object with references to corporate-business objects.

A means of addressing the above issue is to use an object request broker as the means for managing the references to objects across process-and-hardware boundaries. The ORB can manage multiple references to a single object. One should not always defer addressing such issues to the implementation infrastructure, however, but should make handling object identity a key issue in architecture design, especially where a four -layer model is being used and where the above scenario may exist.

📖   Explicitly address the issue of object identity throughout the architecture-design phase. If an assumption is made that the implementation infrastructure will ensure that references are supported, then explicitly state this in the architecture document. Failure to do so could mean problems later.

5.5.5 Managing Different Business Views of CBOs

Different views of CBOs are sometimes found through the views that different users have. Figure 5.24 shows the different views of a "Client," which may be held by Account Managers and Accountants of a financial services firm.

The Accountants are interested in a client's name, account number, balance, and credit history, whereas the Account Managers are interested in the name, the stocks held by that client, and the trade history. Each group of users has a different view of the same "concept" and some additional information, although they may both refer to the concept as the client. A novice modeler may try to combine

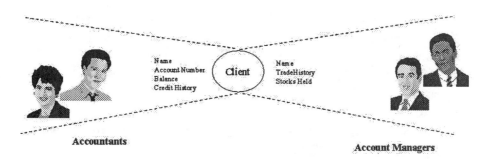

Figure 5.24. Different business views.

the two different views into one object, but this would be inadvisable as it will lead to incorrect models.

Alternatives to the single object could be representing the concept through objects with relationships or perhaps some form of generalization–specialization hierarchy. The modeler needs to be conscious of this phenomenon to avoid modeling problems.

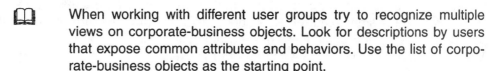 When working with different user groups try to recognize multiple views on corporate-business objects. Look for descriptions by users that expose common attributes and behaviors. Use the list of corporate-business objects as the starting point.

5.6 Summary

In this chapter we have described an increasingly important phenomenon in constructing systems—architecture. Objects allow us to describe, discuss, and reason about software systems in a way that previous paradigms never did. This is not to say that architecture was not an issue until objects came around, but the increasing attention being given to objects has been in line with the increasing awareness of architecture as an important aspect of system construction.

We examined the importance of the role of the software architect and then identified a core set of skills that an architect must possess:

- The ability to balance the practical experience and ideas of system building with a vision.

- An architect must have good listening and communicating skills.
- Probably the key requirement for an architect is experience in designing and implementing systems, preferably of a diverse nature.
- As well as being experienced in design and implementation, an architect must be well versed in systems he or she has had no experience in constructing.
- An ability to understand and allow for the use of microarchitectures within the larger framework of the system.
- The architect must have the vision to share concepts, designs, and code across projects and he or she must have visibility within the organization and across projects to be able to recognize commonality.
- The architect must provide direction in mapping the architectural vision to a practical implementation.
- The architect must possess the ability to approach problems in a considered and thoughtful manner.

We have outlined a generic iterative architecture-design process and some of the typical work-products that are created during that process. The principal inputs to the process were: system requirements and constraints, architectural vision and principles, and experiences and ideas of the team members.

The architecture is specified by a number of models:

- high-level logical software architecture
- physical architecture
- component-interaction models

In addition to the models, it is also possible to create an architectural prototype. This can be useful in demonstrating a proof of concept, experiencing new technologies, and identifying potential problems.

The notion of service-based architecture (SBA) was also introduced. This macroarchitecture is a means of constructing applications from business functionality that utilize reusable services from across the enterprise. The heart of the SBA is the service object, which provides, manages, and tracks a service to requesters based on a contract of services.

The four-layer architecture built on service architectures was described, and some examples demonstrating how the object paradigm can work in a client–server environment were presented.

References

Anderson, B. (1995). Building organizational competence in software architecture. *ACM SIGSOFT Software Engineering Notes, 20(2)*, 25, 28.

Berson, A. (1992). *Client/Server Architecture*. New York: McGraw-Hill.

Booch, G. (1996). *Object Solutions: Managing the Object-Oriented Project*. Menlo Park, CA: Addison-Wesley.

Daniels, J. (1996). ORBs at your service. *Object Expert, 1(4)*, 41–42.

Foote, B. (1988). *Designing to Facilitate Change With Object-Oriented Frameworks*. Unpublished master's thesis, University of Illinois at Urbana-Champaign, Urbana.

Frost, S. (1996). *The SELECT Perspective*. Technical Report. Santa Ana, CA: SELECT Software Tools.

Gamma, E., Helm, R., Johnson, R., & Vlissides, J. (1994). *Design Patterns: Elements of Reusable Object-Oriented Software*. Reading, MA: Addison-Wesley.

Gossain, S. (1990a). *Object-Oriented Development and Reuse*. Unpublished doctoral thesis, University of Essex, Colchester, UK.

Gossain, S. (1990b, April). RApp: An application framework for VLSI routing. In *Proceedings of the Spring European Unix User Group Conference*, Munich, Germany.

Gossain, S. (1995). Designing object interactions, *Report on Object Analysis and Design, 1(S)*, 39–41, 45.

Madany, P., Campbell, R., Russo, V., & Leyens D. (1989). A class hierarchy for building stream-oriented file systems. In *Proceedings of ECOOP '89*, Nottingham, UK.

Schmucker, K. (1986). MacApp: An application framework. *Byte*, 11, 189–193.

Wirfs-Brock, R., & Johnson R. (1990). Surveying current research in object-oriented design. *Communications of the ACM, 33(9)*, 104–124.

CHAPTER 6

DESIGNING OBJECT SYSTEMS

T HE TWO PHILOSOPHIES of development introduced in chapter 2—translation and elaboration—have different views of the meaning of design. In elaboration, design is the continued refinement of analysis models such that they meet all the design goals. In the translational approach, however, design is the creation of an architecture that addresses the design issues that serve as a mapping from the analysis to the implementation. The two approaches have different philosophies but common goals.

Even though in the two philosophies design can take on different forms, some of the activities undertaken are the same. In both cases objects identified in analysis must be represented in some way in the design paradigm, relationships in the object models must be mapped to some design construct, and the designer must decide how to support attributes in the design. For each of these decisions a number of alternatives exist. Each must be considered in the light of a number of criteria.

Therefore, one can consider design to be the decision of which alternative is appropriate and under what circumstances that alternative is selected, based on particular criteria. This chapter provides a discussion of the issues that must be addressed in designing object systems.

6.1   Mapping Structures

When moving from analysis to design, the modeling constructs of analysis must be mapped in some way to design constructs. This will answer numerous questions, such as the following:

- How will this object be represented in the design?
- How will this active object map to a design construct?
- How will states be supported in this system?
- What will this attribute be in design?
- What data type supports this attribute?

In answering the above questions and many others that are similar, designers need to know how to address performance, how to deal with data access, how to use patterns, and how to incorporate reusable components where appropriate. The answers go into deciding which mapping should be used.

Let us look at some of the mapping options in turn, and explore the situations in which they would be used.

6.1.1   Objects to Classes

Perhaps the most fundamental decision one must make is to determine what design structure each object in the analysis should be mapped to. If following an object-oriented design, the class structure is the most obvious answer. Should one object map to one class in the design, however, or one object to two classes? Or perhaps some other alternative is more appropriate.

6.1.1.1   One Object to One Class

The most obvious and direct way of mapping is to map one object to a single class. Attributes can thus be mapped to constructs that correspond to this object, as can operations. The difficult question is how to decide if this is appropriate. Perhaps this should be approached as the default mapping, unless the object is included in either of the options described below.

6.1.1.2 Two or More Objects to One Class

This mapping is for two or more objects in the analysis mapped to a single class structure in the design. There are a couple of reasons why this may be an attractive move:

1. *Strongly cooperating objects.* If there are two or more objects in the analysis that have strong intercommunication, then they might be more suitably designed as a single class. Such a move then minimizes the amount of communication between the two classes at run time. The messages from one class to another can then be replaced with simple sequential statements.

2. *Tight relationships between objects.* Sometimes there are objects that have strong relationships between them. A good example of tight relationships would be two objects participating in more than one different relationship with each other in the model. These references may need to be traversed quite often in the models in order to determine which instances are related (for example, in a many-to-many relationship). This can be quite a constraint on the implementation, as each object looks through the list of instances of the other object.

6.1.1.3 One Object to Two or More Classes

This mapping is for one object in the model mapped to two or more classes in the design. This is a very rare requirement that I personally have never come across.

6.1.2 Relationships

There are numerous ways in which a relationship on the object model may be mapped to a design construct. The mapping you choose is dependent on a number of factors including the usage in the analysis and the potential distribution of objects. Different schemes can be employed based on the cardinality of the relationship.

6.1.2.1 One-to-One Relationships

Examples of the different types of one-to-one relationships are shown in Figure 6.1, which shows the relationship between an Owner and a PurchasedCar, such that a PurchasedCar always has an owner and vice versa. The lower part of the fig-

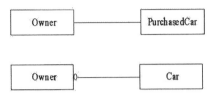

Figure 6.1. One-to-one relationships.

ure shows that a Car may be owned or not owned, hence the relationship between Car and Owner being 1:0,1

There are two ways to design this relationship.

Two-way reference. This is a way for each object instance in the relationship to have a reference to the other participant of the relationship, as shown in Figure 6.2..

This mapping option should be used if the object-interaction diagrams reveal that the relationship is accessed from both directions. For example, for a domain in which a reference to a PurchasedCar is used sometimes to find the Owner, and other times the Owner is used to find the PurchasedCar he or she owns, then the choice of two-way references would be the optimum choice.

If using this mapping, then operations by classes will need to ensure that integrity of reference is maintained. This option introduces a need for checking that must be performed by each object instance when a relationship is created and/or deleted. For the 1:1 relationship shown previously (between Owner and PurchasedCar) this is not such a major issue, as each time either of those objects is created there must be an instance of the relationship.[1] Similarly when instances

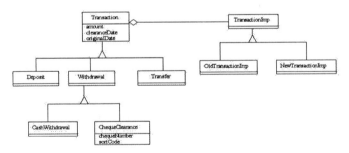

Figure 6.2. Two-way reference.

---

[1] This can often be overlooked. Every time an object in an unconditional relationship is created, it must assign references to the other instances it has relationships with. If these instances do not exist, then this can be problematic because they need to be created.

are deleted, other instances must also be deleted in unconditional relationships. When the relationship is a conditional one (as with Owner and Car), however, there will be references on one side that are unresolved. For the third type of optionality, in which either side may be conditional (say between Person and Car), there may also be references.

Because of the extra overhead two-way references can impose on the programmer in performing this additional checking, the extra storage required, and the greater chance of error, it is worthwhile to review the object-interaction diagrams to see if it is really necessary to have access from both directions, and perhaps even to change some of them if possible so that access is limited to one side only.

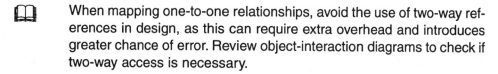

When mapping one-to-one relationships, avoid the use of two-way references in design, as this can require extra overhead and introduces greater chance of error. Review object-interaction diagrams to check if two-way access is necessary.

Be cautious if objects reside in different address spaces. If these objects are separated into different address spaces (such as when distributing them over a physical environment), then such references will need to be even more carefully managed.

One-way reference. The alternative of keeping references on either side of the relationship is just to keep the reference to the other instance on one side (see Figure 6.3).

This method should be chosen if the access path to navigate the relationship is always from one side. For example, throughout the object interaction diagrams, any time a PurchasedCar is searched for the Owner, then a one-way relationship from Owner to PurchasedCar would be appropriate. For those relationships that are conditional, keep the reference on the side of the instance that is always involved in the relationship. So for Figure 6.1 this would be on the side of the Owner and not the Car. One-way references are easier to deal with during design and implementation, as they make it easier to maintain the integrity of the reference.

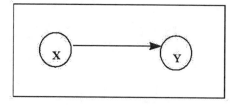

Figure 6.3. One-way reference.

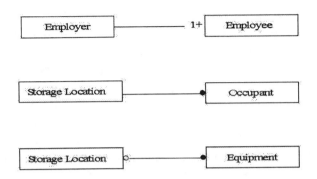

Figure 6.4. One-to-many relationships.

Use one-way references for cases in which access is always from one side. Keep the reference from the side used in the search. For conditional relationships keep the reference handle on the side of the instance that is always involved in the relationship.

6.1.2.2 One-to-Many Relationships

Figure 6.4 shows some examples of one-to-many relationships. The first illustrates an unconditional relationship between Employer and Employee, in which one Employer has one or more Employees. The next two relationships involve optionality, the first shows StorageLocation having zero or more Occupants, and the other shows StorageLocation storing zero or more items of Equipment, and some items of Equipment being stored in zero or one StorageLocations.

There are two principal ways in which to design this relationship.

References on the many side. This first approach has a single reference in each of the object instances on the many side (see Figure 6.5). Therefore, each instance of Equipment will have a reference to the StorageLocation in which it is stored.

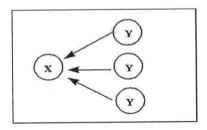

Figure 6.5. References on the many side.

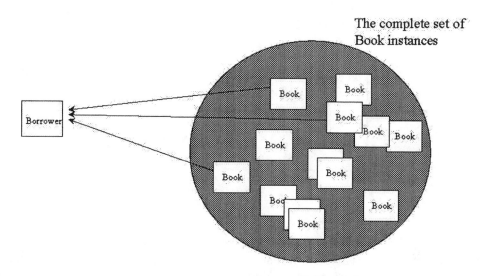

Figure 6.6. One-to-many relationship.

This mechanism should be used in those cases in which the reference on the many side seems practical. As with the one-to-one relationship, access paths are a key determining factor in deciding if this scheme is appropriate. For the third relationship in Figure 6.4, references on the many side may seem inappropriate, as one could argue that an item of "Equipment" should not know where it is stored. This issue, which is primarily one of roles and responsibilities of objects, however, should already have been addressed during modeling and should not need to be considered at this stage of design.

If any access is from the instance on the one side, then this mechanism can prove very compute-intensive, as the object on the one side will have to search through the *complete* list of instances to find which ones it is related to and then determine which particular one it is looking for (see Figure 6.6). The figure shows a Borrower instance having three Books on loan. Because the reference is from Book to Borrower, however, the Borrower has no knowledge of which Books to search to find the three Books she or he has loaned, and must therefore search the complete set. For systems in which there are large numbers of instances, this can impose some significant performance penalty on the system.

For one-to-many relationships, do not use references on the many side if there are significant accesses from the one side. Examine the object-interaction diagrams to check.

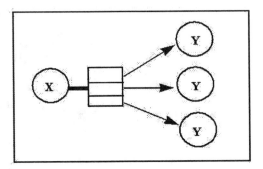

Figure 6.7. List of references on the one side.

List of references on the one side. The alternative method requires the object on the one side to maintain a list of instances of the many side. Therefore, Storage-Location will keep a list of items of Equipment stored there. Again access paths should be used to determine if this is appropriate (see Figure 6.7).

This approach is more attractive than the previous one, as it will limit unnecessary searches from the one side. Any accesses from the many side will have to go through all instances of the object on the one side, however, to find the one involved in the relationship.

The third alternative is to have two-way relationships. The issues around this are similar to those identified in the previous section.

6.1.2.3 Many-to-Many Relationships

Figure 6.8 shows two many-to many-relationships. The first shows a Satellite being used by zero or more GroundStations, and vice versa. The second shows an unconditional form of the many to many with a Radio being used to receive many RadioStations and vice versa.

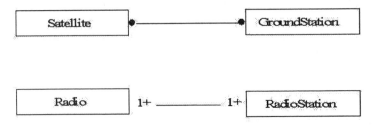

Figure 6.8. Many-to-many relationships.

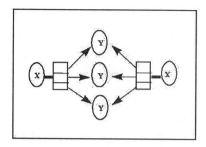

Figure 6.9. List on one side.

List on one side. If the access to other instances is predominantly from one side, then that set of instances should keep a list of references to the other side, as shown in Figure 6.9, where access is from the X side. If there are some occasions when access is from the other side, however, then it may be worth considering keeping a list on both sides. It is not just the number of object-interaction diagrams that need to be used as a guide, but the number of times the scenarios are expected to be supported by the object-interaction diagrams.

List on both sides. This scheme can get rather complex at implementation, when each list of references requires updating when instances are created and deleted. This design will mean heavy iteration of each list if instances are continually entering and leaving this relationship. It is only recommended for critical relationships in which access must be rapidly available from either side equally, or when it is necessary to have references kept on either side. As Figure 6.10 shows, the whole picture can get rather complex, and can lead to memory problems during implementation if not carefully managed.

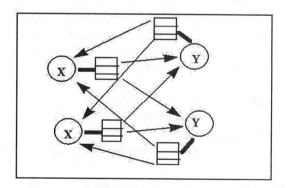

Figure 6.10. List on both sides.

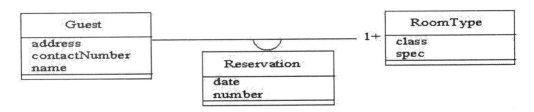

Figure 6.11. Associative object.

6.1.2.4 Associative Objects

The use of objects to capture attributes and relationships was recognized as a powerful modeling tool in chapter 3. The associative object represents the instance of a relationship between two objects. So for Figure 6.11, Reservation describes the attributes of the booking of a RoomType by a Guest.

During modeling, associative objects are treated just like any other objects in that they participate in object-interaction diagrams, are involved in other relationships, and can have life cycles, and so on. Their creation and destruction are intimately linked to that of the relationship, however. Designing how references are stored for these relationships is usually done by storing references to each of the participants in the associative object. Thus, for the above example, Reservation stores a reference to an instance of Guest and an instance of RoomType.

Access from Guest to RoomType say, must then go through Reservation, and this can result in significant overhead if the access is frequent. It is possible to speed up access at run time by indexing and hash tables but this is an optimization and should not be a first-time decision. It is possible to eliminate, or at least reduce, overhead by also keeping direct references in one of the objects participating in the relationship, thus avoiding the need to go through the Reservation instance for some of the queries. Such a decision is not made easily, however, and may be an optimization more than an up-front decision.

> When designing associative objects, store references to each of the instances participating in the relationship. If there are frequent accesses from one of the sides of the relationship, consider adding in an additional reference from that instance to the associative-object instance.

How is the Reservation object reached? Is it reached from either object or by one specific path? Again, looking at data access in the object interaction diagrams

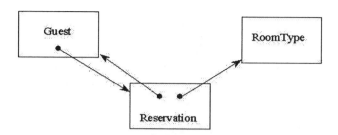

Figure 6.12. An example of an associative-object design.

we can gain much information that will help us decide the best way to design this relationship. In this example Reservation is usually searched for by Guest name as opposed to RoomType, therefore it might be better to keep the Reservation reference accessible from the Guest object. If this was a very frequent access we might want to provide a facility for storing references from Guest to Reservation (see Figure 6.12).

6.1.2.5 Subtype–Supertype

The inheritance structure of object-oriented design is the most straightforward means of mapping a subtype–supertype structure in design. Consider a hierarchy of banking transactions. Figure 6.13 shows a structure that can be mapped directly to an inheritance structure with a one-to-one mapping between objects and classes.

There are alternative methods for mapping these structures to design structures, and these are adequately identified by Martin and Odell (1996), among others. Whereas sometimes one would want to map to a different design structure that exits in the model (e.g., if implementing in a nonobject-oriented language), my preference is to create an object-structure model that can be mapped directly to a design structure. This is because the rationale for creating new subtypes during the modeling process should be such that all decisions to create a new subtype are validated, specifically for those reasons described in chapter 3. Namely, because there are characteristics that are different or there is behavior that is different across subtypes. If there wasn't a good reason for creating a subtype, then it should not exist at this stage of the life cycle.

6.1.2.6 Migrating Subtypes

Migrating subtypes were introduced in chapter 3 as a means of using subtyping to capture changes in the state of an object in which each state may have different

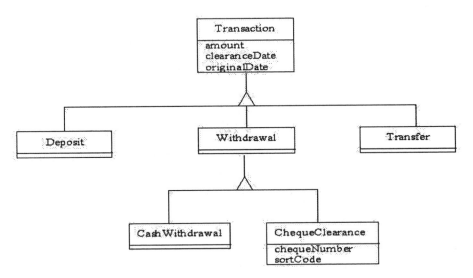

Figure 6.13. A subtype-supertype structure using inheritance.

attributes and/or different relationships. Figure 6.14 shows a Reservation object with three migrating subtypes.

There are two principal ways in which this modeling construct can be mapped to a design: a direct mapping of the model into the design or a mapping that hides the subtypes using delegation.

Direct mapping. The first method is a direct mapping of the structure to a design structure using classes. For the above example, a superclass Reservation will be created with three subclasses: BookedRes, ConfirmedRes, and CancelledRes.

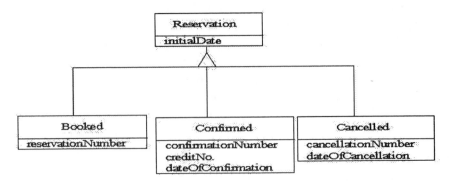

Figure 6.14. Migrating subtypes.

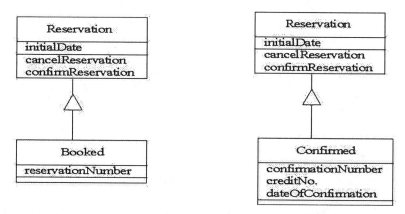

Figure 6.15. Migration from Booked to Confirmed.

When the initial reservation is made by the system operator, an instance of the class BookedRes is created. Once the booking becomes confirmed, the instance of BookedRes must be deleted and an instance of ConfirmedRes must be created (see Figure 6.15).

This transition (migration) must be coordinated in an operation in the Reservation class (say, Reservation::confirmReservation()). This operation must perform the following steps:

1. Lock current class Reservation.
2. Create a temporary copy of all data in BookedRes (includes superclass data, including those providing references to relationships that exist at the superclass level).
3. Create a new instance of ConfirmedRes, passing in new data and existing references at the superclass level (this should copy all of the data to instance of ConfirmedRes, and create a new instance of Reservation).
4. Unlock the original class and delete (this should remove all existing relationships at the subclass level, etc.).

As one can see these steps are nontrivial, for the following reasons:

- The Reservation object may have references to other instances for relationships in which it may be involved. If the references are *from* the Reservation *to* other classes this is easier to handle than from other classes to the Reservation.

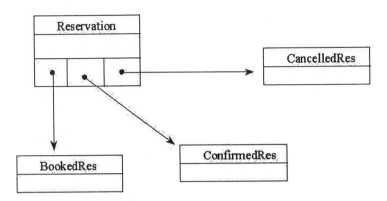

Figure 6.16. Designing migrating subtypes using subtype hiding with delegation.

- It is necessary to lock the class when managing this transition, as it may be accessed by other objects (say a status check on all Reservations).
- The identity of the original Reservation is lost.
- It can become a compute-intensive task if frequently performed.

Given the above reasons, a direct mapping is not the preferred option.

Subtype hiding using delegation. A more elegant means of designing structures to map from migrating subtypes is to create a class for the supertype and a separate class for each migrating subtype, but to have the superclass hold references to each of the subclasses, rather than use inheritance (see Figure 6.16). At any one time, only one subclass exists along with the superclass. The subclasses cannot be seen by the clients of the Reservation class. This method of using delegation and hiding subtypes also requires some work on the part of the programmer to manage the transition. The difficulties in managing the transition are a little easier than in the direct mapping, however.

So the previous example of migrating from a BookedRes to a ConfirmedRes requires the operation (again, Reservation::confirmReservation()) to perform the following tasks:

1. Delete the instance of BookedRes (this should terminate any relationships ate the subtype level).
2. Create an instance of ConfirmedRes passing in data as necessary.

We can see that this method is simpler than the previous one. Any polymorphic messages used in the analysis must be handled by the supertype, however, and then forwarded to the instance representing the subtype, as an instance of the subtype never actually exists (with the subtype–supertype structure being implemented using delegation).

> When implementing migrating subtypes, use subtype hiding with delegation, rather than a direct mapping.

6.1.3 Attributes

During the object-modeling activities, attributes are derived from characteristics of the objects in the real world. Attributes can be single or multivalued. The task during design is to decide how these attributes are to be mapped to a design construct. Figure 6.17 shows an object in modeling where the attributes need to be mapped to some design structure.

Attributes as functions. In some cases it is appropriate to have an attribute in the object model represented by a function during design. Thus when an attribute is used in an action of that object it is computed rather than used from a reference to some stored data.

This would be appropriate in situations where the value needs to be up to date and cannot be properly represented by a stored attribute. For the Portfolio object shown in Figure 6.17, it may have its attribute currentValue computed in real time and thus mapped to a function, as it can change from one moment to the next. As another example, altitude for an airplane-control system may be computed in real time when needed by various algorithms, rather than stored and updated at regular intervals.

> Represent attributes as functions/operations in design where the value must be computed in real time.

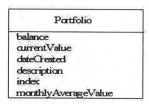

Figure 6.17. An object needing to have its attributes mapped.

Attributes as values. This is probably the most straightforward mapping, taking an attribute in the model and representing it as a value in the design. For example, the Portfolio object will most likely have the attribute dateOpened stored as a value. This is a one-off attribute and is not likely to change much.

Attributes as classes. Although it may not have been recognized as an object in the model, a class (or a data structure if not using a pure object-oriented language) may be the appropriate mapping for a multivalued attribute. For example, address is commonly an attribute of a customer or person object in models. This attribute can be represented by a class Address, which allows for different types and values as part of its structure.

> Consider using classes to represent multivalued attributes in a design.

6.2 Mapping Behaviors

In addition to the mapping of the structure models to design constructs, the behavioral concepts of models must also be mapped to design constructs. These behavioral models include the different forms of object interaction and object-state models.

6.2.1 Object Interactions

During the object-modeling activity, object interactions were modeled using object-interaction diagrams. These diagrams describe how an object instance interacts with another instance through message passing. In chapter 4 we identified the need for two types of communication:

1. *Synchronous:* A communication between two objects whereby the object sending the message, A, relinquishes control to the object receiving the message, B, until object B relinquishes that control. An example of a synchronous communication in implementation would be a member function invocation in C++.

2. *Asynchronous:* A communication between two objects whereby an object A sends a message to object B. Object A continues its processing, whereas object B, on receipt of this message, also begins processing. An example of an asynchronous communication in an implementation environment may be some form of interprocess communication.

The principal purpose for making the distinction between asynchronous and synchronous communication is twofold: (1) to ensure the modeling does not preclude any object distribution decisions, and (2) to fully exploit the natural concurrency of the problem domain when modeling interactions.

When moving to design, each of these two forms of communication must be mapped to a construct that is supportable by an implementation. This actual mapping cannot be completed until the object-distribution issues have been decided, which is described in chapter 7. The forms the mapping may take can be discussed, however. Let us look at the possibilities for each.

6.2.1.1 Synchronous Communication

Synchronous messages can be mapped most directly to method/operation invocations in the target environment. A C++ member-function invocation would be a prime example. Such a call requires that the class instance whose member function is being invoked is capable of receiving such a message. Any instance outside the process boundary must be invoked using whatever form of interprocess message communication is being used (see chapter 7).

> Map synchronous calls to simple method invocations when instances are within the same processing boundary.

An alternative mapping is to use callbacks. This is useful in those cases in which the instance receiving the first message does not need to know the identity of the sender, and hence the destination of the return message. This style of communication has been used for many years and has similar usage in object systems.

6.2.1.2 Asynchronous Communication

Asynchronous messages can be mapped to synchronous communication if the architecture and distribution of the system is such that an asynchronous communication is not necessary or is unsupported, or can be mapped to an asynchronous message if the implementation environment supports such communication.

> If two objects in an object-interaction diagram communicate via an asynchronous message and are located in different process spaces, then the asynchronous message should be carried through to implementation.

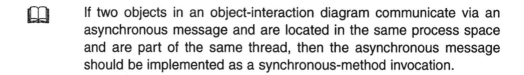   If two objects in an object-interaction diagram communicate via an asynchronous message and are located in the same process space and are part of the same thread, then the asynchronous message should be implemented as a synchronous-method invocation.

6.2.1.3 Broadcast Communication

This type of messaging is used when an object sends a message to all other objects without directing the message at any objects in particular. In fact whether the message is received or not is of no concern to the sender. It has performed its responsibility by sending the broadcast message. This message is a like a radio signal being broadcast in a certain region, and anyone interested in the music can tune in if he/she wishes.

    Broadcast messages need to be supported by the implementation environment if they are to be implemented as broadcasts. If not then the design needs to ensure that there is a list of all instances available so that a number of asynchronous messages can be used as a means of simulating broadcast communication.

6.2.1.4 Publish–Subscribe Communication

This messaging mechanism can be considered a specialized form of broadcast. A sender sends a number of messages to receivers who have registered an interest in receiving the message. The sending object accepts subscribe messages and then publishes results to subscribers. The sending of subscription messages is usually modeled as synchronous communication, whereas the publication of information is typically asynchronous, although synchronous communication can be employed. Use the guidelines of Sections 6.2.1.1 and 6.2.1.2 to determine which construct is appropriate in design.

6.2.1.5 Request–Reply Communication

The request–reply form of messaging occurs when an object requests some information from another by sending a message and receives a reply. It is possible to have one request with numerous replies, as opposed to a single reply. This would require asynchronous communication. It is also possible to have one request serviced by no reply, again requiring asynchronous communication or some time-out in the absence of a reply with some synchronous communication.

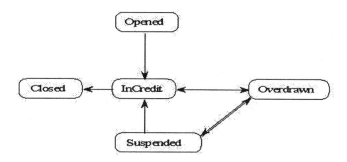

Figure 6.18. Example state model of an object, Account.

Depending on the type of request–reply being modeled, use asynchronous or synchronous communication. Use the guidelines of Sections 6.2.1.1 and 6.2.1.2 to determine which construct is appropriate in design.

6.2.2 State Models

If state modeling has been used to represent the life cycles of some objects, the object-state models need to be designed. Figure 6.18 shows an example of a basic state model for an Account object.

There are two principal means of providing a design structure to support object-state models. These will now be described.

Each active object is a finite state machine. This approach maps the state model of an object to a finite state machine in the design. There are a number of ways in which to do this. One method is to use a set of base classes that provide the facilities of finite-state machines, transitions, guards, and so on. These properties of the architecture framework can then be inherited by those classes with state models.

> For the most straightforward approach to designing state models, use a set of base-class libraries that provide much of the finite-state machine functionality.

There are fine examples of mechanisms in the literature that support this approach. Shlaer and Mellor (1990), and de Champeaux, Lea, and Faure (1993) are two such examples.

An alternative method is to use delegation to mimic the inheritance of the base classes. Each model object with a state model is mapped to a class containing a finite-state machine, which it uses to execute its state model.

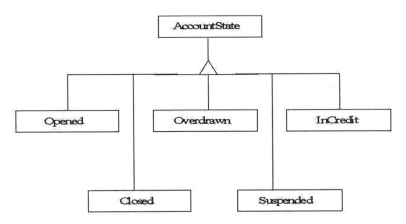

Figure 6.19. Each state is a class in design.

Each state is a class. In this approach each state of an object's state model is represented by a class in the design. So, for the example of Figure 6.18, the classes in the design become that of Figure 6.19.

Interestingly, de Champeaux et al. (1993) note that it is possible, and sometimes advantageous, to use the same root class for both the abstraction and the states.

> Using states as classes is a useful strategy for designing object-state models, especially when the object must be distributed across its state. It is especially useful for migrating subtypes with life cycles.

6.3   Use of Design Patterns

Design patterns are micro-architectures that can be reused from one application to another. Gamma, Helm, Johnson, and Vlissides (1994) have cataloged some 23 of these patterns, which they describe as "descriptions of communicating objects and classes that are customized to solve a general design problem in a particular context."

In their text Gamma and his colleagues provide an example of how design patterns can be used during design through the use of a case study of a Document Editor. This example nicely describes how the patterns can help in this particular design at a microlevel, but it does not provide any description of a process that allows the systematic application of such patterns on projects. This is left to the reader to determine, although the authors do provide some useful hints on how to use patterns.

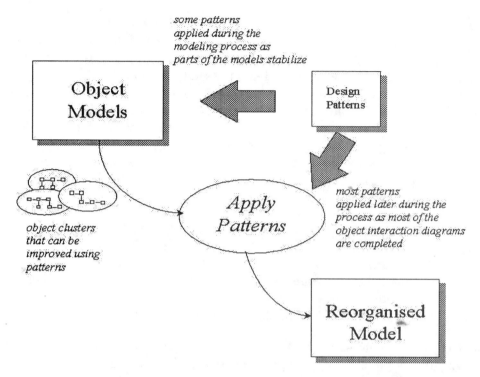

Figure 6.20. Using patterns with an object-oriented method.

When developing object systems in tight time scales and with teams of designers with varying levels of experience, design patterns are not as easy to use as perhaps the authors would wish. In many projects the team may not have the requisite experience and knowledge of how to use patterns, or may not feel confident enough in the process of using such patterns. After all, patterns should be used to apply a proven design structure to a common problem, and not be used as an end unto themselves. Figure 6.20 describes a process in which design patterns can be used within the boundaries of an object-oriented method, an issue that Gamma and colleagues do not address in their text.

It is generally difficult to apply patterns in large group sessions. I have seen them best applied by individuals when working on the parts of the models for which he or she is responsible. Assigning work based on clusters of objects and classes seems to work well in such scenarios.

Each cluster represents a group of related objects that are assigned to an individual or small team of individuals to work on. The object models related to these objects (static structure model, object-interaction diagrams, etc.) can then be matched against the pattern descriptions and if appropriate the pattern can be applied. Changes to other objects outside the grouping to which the patterns have been applied need to be documented and passed on to others.

This use of patterns can be attempted during the modeling process, as some patterns can be applied as models begin to stabilize. Gamma et al.'s (1994) book has a useful template for determining the applicability of a pattern in the pattern description and this is especially useful in judging whether or not a pattern is appropriate. Many patterns, however, are best applied later in the process during design, when the models need to be adjusted and reorganized to map to design constructs.

> When applying patterns, work on small clusters of objects in a small team or individually. Evaluate the models against the description of the pattern, the applicability, and the consequences. If appropriate, use the pattern to reorganize the model accordingly. Note any changes to potential objects outside your cluster, however, and discuss these at the next team session. It may be necessary to undo the pattern's changes due to incompatibilities.

As an example let us look at the use of a pattern to redesign a small cluster. Let us revisit the mapping of an analysis model to a design structure where inheritance was used to map from a subtype to a supertype structure This example was provided in an earlier section (Section 6.1.2.5). After deciding on the mapping, the team agreed that it was necessary to be able to change the implementation of transactions easily, but still use the design. This requirement emerged late in the process, as there were to be multiple implementations of executing transactions.

Once this requirement was identified (late in the process!) the affected class cluster was assigned to a small group of people who investigated the problem. Their investigations identified that the Bridge pattern described by Gamma et al. (1994) would be well suited for this problem. The Bridge pattern is used to "decouple an abstraction from its implementation so that the two can vary independently" (Gamma et al., 1994, p.151). This is achieved by having the abstraction and the implementation in separate class hierarchies, thereby achieving the decoupling.

The team then set about applying the pattern to the class cluster and making changes as necessary. The hierarchy of Figure 6.13 was then modified to that of Figure 6.21. The bridge is between the Transaction (the abstraction root class) and TransactionImp (the implementation root class).

We can see from the diagram that an OldTransactionImp provides one implementation and NewTransactionImp provides another.

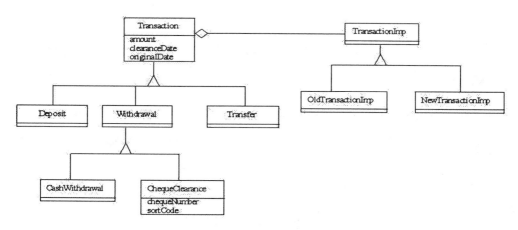

Figure 6.21 Application of the Bridge pattern.

The above example is a real example that demonstrates that the use of patterns can be effective after some design decisions have been made. The successful use of patterns requires knowledge of those patterns beforehand and the ability to recognize when and how to apply them successfully. For an inexperienced team of designers this is not always that simple. It can be helpful to identify one person in the team to be the guardian of patterns and to be responsible for determining if and when the use of a pattern is appropriate. The team can benefit from this person's viewpoint and learn as the patterns are applied. After a while, their confidence in patterns will increase and of course their inexperience will decrease.

> If you are interested in applying design patterns, identify one person in the team to be the guardian of patterns, whose responsibilities include determining if and when patterns are appropriate. The person should have a good understanding of patterns or at least the capacity for a good understanding.

> The pattern guardian should also be responsible for distributing knowledge about patterns to others in the team. Hold regular briefings to share such knowledge.

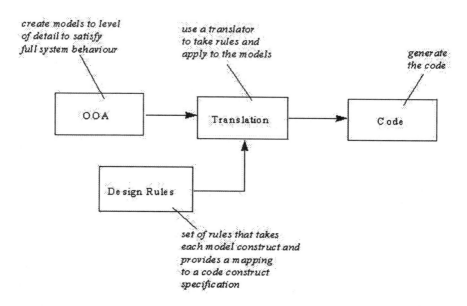

create models to level
of detail to satisfy
full system behaviour

use a translator
to take rules and
apply to the models

generate
the code

OOA

Translation

Code

Design Rules

set of rules that takes
each model construct and
provides a mapping
to a code construct
specification

Figure 6.22 The translational approach.

6.4 Performing the Mapping

The previous sections of this chapter have described some techniques for mapping object structures and object behaviors to design structures, which can then be implemented. These techniques can be used equally well in both translational and elaborational approaches. It is the process in which they are applied that differentiates the design of the two approaches, however. In this section we shall look at the processes and some of the issues surrounding each of the two approaches.

6.4.1 Translation

Chapter 2 outlined a process for the translational approach. It is shown again in Figure 6.22. In this context, design does not really exist. It can be viewed as the creation of a set of rules that will be used in the process of translating the analysis models into code.

The contents of the previous sections of this chapter are still applicable to this approach. However, they are used in creating the rules by which the models are translated. The key decision in creating a rule is deciding which mapping should be used for each type of a possible construct.

We shall use the example of mapping a 1:M relationship to illustrate some key points. Deciding which mapping will be used for 1:M relationships on the object-structure model, and also deciding under what conditions a particular mapping will be used is the goal of the rule set. An example rule would be:

> For all 1:M relationships on the object-structure model, create a reference on the M side that refers to the instance on the 1 side.

As we identified earlier, this may not be the most suitable structure for all 1:M relationships. If this is the case, then the rule must be qualified further. For example:

> For all 1:M relationships on the object-structure model where more than 75% of access is from the M side, create a reference on the M side. For all other 1:M relationships, create a list of references to the M side instances, in the 1 side.

The above rule specifies the mapping (keeping reference on the many side or a list of references on the one side), and also the criteria for using a particular mapping (dependent on the percentage of accesses from a particular side). Other criteria may be used instead, or may be added to the existing one to fine tune the rule.

The implementation of this rule has a number of implications that affect class behavior:

- *The creation of the instance containing the reference:* The instance containing the relationship reference needs to be set up such that its structure will allow it to store, update (if necessary), and delete references.
- *The population of references as the relationships are created:* Depending on the choice of mapping there will need to be some logic that handles the population of the reference identifying the relationship.
- *Traversing references in either case:* How relationships are traversed (that is, how it is possible to identify the other instances in the relationship) is dependent on the structure of the relationship. A list of instances on the one side could require some iteration through the list, whereas a reference on the many side would require some means of traversing all instances in existence to find the particular instance involved in the relationship. Whichever mechanism is used, some standard logic can be provided to handle each of the cases.
- *The deletion of references:* When a relationship ends the reference must be deleted.

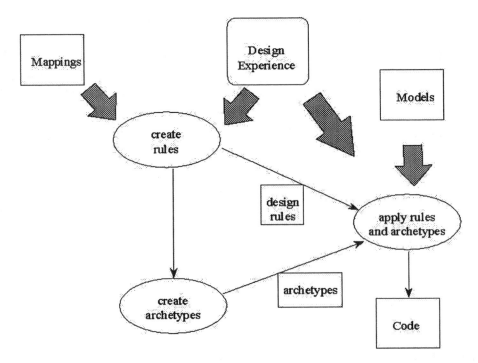

Figure 6.23 Creating rules and applying them.

Given the above implications it is not too difficult to imagine standard constructs that can be used as templates to apply the mapping based on the choice of mapping. This is possible through the creation of archetypical structures that can be used once the rule has been executed. Shlaer and Mellor (1990) identify archetypes as a set of standard template constructs that can be applied to objects on the model conforming to a particular rule. This template is essentially a series of code frames that provide the necessary infrastructure needed to support the implications of a rule.

The process of creating and using rules is shown in Figure 6.23.

Similarly, it is possible to create rules for other aspects of the object model. A state model, for example, may have a standard structure in the design, or there may be a choice of two, based on some criteria. Earlier we defined two possible mappings for state models so either of these could be a possibility attached with some criteria. It is possible to create a set of rules for all types of structures (objects, relationships, attributes, state models, etc.) that are applied according to the criteria that eventually become part of the rules.

The rules may be written down on a piece of paper, and executed manually, or one may create an intelligent translator, which takes rules as one set of inputs and the object models as another, and outputs code that conforms to the rules. More sophisticated translation engines and rules may also be created, or even purchased.

Performance tuning in this approach is done by editing the rules and reapplying them to the models. This means that in this paradigm the code is not the real asset: the models and the rules are. The code is "disposable." As Shlaer and Mellor (1993, p. 20) point out:

> We have seen a case where the real challenge was in achieving adequate performance. . . . On this project the application modules were complete and stabilized for a significant period of time while the designers iterated through a series of software architectures, searching for one that could meet the real-time requirements. The transformation engine made it possible for the designers to experiment with many creative tasking strategies and the like to arrive at a satisfactory solution.

The use of the term "architecture" above refers to the set of rules used to map from models to implementation. Architecture is Shlaer and Mellor's term. As mentioned in chapter 2, in a translational approach the rules are the essence of the design. The real challenge in writing the rules is deciding on the criteria of how to apply them.

When creating rules, go through all possible mappings for all constructs and determine under which circumstances each mapping would be used. The architect should be a key part of this effort.

6.4.2 Elaboration

Figure 6.24 describes the process of elaborating analysis models to code. It is the same process that is shown in chapter 2. In the translational approach, design does not exist, but is replaced by the writing of rules. In the elaborational approach design is more of an extension of the modeling, where the analysis models are extended and transformed to take into account design decisions and architecture.

Let us look again at the design of a 1:M relationship. In this approach each individual 1:M relationship will be assessed and the decision on which mapping to use will be made. So for some relationships we will choose to keep a reference on the M side and on others we will keep a list of references on the 1 side. Once the decision has been made, we will extend the model to record that decision and move on.

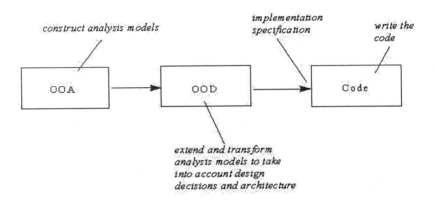

Figure 6.24 The elaborational approach.

The process of elaborating the models can be a systematic one or an ad hoc one depending on the rigor and thoroughness of the people carrying out the process. It is essentially a manual process that will depend on the individuals executing it.

Elaboration is an additive process that requires a gradual shift in the approach from analysis models to design models to creating the code. As Rumbaugh (1996) points out:

> The development process is a series of decisions. The best kind of model is one in which the individual design decisions are captured directly in an additive form, i.e., successive decisions are represented by separate modeling elements that add to, rather than replace, modeling elements representing earlier design decisions.

Performance tuning in such an approach is achieved by making adjustments to the models. Changes could include: using different mappings for structures, reorganizing subtype–supertype structures, algorithm optimization, and so on.

6.4.3 Performance Issues

The decisions made during design have a major impact on the performance of the system. During design it is difficult to predict the performance of the system except with the use of limited-value tool sets, such as simulators and prototypes, but these only provide an indication of performance expectations and not a detailed analysis. The aforementioned comments notwithstanding, there are some areas to be aware of that can drastically impact performance:

- *Traversal of relationships:* This is one of the biggest impact decisions on performance. Because relationships are so central to object systems, the iteration through lists and traversal of references can be very computationally intensive tasks. It is worth taking the time to determine the optimum mapping for each relationship on the model.

  Keeping records of how relationships are accessed, etc. as the modeling proceeds is a good way of being prepared for design decisions at this time.

- *Broadcasting messages to numerous receivers:* Broadcasts require sending messages to all instances. This should be used very rarely as a single broadcast can affect all instances in a system or a broadcast region.

- *Excessive communication between objects:* Object systems are rich in communication, and designers should be aware of objects that interact heavily. It may be a case of their being in the same address space, or even being combined into a single design structure.

- *Inappropriately distributed objects:* This will be addressed in the next chapter, but inappropriate distribution can lead to systems that have too much interprocess communication, are continually swapping new tasks in and out, or are very compute-intensive.

- *Inappropriate mappings:* Choosing the right mapping for a relationship or an object is very important. The designers should be guided by experienced resources, such as the architect.

- *Object creation and deletion:* An object-oriented system may contain thousands of objects. Object creation can be very compute-intensive tasks as they are initiated, relationships created, and so on. Similarly, deletion can also be very compute-intensive.

- *Algorithms:* Complex objects that perform detailed and complex algorithms can have a negative effect on performance. Optimization of such algorithms may be necessary.

- *Messaging mechanisms:* Using synchronous access, for example, for external systems, when asynchronous access is preferred, can have a performance impact.

6.5 Summary

This chapter has presented a discussion of issues that are relevant in designing object systems. A series of mappings for object structure and object of relevant behaviors were presented. They addressed the following:

- Mapping objects to classes. Two approaches were introduced: One object to one class and more than one object to one class.

- Mapping various relationship forms to design structures. One-to-one and one-to-many forms were described, with a number of schemes for each presented.

- Mapping migrating subtype structures. Two approaches were presented: A direct mapping with subtypes being created and deleted during migration, and a delegation-based approach with hidden subtypes.

- Mapping attributes. Attributes can be mapped to values, functions executed at run time, or even classes where appropriate.

- Mapping object interactions. The various mappings for the different types of communication were introduced.

- Mapping state models. Two mechanisms were described for mapping state models: representing each state of an object as a class, and using architectural classes to provide state-machine behavior that can be inherited by those objects with state models.

A process for using patterns within the broader context of an object-oriented method was also described.

In describing the methods for design, the elaborational and translational approaches to design were revisited with some key issues being addressed in each section. In addition to this some of the design decisions affecting performance were introduced. They were as follows:

- traversal of relationships

- broadcasting messages to numerous receivers

- excessive communication between objects

- inappropriately distributed objects

- inappropriate mappings

- object creation and deletion

- algorithms

References

de Champeaux, D., Lea, D., & Faure, P. (1993). *Object-Oriented System Development.* Reading, MA: Addison-Wesley.

Gamma, E., Helm, R., Johnson, R., & Vlissides, J. (1994). *Design Patterns: Elements of Reusable Object-Oriented Software.* Reading, MA: Addison-Wesley.

Martin, J., & Odell, J. (1996). *Object-Oriented Methods: Pragmatic Considerations.* Upper Saddle River, NJ: Prentice-Hall.

Rumbaugh, J. (1996). Layered additive models: Design as a process of recording design decisions. *Journal of Object-Oriented Programming, 9(1).*

Shlaer, S., & Mellor, S. (1990). *Object Lifecycles—Modeling the World in States.* Englewood Cliffs, NJ: Prentice-Hall.

Shlaer, S., & Mellor, S. (1993). A deeper look..at the transition from analysis to design. *Journal of Object-Oriented Programming, 5(9),* 16–21.

CHAPTER 7

CLIENT—SERVER AND OBJECT DISTRIBUTION

W ITH THE GROWING GEOGRAPHICAL distribution of today's businesses and the need to access information from a wide variety of systems, the need for distributed systems is increasing considerably. Client–server is the architecture of many distributed systems. This chapter looks at two key issues involved in building object-oriented client–server systems, namely, object distribution and accessing legacy systems.

7.1 The Client—Server Model

The client–server model emerged as an extension of shared device processing typically found in local-area-network environments. As the desktop became more powerful and so did the file servers, people started using file servers for more than just file-and-print services, and desktops for more than just presentation. Application processing was no longer resident on large hosts but was now distributed across platforms—clients and servers. Berson (1992) provides a good description of client–server history and technologies.

Some of the advantages of client–server are as follows:

- allows leveraging of emerging technologies
- processing can be close to source of data
- facilitates use of graphical user interfaces available on powerful workstations and desktops
- can make leverage the use of functionality on existing systems
- allows distribution of functionality as needed

A few of the major disadvantages of client–server are as follows:

- complexity can increase as the system becomes distributed
- cost—clients, middleware, servers, and so on
- servers can become potential bottlenecks

Original client–server systems were said to be "two-tiered." That is, they were essentially made up of a tier of presentation logic tied to a tier of data logic, with processing of business rules either achieved on the client and/or the server.

A "three-tier" client–server architecture provides a considerable number of advantages over two tiers and alleviates some of the issues of two-tier architectures: Specifically, difficulties in scaleability and the difficulty of changing business rules. The three-tier architecture separates the business logic as a separate logical tier, thereby decoupling the presentation and data, allowing ease of change of any one tier without affecting both others. Figure 7.1 shows a logical two-tier architecture and a three-tier architecture.

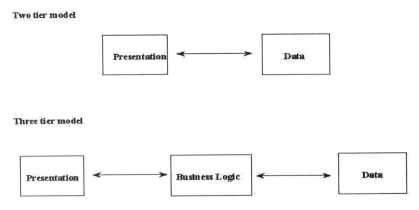

Figure 7.1. Two- and three-tier architecture models.

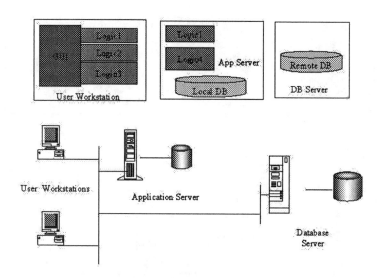

Figure 7.2. Mapping a three-tier logical environment to a physical one.

One of the major advantages of a three-tier model is that it can be mapped to a number of different physical environments, as shown in Figures 7.2 and 7.3.

We can see from these figures that business logic, data access, and presentation can be partitioned and mapped to different physical environments. The business-logic functionality will be a series of objects interacting to provide the functionality. As we can see these can be distributed in a number of ways when the logical structure is moved to a physical environment.

The message-passing paradigm of object technology fits in well with the client–server model as both rely on communication to another entity to perform a task. Objects send messages to each other and perform tasks on receipt of a message. Clients send requests to servers who fulfill those requests. In this way we see that objects are clients, clients are objects, servers are objects, and objects are servers.

7.2   Object Distribution

It is the distributed nature of client–server systems that pose a challenge to the system design and development teams—namely, how to distribute objects in a client–server environment?

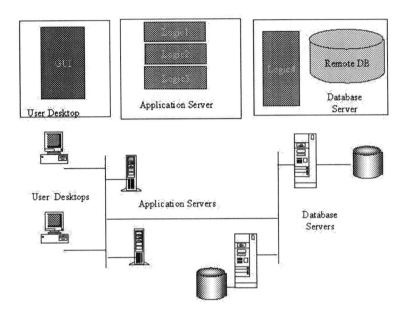

Figure 7.3. Another mapping of a three-tier logical environment to a physical one.

The unit of distribution as used in this book is the cluster. A cluster is a group of classes that have been allocated together to be considered collectively in distribution. A cluster could be considered a large-grain object that has a number of responsibilities for its constituent members. They are as follows:

- *Manage memory:* The instances of the classes identified in a cluster will have certain memory requirements as they are created, create and delete other instances, and are themselves deleted. The cluster can be responsible for allocating and deallocating memory for its constituent instances.

- *Group objects together:* The cluster is a unit of grouping for objects.

- *Provide a single address space:* Object instances within the cluster reference each other directly using unique addresses within a single address space.

- *Provide an operating environment:* The cluster provides an environment in which objects may be created, deleted, and may carry out their responsibilities.

- *Deliver messages to the individual members:* The messages to a particular member of a cluster can be sent to the cluster with the appropriate index provided to uniquely identify the member. The cluster is then responsible for delivering the message.

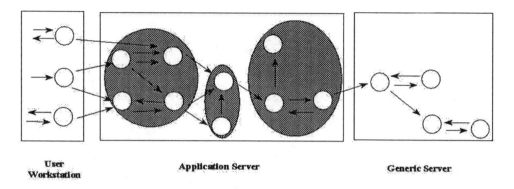

Figure 7.4. Objects distributed across a three-tier physical architecture.

7.2.1 Distributing the Objects

Unfortunately, there is no cookbook approach to distributing objects. There are a number of different criteria against which objects can be distributed, and a number of different distribution schemes that can be employed. In a three-tier architecture the goal is to distribute objects across hardware boundaries, and if operating in a multiprocessing environment, also across process boundaries. The distribution is done after the object models (both static and dynamic) have been created, prior to any implementation. In an elaborational approach the distribution is typically done manually after the design issues have been incorporated into the models. Whereas in a translational approach the distribution is carried out as part of the translation rules.

Figure 7.4 shows a number of objects distributed across a three-tier architecture. The boxes represent different hardware and the shaded ovals represent processes within a particular server.

In determining how to distribute objects there are a number of guidelines we can follow. Figure 7.5 illustrates a general process that can be followed for distributing objects.

Let us look at each step in turn.

7.2.1.1 Start with Defaults

The first step begins with a listing of the basic requirements and constraints in which the system must operate, along with some of the "given" decisions. These

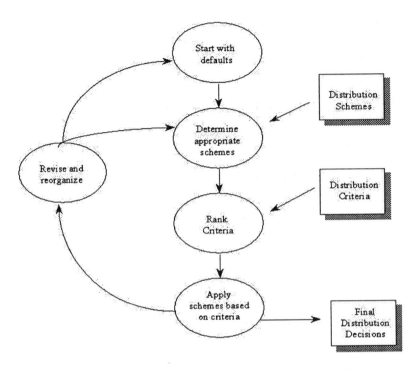

Figure 7.5. High-level process for object distribution.

decisions are those partitioning choices that are the initial defaults used to provide an initial straw model. Some of these are as follows:

- User-interface objects are most likely to be placed on the desktop client.
- Identify object groupings that perform a well-defined service, as these will likely be clustered together and distributed together.
- Objects that directly communicate with devices on some hardware should be grouped together into a cluster, and should reside on a platform as "near" to the device as possible.
- Distinguish between asynchronous and synchronous communication when distributing objects.

Part of this initial set of defaults involves calculations around the use of the network because the availability of a network can so heavily affect a client–server system. As a result, network capacity and utilization play an important part in the performance of the application, as well as in the capacity of the distribution to work. Therefore, at this stage coarse-grain calculations are used to identify high-level network issues. On large systems, performing this at the object level is futile. Performing such exercises at the subsystem level is worthwhile, however, as figures may reveal communication problems that may require the movement of whole groups of objects.

Some of the calculations worth looking into are as follows:

- *Estimate the amount of communication under typical and extreme usage.* It is worthwhile to estimate the amount of interobject communication that may exist in the system under typical and extreme usage. Working with estimates of average number of users, average work rate for a user, typical tasks for users, and so on helps to begin the process by which these numbers are arrived at. These are then used as input to calculations that will lead to number of messages across the network, and so on.

- *Estimate the number of instances of objects and creation-and-deletion rates.* In order to determine whether or not object creation and deletion will have an effect on the distribution, it is worthwhile to estimate the average number of objects being created and deleted over a period of time. Create-and-delete events can require establishing and closing references to other objects for managing relationships. This may require communication to these other objects thereby affecting the network.

- *Estimate the frequency and quantity of updates that will affect network traffic.* There may be regular real-time updates to objects in some environments, such as financial services with publish-and-subscribe services. These may have an impact on the network traffic.

7.2.1.2 Determine Appropriate Distribution Schemes

There are a number of schemes that can be used to distribute objects. We will use the partial-object model of an order-entry system, shown in Figure 7.6, as the basis for our discussion on the description of schemes.

By object type. This scheme distributes objects according to type. Therefore, all instances, or some defined subset of instances, of a particular object type will be located in a cluster. There may be other object types that are also part of that cluster. In this scenario, there will not be any instances of a particular object type outside that cluster. Its usage is illustrated in Figure 7.7. We can see that cluster 1 contains instances of type CustomOrder, OrderItem, and StockItem, whereas cluster 2 contains instances of Customer, CorporateAccount and IndividualAccount.

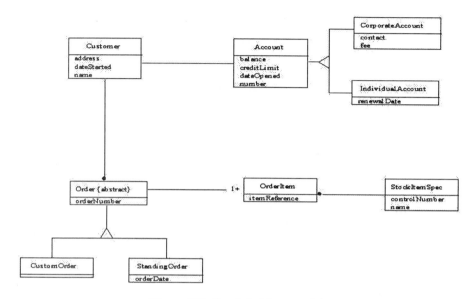

Figure 7.6. Partial object model.

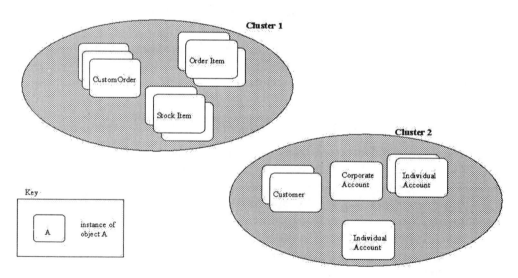

Figure 7.7. Distribution by object type.

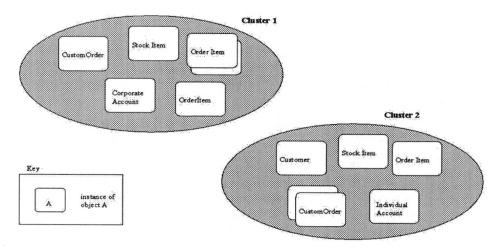

Figure 7.8. Distribution by object instance.

Distribution by object type is good for objects with strong relationships that need to be grouped together. It is especially useful for structural criteria (see below).

The problem with this form of distribution is that it usually requires a great deal of communication across clusters. This is because most systems do not have objects of the same type communicating as often as objects of different types.

By object instances. This is the most commonly used scheme that groups together instances of objects in a cluster. The grouping is determined by the instances that exist according to some situation, typically in one-or-more-communication scenarios, rather than the type of object they belong to. Its usage is illustrated in Figure 7.8. We can see that cluster 1 has instances of CustomOrder, StockItem, CorporateAccount, and OrderItem. Cluster 2 has similar instances.

Distribution by object instances is especially suited for systems with high object-communication profiles.

By object states. This scheme is sometimes used for objects with state models. It is also possible to use the above schemes for objects with state models, but sometimes this approach is more suitable. Using this approach, it is possible to locate some states of an object in one cluster and some other states in another cluster. This approach splices an object into a number of pieces, with each piece

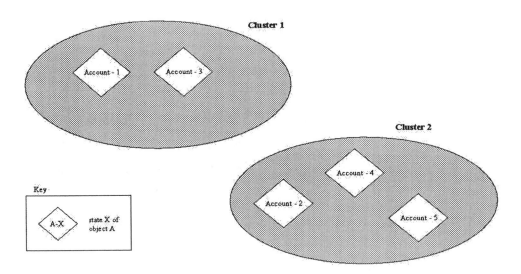

Figure 7.9. Distribution by object states.

being represented either as a class or as some other construct in nonobject-oriented designs. It is especially useful for distributing an object when it has been designed such that each state is a separate class (see chapter 6). This scheme is more likely to be used in a nonobject-oriented design, however.

Figure 7.9 shows states 1 and 3 of Account in one cluster and states 2, 4, and 5 in another. There will be other objects in these clusters also,[1] although they are not shown. The split by states could occur for a number of reasons: One is because some states have closer links to certain objects than others. Another is because some states may require more power to compute, as they may be performing complex tasks, and so must reside in a different machine.

These three distribution schemes—type, instances, and states—are not mutually exclusive and typically one uses a combination of these schemes. The process of determining which schemes are appropriate for which clusters needs to be driven by the architect. This is done by analyzing the various modeling work-products, such as the object-structure model, the object-communication model (which summarizes all the object-interaction diagrams), and the object-state models. The architect should drive the process of investigating distribution schemes by working through communication-prototype schemes and investigating their suitabilities against the scenarios most likely to occur.

---

[1]These objects may or may not be split by states.

7.2.1.3 Rank Criteria

Objects can be distributed according to a number of criteria. For example, object communication may be a major issue in a system and therefore is used as a primary factor in determining how to distribute the objects. For another system, the availability of compute power may be of primary importance. Therefore, for that particular system, issues that affect computation will be high on the list of criteria. The distribution thus varies from system to system.

Once the schemes have been investigated it is necessary to rank the criteria. Then, using the criteria, objects are grouped into clusters according to the scheme identified. So if using states for some objects, then a cluster of object states will need to be created and the nature of how it will communicate, and so on will need to be determined. For other schemes such as communication, the procedure is more straightforward as whole objects are grouped together into tightly coupled communication clusters, which form the units of distribution.

Some of the more common criteria are listed here.

- *Structural:* Objects closely related should be grouped together. For this it will be necessary to look at the object-structure model and group objects together based on their relationships. Subtype–supertype structures are usually kept together in such a scheme, as are associative objects.

- *Communication:* This is directed at objects that heavily interact. Examine object interaction (using an object-communication model) to identify those objects that are in heavy communication with each other.

- *Tasks:* Objects in a single threaded task should be grouped together.

- *Collections:* Objects that may be part of the same collection can be grouped together.

- *Computation:* Any group of objects requiring substantial, simultaneous compute time may be grouped in order so that the grouping may be distributed separately.

The above list consists of the categories I have used. De Champeaux et al. (1993) also provide a good list of clustering criteria. As they point out: "Because clustering remains something of a black art, it is very convenient to use a prototyping tool to assist in the evaluation of clusterings." Object distribution is certainly more of an art than a science at this point in time.

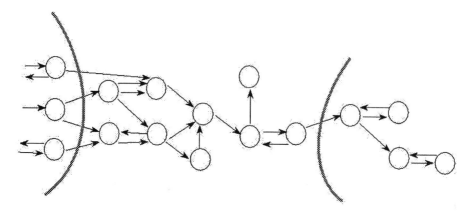

Figure 7.10. The object-communication model can be used as part of the first pass of partitioning.

7.2.1.4 Apply Schemes Based on Criteria

Once the criteria have been ranked and the schemes identified, they can be applied to the objects. For example, if using a communication-based criteria with whole instances for the items being distributed, then an object-communication model can be used as the input to the decisions. Figure 7.10 provides a high-level illustration of this idea.

After these objects have been partitioned one can look at the partitions to determine where they will reside and if they have to be further partitioned into processes. If so, then we return to the schemes and criteria for our grouping into clusters for processes.

7.2.1.5 Revise and Reorganize

Once the stakes have been put in the ground and explored, it is worth using tools to help determine if the distribution scheme is worthwhile. Here some of the newer second-generation client–server tool kits (see section 7.3) may help, or, as an alternative, one could use simulation tools.

It is then worth revisiting the decisions, and iterating back to the earlier stages to go through the process again. It is unusual to get it right the first time around. Finally, if bottlenecks still exist or you are limited by hardware choices, you may need to revisit your initial decisions, as outlined in section 7.2.1.1.

7.2.1.6 An Example Following the Overall Process

The overall distribution process is not always straightforward, but if one begins with the defaults and the basic ideas, it is possible to decompose a fairly large system into some initial clusters, and gradually reduce the numbers of objects still to be distributed. There is a notion of trial and error but also of "common sense" throughout the process.

For example, let us say we are distributing objects for an order-entry system that will use PCs as the desktop clients, UNIX servers for logic and local database access, and will access an ES9000 mainframe for some functionality. We decide to use communication-based criteria along with structural criteria, and partition by instances as the scheme, we may decide on the following when going through the process:

1. **Start with defaults.** Our high-level structuring decisions lead us to decide that we will move all user-interface logic to the PCs; and all business logic will be on the UNIX server, except those that access the mainframe functionality, which will be a series of object-based access methods using an ORB (object request broker). The data-access functionality will also reside on the UNIX server, as we are using a relational DBMS (database management system).

2. **Determine appropriate schemes.** We decide that instance-based schemes are most appropriate as we have strong communication links between objects.

3. **Rank criteria.** The most important criteria are the communication-based ones, then come structural criteria, which are followed by the others.

4. **Apply schemes based on criteria.** We conduct an analysis of the object-communication model and partition the objects based on communication. Using a set of instance diagrams and interaction diagrams we identify instances that are tightly bound together along communication paths and group them into a cluster.

   Looking at the object-structure model identifies clusters of objects that have many relationships within the clusters. We see that objects related to Customers and Accounts in the same cluster, and another major cluster is formed around Orders, Line Items, and Stock.

   The deliverable is a document illustrating the clusters, their groupings, and their locations. The rationale for decisions must also be recorded.

5. **Revise and reorganize.** Having performed the initial distribution, we now need to look in detail at the clusters to look for process-boundary definitions. This will require another iteration, and a more detailed examination of object-interaction diagrams and instance diagrams.

7.2.2 Access to Objects

A key feature of distributed systems is the sharing of objects across multiple clients. Access to objects that are shared, such as service objects, must be carefully controlled. Use of an object request broker as the middleware will help make things easier. In some of the initial systems in which I have been involved, however, such facilities were not available. In order to highlight some of the issues, I shall explain the issues surrounding that project.

The objects to be shared were service objects. The pricing service was one of the most heavily used service objects. As a result there was a need to introduce locking and unlocking during design. This was because the protocol for locking and unlocking would impact some of the later decisions about the design of these objects. Figure 7.11 shows a pricing-service object and its contract with a client. The service-provision contract consists of five key steps:

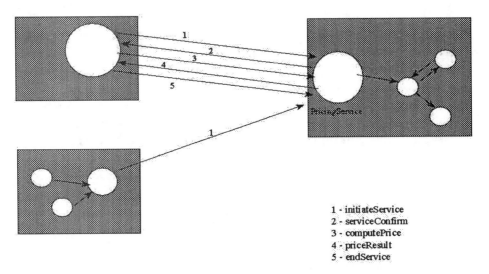

1 - initiateService
2 - serviceConfirm
3 - computePrice
4 - priceResult
5 - endService

Figure 7.11. Access to service object PricingService.

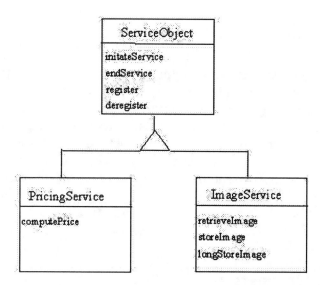

Figure 7.12. Abstract class ServiceObject and subclasses.

1. *initiateService:* Identifies requester and locks object so only this requester can access service object from here on (time out ensures safety in case of client failover).

2. *serviceConfirm:* Reply from service object to initiate request.

3. *computePrice:* Client sends request and references to data. Service object performs calculation.

4. *priceResult:* Service object returns result to client.

5. *endService:* Sign-off by client; this unlocks service object.

During the communication between requester and service object no other object was permitted to communicate with the same instance of the service object. This means that the service object has to initiate some locking mechanism that will ensure it will not respond to any other requests. An abstract class ServiceObject provides such a mechanism to ensure such functionality, as shown in Figure 7.12.

The locking and unlocking of shared objects needs to be performed for all shared objects in a distributed system.

7.3   Accessing Legacy Systems

Many client–server systems are being used to leverage existing functionality on legacy systems while providing a migration path from those systems. As such, much of the functionality of a client–server system in its first phase may still actually be executed on a legacy system, such as a mainframe. It is therefore necessary to provide a means of accessing that functionality and data, and also providing an interface such that migration from the legacy system can be possible. Most legacy systems are functionally oriented, and providing an object-oriented interface to the functionality can be challenging. The most popular technique, which has numerous variations, is to use *object wrappers*. An alternative that is sometimes more appealing is to use an object-based approach.

7.3.1 Object Wrappers

An object wrapper, as described by Mowbray and Zahavi (1995), "allows us to provide access to legacy system through an encapsulation layer. The encapsulation exposes only those attributes and operation definitions desired by the software architect." The wrapper essentially provides a link between old and new, with one side implemented using the legacy system's communication mechanisms and the other side providing an interface to the new application.

When wrappers were first used, the method was to create one or two classes that would access the legacy-system functionality; provide arbitrary names for these classes, say LegacyAccess; create one instance of each class, which would then have as its interface a series of operations mapping directly to the functions it is wrapping (see Figure 7.13).

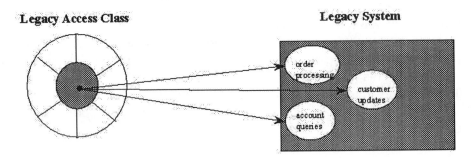

Figure 7.13. Single wrapper class with no semantic context.

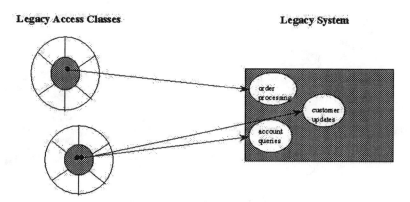

Figure 7.14. Multiple wrapper classes with semantic context.

Although this approach works fine in the short term and does provide an interface to the legacy system, it is not a recommended approach because it does not provide any real semantic context to the messages being sent to it and those it will subsequently call. It is really just a series of operations that happen be provided by a class. It is better to separate the functionality of the legacy system and map it to a set of objects with a semantic link. Use of a meaningful set of classes also means that the functionality of the legacy system can be gradually migrated in coherent pieces of functionality.

The value of a semantic context to the legacy-system interface is especially important for those that are providing multiple services to the new system and thus need to be distinguished from each other. For example, grouping a series of calls for order processing, account inquiry, and customer record updates is not worthwhile if in the future the next step is to migrate customer record updates off the legacy system and onto the new system. Creating separate classes for certain areas will make it easier to separate these services into several wrapper classes with semantic context, thus making a cleaner interface and allowing for an easier migration (see Figure 7.14).

> When wrapping legacy-system functionality, perform some analysis on the functionality to be accessed and map to a set of objects that reflect the objects within the existing system.

Wrapper performance can sometimes be a problem. Some wrapper implementations block the client when making calls to the legacy system. This means the processing is stopped on the client while the legacy operations are being execut-

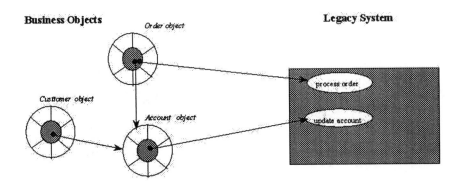

Figure 7.15. Object-based access.

ed. This can lead to performance problems because other tasks that could have been executed in parallel cannot be carried out, and have to wait for the legacy call to return, which creates an unnecessary delay. One possibility of averting this is to use asynchronous calls to the legacy system where possible, thus allowing the client to continue processing until the functionality being executed on the legacy system has been completed. Such a mechanism would, of course, need to be supported by the implementation environment.

7.3.2 Object-Based Access

This alternative, but similar, approach to accessing legacy systems also uses objects with semantic context to access legacy systems. It does not, however, use a single interface or a small set of classes to access the legacy system, but utilizes a scheme whereby the legacy system is accessed as needed throughout the business objects. The interface thus being accessed across the business objects is illustrated in Figure 7.15.

The difference between this approach and the previous one is that the legacy-system functionality is accessed throughout the system by the business objects as part of their processing rather than being provided by a separate series of objects whose sole existence is to provide an interface-object layer. Previously the business objects would send a message to an object wrapper, whereas now they can access the legacy system directly, or, even better, through a thinner wrapper layer.

This approach can be taken even further now that it is possible to purchase object request brokers that run on legacy systems such as mainframes (Kei Stewart,

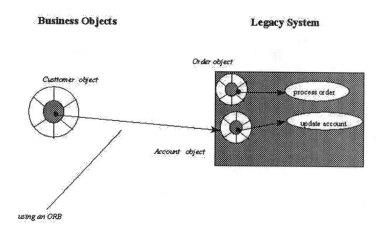

Figure 7.16. Objects on legacy systems.

1996). Where considerable functionality is to be executed on a legacy system, it is possible to have objects executing on that mainframe that provide the link to the functionality. This is illustrated in Figure 7.16.

Using this approach does require a more detailed understanding and integration of the functionality of the legacy system. Therefore it is necessary to carry out an object-oriented analysis of the existing functionality to be able to create the "right" objects.

7.3.3 Using the Bridge Pattern for Accessing Legacy Systems

The Bridge pattern, described briefly in an earlier chapter, and described fully by Gamma et al. (1994), can also be used to provide wrappers. The principal use of the Bridge pattern is to decouple an abstraction from its implementation, thus facilitating ease of change. This is achieved through the use of separate abstraction-and-implementation hierarchies. Clients only "see" the abstraction hierarchy.

Figure 7.17 illustrates how the legacy-system access, carried out by the Order-Legacy class, can be separated from clients. When wishing to migrate away from the Legacy system, the class OrderLegacy can be replaced with a new implementation.

Use the Bridge pattern to provide an object-based access to functionality currently executing on a legacy system, in cases for which you wish to later migrate the implementation away from the legacy system.

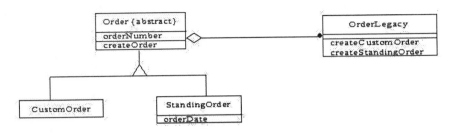

Figure 7.17. Using the Bridge pattern to access legacy systems.

7.4 Summary

This chapter introduced the client–server model and two key issues that must be addressed in constructing such systems: object distribution and accessing legacy systems.

A general process for object distribution was presented with five key steps:

1. start with defaults
2. determine appropriate schemes
3. rank criteria
4. apply schemes based on criteria
5. revise and reorganize

In the description of this approach a number of key issues were identified:

* There is no cookbook process.
* There are three primary ways of distributing objects, which can be used together.
  1. by object type
  2. by object instance
  3. by object state
* Numerous criteria exist for making distribution decisions. They are not mutually exclusive and are often used in combination. They can be ranked, however, based on the particular system needs.
* The object-distribution process is iterative and is subject to trial and error.

Accessing legacy systems is a key issue for many organizations today. Two methods for accessing legacy systems were introduced:

1. *Object wrappers:* Simple wrappers are of limited value; wrappers with semantic context are far more valuable.
2. *Object-based access:* This allows for a more distributed interface but a richer migration path.

References

Berson, A. (1992). *Client/Server Architecture*. New York: McGraw-Hill.

de Champeaux, D., Lea, D., & Faure, P. (1993). *Object-Oriented System Development*. Reading, MA: Addison-Wesley.

Gamma, E., Helm, R., Johnson, R., & Vlissides, J. (1994). *Design Patterns: Elements of Reusable Object-Oriented Software*. Reading, MA: Addison-Wesley.

Graham, I. (1994). *Migrating to Object Technology*. Wokingham, UK: Addison-Wesley.

Kei Stewart, M. (1996, July). Executive briefs: Orbix moving to MVS. *Object Magazine*, 9.

Mowbray, T., &. Zahavi, R. (1995). *The Essential CORBA: Systems Integration Using Distributed Objects*. New York: Wiley.

CHAPTER 8

PUTTING IT TOGETHER AND MAKING IT ALL WORK

A LL THE TECHNICAL strategies, techniques, and idioms in the world will not guarantee a successful project if the project is not managed correctly. This is not a book on project management—there are others covering that topic. This final chapter presents, however, a number of strategies and ideas on putting it all together and managing the process.

We begin with a description of the core roles involved in an object project and their activities during each stage of the process model, which was described in chapter 2. The description of roles and activities was not covered earlier because it requires an appreciation of the rest of the context of the book for it to be of maximum value.

Tracing requirements is an essential activity in a project with respect to quality and is also a means of measuring success for the project as a whole. With many organizations still employing a requirements-specification-type approach, some ideas and strategies on how to address this approach are presented.

We conclude this chapter, and this book, with some strategies on managing the project, tracking progress, and running workshops. We close the chapter with the six most critical success factors of object-oriented projects.

8.1   Team Structure and Roles

There are a number of different people involved on an object-oriented project, from the project manager/team leader to the quality assurance expert. Not all roles are full-time roles, and one person may play multiple roles. There are, however, a number of core roles that are worth describing. They are as follows:

- *System Architect:* Discussed in detail in chapter 5, the system architect is responsible for creating the macroarchitecture of the system, maintaining the architectural integrity of the software, and consulting with various design, implementation, integration, and quality-assurance teams.

- *Object Modelers:* These are the key individuals involved in creating the object models. There should be two types of experienced object modelers on a project: object modeler and senior object modeler.

  An object modeler should have a good grasp of object concepts and solid experience with at least one object-oriented methodology. The object modeler should also have participated previously in the full life cycle of at least one complete object development. The primary tasks of the object modeler is to participate in modeling activities and to mentor the inexperienced modelers on the team.

  A senior object modeler has been an object modeler on at least two other projects; is an expert of at least one object-oriented methodology; can mentor the team concepts and techniques; and can direct the modeling process, involving the team. The senior object modeler and the system architect may be the same person, but these are two distinct roles. The primary tasks of the senior object modeler on a project is to ensure the integrity of the models and to mentor and grow the other modelers on the project.

  Project Manager: The project manager in an object-oriented project plays a role similar to that of other projects. He or she is responsible for the project being executed in an efficient manner and completed on time and within budget. It is not essential that the project manager of an object-oriented project has experienced an object-oriented project before, as long as she or he is surrounded by people who have had experience, and there is a mentor from whom he or she can seek guidance.

If the project manager has not had any exposure to object projects, then he or she should be mentored by someone with extensive experience in the management of object-oriented projects. This mentor may be the architect or a senior object modeler.

- *Domain Experts:* A domain expert is an expert on the system. A domain expert is not necessarily the person who will be the prime user of a system; for example, a qualified expert on insurance policies may not be the primary user of a system used to provide car-insurance quotations to customers over the telephone. He or she will, however be the expert on the business domain and the rules and policies of that subject matter.

  A variety of domain experts will be needed in the life cycle, both for variety and different perspectives on the same domain, and also for information on the different domains that make up a system.

- *End Users:* The involvement of end users in the development process is essential for the construction of systems that will be used, and will be what the user wanted. Too many tales exist of systems being rolled out and remaining unused; this has been a factor in creating more user-driven development processes.

  The end user is the final user of the system—someone who will interact with the interface of the system. For most medium to large systems this will usually be a group of people who hold a variety of roles in their organization who represent the broad base of users.

  A recent report by the Standish Group (1995) points out that the lack of user involvement is the top reason for project failure. The involvement of users cannot be ignored.

- *Designers:* In a translational life cycle, the designers are responsible for creating the design rules of the system, which are the rules for mapping the analysis models into an implementation structure. In doing so they are responsible for extracting their design knowledge and experience and codifying it into a set of rules that can be used and reused where appropriate. Therefore, the designers should be the some of the best designers that an organization possesses. A team of designers should be knowledgeable in system architecture, physical system design, distribution, and other areas concerned with mapping a set of logical models into a physical environment.

  In an elaborational life cycle the designer is also involved in the modeling, as the models are refined and added to until they become an implementable specification. It may be necessary, however, to draw on people experienced in the area of implementation when reorganizing and restructuring object models to meet design criteria.

- *Reuse Coordinator:* The reuse coordinator for a project is the conduit into the reuse organization. This person should be knowledgeable on the contents of the reuse repository and also able to conceptualize how the components may be reused on this project, he or she should also be aware of opportunities for creating components within the context of this project.

- *Application Modeler/Developer:* This role refers to people involved in modeling during the modeling activities, who are also involved in design in an elaborative approach, and responsible for implementation during the coding parts of the project. In a translative approach theses modelers would be involved full time during modeling, but may not be involved after translation depending on the size of the project. She or he may be used in testing, and so on.

It is my experience that the use of separate teams for modeling and implementation is simply ineffective. There may be people who join the project during implementation who were not part of the modeling, and there may be those who leave the project after modeling, however, the era of using different analysts, designers, and developers does not work in today's rapid application-development environment.

In constructing a team, a ratio of 1:1:3 or 1:1:4 (senior object modeler: object modeler: application modeler/developer) is the optimum ratio of roles. It allows transference of knowledge from the experienced to the inexperienced and allows for a balanced team.

In understanding the different core roles on a project and which roles are important in which phases, let us take a look again at the process model we outlined in chapter 2, which is shown in Figure 8.1.

Table 8.1 identifies which core roles are involved in each phase of the life cycle and the extent of that involvement. The content of the table is largely drawn from different parts of this book, but serves as a useful summary. Some cells in the table begin with "Elab": the description in these cells applies to the elaborational approach. Similarly, text in cells beginning with "Trans" applies to the translational approach.

8.1.1 Seeding Teams

It is now well recognized that becoming even moderately proficient with object analysis and design can take up to a year (the average seems to be 6–12 months), and to become advanced can take up to 2 years depending on projects and level of involvement (Goldberg & Rubin, 1995). This proficiency is best obtained on projects, as opposed to just taking training courses and/or learning from books.

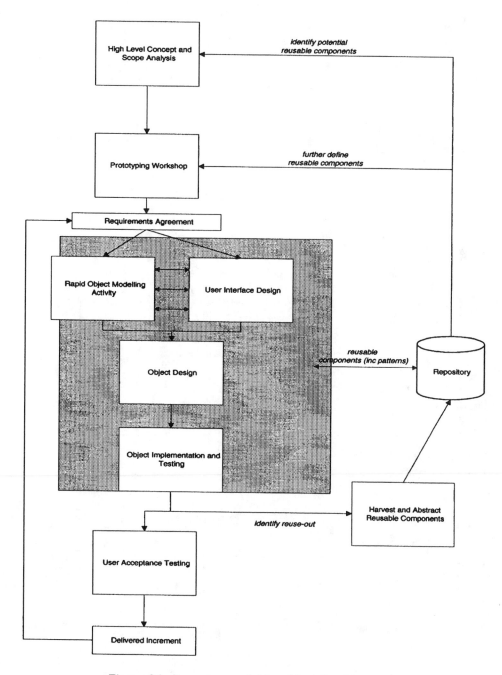

Figure 8.1. A process model for object development.

Table 8.1. Core Roles and Responsibilities Throughout the Life Cycle Function

	System Architect	Modelers	Domain Experts	End Users	Designers	Reuse Coordinator	Application Modelers/Developers
High-level Context Analysis	Provides initial vision of system	Construct high-level object models. Prelim use cases	Provide context knowledge for subject matter	High-level input to context analysis	—	Identify opportunities for reuse	Help construct initial object models
Prototyping Workshop	Further define initial vision of system	Refine high level models, identify prelim use-cases	Provide business logic details for prototype	Provide details of scenarios for workshop	—	Further identify opportunities for reuse (into project & out of project)	Work on prototype. Work on models
Rapid Object Modeling	Define high-level architecture	Model domains; use strategies as appropriate	Involvement in object modeling as much as possible. Validate models	Participate & provide input to modeling workshops as nec.	Trans-Create preliminary rules for translation of system	Identify reusable models where appropriate. Provide access to reusable components	Model domains use strategies as appropriate
Interface Design	Understand users' needs where it may impact architecture (e.g., performance) (minimal involvement)	Work with users to identify screen flows & user processes	Understand user view of system	Work with team to create vision of system & design screens & scenarios	—	Identify opportunities for reuse, providing access to components where appropriate	Work with users to identify screen flows & user processes

Table 8.1. (continued)

	System Architect	Modelers	Domain Experts	End Users	Designers	Reuse Coordinator	Application Modelers/ Developers
Object Design	Refine architecture & work through scenarios	Elab—use patterns to refine & reorganize objects	Validate models are meeting domain requirements	—	Trans—refinement of rules. Work on distribution rules	—	Design of objects
Object Implementation & Testing	Validate architecture throughout implementation	—	—	—	Trans—apply rules to models to create code	Provide support to re-using code components	Implementation & testing
User Acceptance Testing	—	—	—	Ensure system is as expected	—	—	Change as necessary
Harvest & Abstract Components	Identify reusable components from architecture	Identify reusable models & patterns	—	—	Trans—abstraction of rules where appropriate to reuse library	Work with team to harvest components & plan abstraction	Identify reusable model, patterns, & code components

Because of this need for on-project learning, mentoring programs have been very effective in managing this knowledge transfer from experienced object people to inexperienced ones.

Many organizations have only a few people experienced in object technology and it is important for them to effectively utilize these resources. A means of using them as mentors on projects can be accomplished by using them as "seeds"on projects. These people would be expected to mentor others and contribute heavily to the modeling, in many cases leading the modeling activities. For example, one experienced person and one other member of the first team can become resources with others on a subsequent project. For projects with small focused teams, a ratio of 1:1:4 (very experienced object person : mildly experienced person: inexperienced object person) should be aimed for on projects. Similarly, other projects can be seeded with people from the first project, and so on. As pointed out in Section 8.4, the need for experienced full-time modelers during development is essential for the success of a project.

📖   In order to fully leverage experienced resources, use small focused teams with a ratio of 1:1:4(very experienced object person: mildly experienced object person: inexperienced object person).

This seeded model (see Figure 8.2) works best for ensuring that existing resources are used most effectively to maximizes the spread of object-oriented experience. The seeded model can be used as part of a migration strategy for an organization, ensuring that real-world object knowledge (gained on projects) is available for as many people as possible.

📖   When only a few people have object experience in an organization, use the seeded project team model to effectively leverage their knowledge on a maximum number of projects.

8.2   Organizing and Managing the Process

In order to fully utilize many of the techniques and strategies identified so far, there are a number of key areas related to organizing and managing the object-oriented project that also need to be addressed. They are as follows:

- *Project management:* Are object-oriented projects different?
- *Allocating the work:* How to allocate work in an object-oriented project?

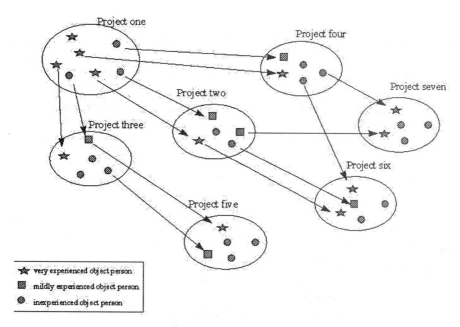

Figure 8.2. Seeded project team model.

- *Tracking progress:* How well is the project going?
- *Workshops:* Strategies for running workshops
- *The wall:* How to get feedback from all interested?

8.2.1 Project Management

Is object project management different? No, not really, as long as there is an understanding of the life cycle. Project management is still all about dividing a large task
into smaller, more manageable ones. The object-oriented project is very focused
on architecture, however, and the overall process is very architecture driven.
Therefore, the project manager must understand the impact an architecture-driven
approach can have on the project and its management. The project manager must
also become accustomed to devolving control to the various subteams that are on
the project.

Earlier in this book we discussed how work can be partitioned along domain
lines. For large projects, a team handling each domain is worthwhile, although the
team size may vary depending on the complexity and size of the domain.

> The system architect who has overall responsibility of the architecture of the system must be regarded as a peer of the project manager and be responsible for the technical vision of the project. As a result we find that project managers and architects must work closely together.

As noted by many authors (e.g., Booch, 1996), object projects spend more time in the earlier parts of the development life cycle. This may be difficult for some project managers who may be accustomed to going very quickly into design and then development. This length of time can be easier to manage in an incremental life cycle, however.

8.2.2 Allocating the Work

In chapter 3 of this book, I recommended that the system be partitioned along the lines of subject matter, and that each subject matter can be analyzed separately for large systems (constructing separate object models for each domain), or can be analyzed together and represented on a single model. This is fine for modeling domains, but does not address how work can be allocated within a team. There are two aspects to this issue:

1. How to divide modeling work?
2. How to map the architecture to the modeling work?

The first deals with the allocation of modeling work to individuals. There are two schools of thought on how this can be managed. The first says that each person on the team should be allocated "ownership" of some object clusters, on which she or he is responsible for completing the modeling. This worked well before use cases became the principal means of driving the process throughout the modeling. Allocating ownership of object clusters requires a great deal of interaction between team members, as they model scenarios through object-interaction diagrams. For example, an object-interaction diagram involving 11 objects could at worst case require involvement of 11 different people.[1]

An alternative is to assign use cases and their related scenarios to team members. This means that a single team member is responsible for modeling a scenario, although he or she may organize a group session to carry out the modeling, irrespective of the number of objects it involves. This approach ensures that there is

---

[1] This is a worst case, but does serve to illustrate the point.

a single perspective across related scenarios, but perhaps could lead to fragmented object definitions. To ensure against such eventualities requires regular object reviews, where object behaviors are checked against the roles and responsibilities identified for them early in the process and the scenarios they are involved in are also reviewed to ensure that they are in accordance with such descriptions.

This two-dimensional approach—individual responsibilities for scenarios and group responsibilities for objects—works well because objects and use cases are orthogonal concepts. Early in the modeling process the group object-modeling activity means there is group ownership of models (although there may be individual detail work being carried out) and this is continued later in the modeling process when the scenarios drive much of the modeling.

> Allocate modeling of use cases and related scenarios to team members. Allow a team member to "own" a set of scenarios for modeling purposes. Ensure that objects do not become "fragmented" by holding periodic reviews of object models and scenarios, reviewing against roles and responsibilities defined earlier in the modeling process.

When moving to implementation in an elaborative paradigm, the above set of responsibilities can be carried through to creating the class specifications. At that time responsibilities can be re-allocated to classes, which are the units of implementation.

The second issue identified above is how to map the architecture to the modeling activity. As outlined in chapter 5, architecture definition is a parallel activity to modeling. One aspect of creating an object-oriented system is that it can support an architecture framework that provides much of the structure and generic concepts of a system. If this is possible for a system, a separate team can be allocated the task of modeling and implementing such a framework, thus allowing other teams to focus on the business functionality.

The core objects and their responsibilities can be identified and agreed on by all early in the architecture definition, and a set of common principles and protocols defined. Once agreed to, these can form the basis for modeling for the architecture-framework team and provide the guiding generic structure for others.

As an example, I worked on a project that used a generic adaptation of the model–view–controller architecture from Smalltalk (Goldberg & Robson, 1983) as a basis for high-level responsibilities and communication protocols. A core set of principles identified what constituted a "model" type object, a "view" type object, and a "controller" type object. Once the principles were agreed to, each team member could then model his or her own set of scenarios, adhering to these principles.

The architecture team could then define the communication paths between objects that would be inherited by the three types of objects.

> 📖   If the generic aspects of a system can be captured by an architecture, allocate your architecture team the responsibility of working on a set of architectural components that can be used by the core functionality. Other team members can model their interactions based on the generic definitions.

8.2.3 Tracking Progress

Two essential areas to focus on when tracking progress are (1) use cases and (2) objects. Use cases provide a thread from the beginning of the project when understanding user's requirements to the end of development when testing the system. When reporting progress it is possible to identify the number of use cases modeled and later to report the number of use cases implemented and tested.

Objects are used in the modeling stages of the life cycle and then subsequently transformed (through elaboration or translation) into design constructs that can then be tracked through reference back to the objects. It is possible to report progress on the number of objects implemented and also on the number remaining. Because objects are orthogonal concepts to use cases either measure does not directly suffer if the progress measurements of the other is flawed.

> 📖   When tracking progress of a project make sure you keep a record of the number of use cases and objects. High-level reporting can then be carried out around these two concepts. For example, "we have completed modeling 12 out of 35 use cases" during the modeling, and "of the 195 objects identified in the modeling, we have completed implementation of around 55, which covers approximately 17 out of 35 use cases."

8.2.4 Workshops

One of the core strengths of the object paradigm is that it focuses on the vocabulary of the problem space when modeling. This language can thus be understood by domain experts, end users, and analysts alike. Couple this with the processes of joint application design (JAD) and you have a very powerful combination. The development process outlined in this book is very workshop based, with their being numerous types of workshops. There are numerous texts describing JAD and workshop techniques, so I am only outlining a few of the more useful ones here.

CRC Cards. CRC (class–responsibility–collaborator) card workshops were described elsewhere in this text as a means of working with domain experts and end users alike in understanding the behavior of a domain.

> 📖 CRC card workshops should be limited to 2 hours each. It is worthwhile organizing a few of these in a week. Focus each session around a few key scenarios that will provide insight into the domain.

When performing these exercises the necessary level of user involvement varies from project to project. There are different ways to work with the users:

1. Identify the objects initially and prepare the cards for those objects.
2. Draw out the cards for one of the scenarios in advance. The first scenario could then serve to validate the prefilled-in cards. Subsequent scenarios would round them out and fill in the holes.

Users do not necessarily need to be involved in a CRC Card workshop. They are useful among full-time members of the team for exploring system behavior by going through role-playing exercises.

Building Blocks. I must say I am not sure where this actually comes from, but my first exposure was from Raj Mistry of Cambridge Technology Partners, who enlightened me on the use of toy building blocks or toy bricks to construct an object model for all to see. The principles are simple: each block, or structure of blocks, represents an object, and a piece of string between two objects indicates a relationship between the two objects (a dependency of some sort).

By exploring different scenarios it is possible to construct a three-dimensional structure that graphically depicts objects and their relationships. Different color string could represent different types of relationships; for example, blue for inheritance, green for a usage relationship, yellow for other relationships.

Building-block workshops can be useful in the early stages of a project when aiming to gain confidence of users and domain experts. It will allow them to appreciate the modeling aspects of the process and also dissolve any misconceptions they may have of the process.

> 📖 Use building-block workshops in the early stages of a project when aiming to gain the confidence of the users and domain experts in the process, and also to allow them some insight into the modeling process.

Whiteboards. Not as dramatic as building-block sessions, but only slightly less effective, a whiteboard is essential for workshop sessions with either end users or with domain experts. As outlined in chapter 2 it is important to get "outsiders" in each of the sessions: getting domain experts involved in user sessions and vice versa.

A whiteboard can be used to draw an object model when it is in its early stages, and also to encourage people to change their minds and be free to delete previous objects and create new ones without becoming too attached to the concepts.

Storyboards. A storyboard is used to graphically depict the activities in one or more use cases. It is possible to construct a graphical depiction of the business activities involved in a business process and describe the system interaction within that process. From then on the use cases can be traced back to the broader business process. The storyboard describes how the user interacts with the system and how the system responds, both from the user's point of view (using screens and screen flows) and also from the modeler's point of view (using object-interaction diagrams).

Storyboarding thus captures the sequence of steps in system usage from which it is possible to construct instance diagrams of objects and their relationships. These can be used, as described earlier, to validate the objects and their relationships, and in some cases can even be used in their construction.

An example storyboard of a customer-order system is shown in Figures 8.3, 8.4, and 8.5. The storyboard in this case is represented in a table. The first column describes the interaction between the system and the user. The second provides a reference to the screen with which the user will interact after the task has been completed, and the third shows the *object instances* (and relationships and attributes) that exist as a result of the interaction. The scenario being acted out is one in which a user (a customer-service representative for a clothing reseller) is taking an order over the telephone.

In the initial scene the user is waiting for a call (Figure 8.3, row 1). There are no relevant instances at this time. Once the call arrives (Figure 8.3, row 2), the customer provides details over the phone (such as her/his name) and these are used to retrieve customer details. The system now displays Screen02, and two instances have been created: Customer (name = John Smith; address = 77 The Crescent; Date Started = June 10th 1996) and Account (number = N12345; balance = $250; credit limit = $5000).

The customer now indicates that he wishes to place an order, which, when requested by the user, results in Screen03 being displayed (the order-entry screen) and a new instance of Order (number = 09876; dateOfOrder = July 27th 1996) having been created, as reflected in the column entitled "Instances."

So far we have seen a number of instances being created as a result of user interaction. It is possible to place the continuing object interaction that causes

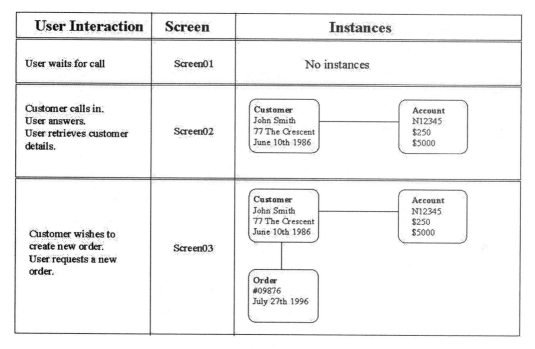

User Interaction	Screen	Instances
User waits for call	Screen01	No instances
Customer calls in. User answers. User retrieves customer details.	Screen02	**Customer** John Smith 77 The Crescent June 10th 1986 — **Account** N12345 $250 $5000
Customer wishes to create new order. User requests a new order.	Screen03	**Customer** John Smith 77 The Crescent June 10th 1986 — **Account** N12345 $250 $5000 **Order** #09876 July 27th 1996

Figure 8.3. Storyboarding, part 1.

these instances to be created in an extra column between the Screen and Instances column. This will certainly provide a complete picture of how the system interacts with the user, and how the objects interact to provide the required functionality.

The instance diagrams are useful as they allows us to ensure that objects and especially relationships have been modeled correctly. For example, the last instance diagram of shows an order with no OrderItems related to it. If this is correct then it tells us that it is possible to have an Order with no OrderItems attached to it, thus requiring a multiplicity of one to zero or more between Order and OrderItems. If this is not allowed (i.e., an order must have at least one order item) then we must correct the instance diagram to show an empty OrderItem instance with a relationship to Order. This will demonstrate our adherence to the rule that an Order must have at least one OrderItem.

The storyboard continues in Figure 8.4 with the customer first ordering a shirt and then a sweater. As the order details are entered by the user, the instances and appropriate relationships are created. The story concludes with the customer changing his mind about ordering the shirt and removing it from the order. The

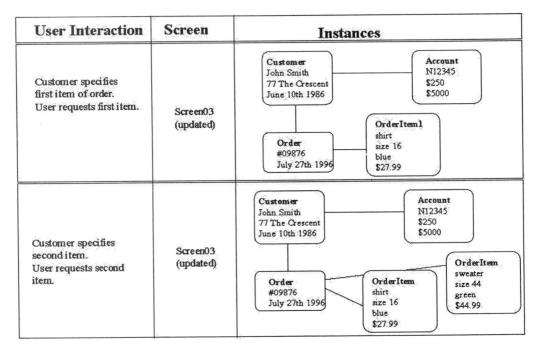

Figure 8.4. Storyboarding, part 2.

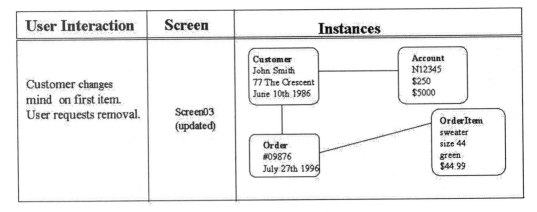

Figure 8.5. Storyboarding, part 3.

corresponding instance diagram of shows the instance of OrderItem for the shirt now having been removed.

Storyboards, easily created on whiteboards and flipcharts, are a useful mechanism for taking complex relationships and scenarios to very low levels of detail during the modeling. This helps to expose incorrect relationships, missing steps in the scenario, and also validates the correctness of the models. The collection of instance diagrams can be transformed into the object-structure model to perform such a validation.

> 📖 Use storyboarding as a means of performing detailed analysis during modeling to validate models. Work with domain experts and object modelers to take a scenario step-by-step to conclusion.

Storyboards are also useful as a group exercise during workshops to show users and other nontechnical individuals what is happening "behind the scenes" in an object-oriented model.

> 📖 Use storyboards during workshops to demonstrate to users the "secrets" of object modeling.

8.2.5 The Wall

The Wall is a social phenomenon that was properly introduced to me by Mickey Smith of Cambridge Technology Partners while we were working together on a project. It is a derivative of wall-charting (Martin & Odell, 1996)—a recognized method of conducting workshops—the wall is a somewhat longer process in that it is used to monitor progress throughout the lifetime of a project not just during a workshop. The goal is to bring together multiple interested parties to review and critique the models being constructed as part of the object-modeling process. It is not only models that can be reviewed but any work-product that would be of interest to them.

The wall is essentially a wall of a room covered with artifacts of the object project (see Figure 8.6). The wall of the project room is usually the most effective place to put the artifacts. An artifact is anything from initial system assumptions, to high-level architecture models, to detailed object-interaction diagrams.

These artifacts are placed on the wall at regular intervals (daily, weekly, or monthly, depending on the rate of change and the speed of the project) and are open for review by all concerned with the project: from business sponsors and executives of the project to the developers on the project.

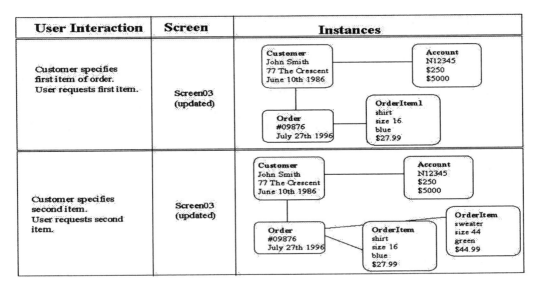

User Interaction	Screen	Instances
Customer specifies first item of order. User requests first item.	Screen03 (updated)	Customer — John Smith, 77 The Crescent, June 10th 1986; Account — N12345, $250, $5000; Order — #09876, July 27th 1996; OrderItem1 — shirt, size 16, blue, $27.99
Customer specifies second item. User requests second item.	Screen03 (updated)	Customer — John Smith, 77 The Crescent, June 10th 1986; Account — N12345, $250, $5000; Order — #09876, July 27th 1996; OrderItem — shirt, size 16, blue, $27.99; OrderItem — sweater, size 44, green, $44.99

Figure 8.6. The wall.

People are walked through the models by team members, or are allowed to browse the models at their leisure and are encouraged to provide input and feedback on the material—usually by writing on or next to the material.

> Use a wall of the project room to display project work to date. Use it as a means of openly recording progress on the project and receiving feedback from all concerned. Encourage all (from business project sponsor to end users) to review the wall, and provide open and honest comments. Update the wall periodically, the exact period is dependent on the rate of the project.

The wall can be used with any object-oriented method. The only real obstacle to be overcome is the notation used on the object models and perhaps some of the semantics of how objects with state models operate. These can easily be addressed by simple explanation as a person sees the wall for the first time.

It is possible to start the wall at the beginning of the process during the high-level context analysis and all the way through the modeling. It is possible to carry it through during implementation, but this would only be really useful for the display of window images.

The models are displayed on the wall of a public place such as a team room, project center, or some other place where there is a great deal of wall space, and that is accessible to the many interested parties.

It is possible to display all the work-products created in any development process including: context models, domain charts, object models, use-case descriptions, event tables, object-interaction diagrams, state models, and so on. Models should be updated regularly, with the frequency of updates depending on the rate of change of the models. In some projects we have updated some models daily because the time frames were so compressed.

It is worthwhile to have an "art-gallery" attitude toward the wall in which one can invite people to view the models. Invite people to provide feedback on the models by writing on them. All comments must be signed.

> One evening a month (or every 2 weeks if preferred) invite people to come to the wall and take a look at the models. Provide "tours" and "viewings" for the guests. Take an art-gallery view of the models, explaining details and issues to those not involved in their creation (business sponsors, some domain experts, etc.).

There are considerable advantages to the use of the wall, both technical and social. Some of the social benefits are as follows:

- Group ownership of models. Everyone involved in any aspect of modeling feels she or he own the models and thus do not feel left out.
- It provides an effective approach to working with users.
- It allows rapid feedback from experts and users. Because users and experts can view the models in their own time and at their own pace they can provide feedback rapidly and in a setting that is removed from organizational hierarchies. Comments are usually more open.
- The wall increases confidence of users. Users involved in the process feel they are contributing to the creation of the system, thus increasing the confidence they have in the system.
- The wall takes the mystery out of modeling. The models are open for all to view, thereby allowing the "mystery" of software development, which many business people feel exists, to be removed. The software-development process is now an open, understandable process to which domain experts and users can directly relate.

The technical benefits to the wall include the following:

- It allows one to reach the real heart of a problem more quickly. Because feedback is more direct and potentially faster and more open, the heart of the problem can be identified much sooner.

- Domain experts and those not directly involved in creating the models can provide their perspective on the models.

- Errors are identified more quickly because feedback can be obtained more rapidly.

- The wall allows for more accurate models. Everyone has an opportunity to contribute and therefore the models are more representative.

- Validation of models is provided, which ensures that the models are correct from multiple viewpoints.

It is important to recognize that the use of the wall does not remove the need for a formal review procedure.

8.3   Requirements Traceability

The classic software-engineering text by Sommerville (1989) provides the following description for a software-requirements definition: "A software requirements definition is an abstract description of the services which the system is expected to provide and the constraints under which the system must operate."

Although the academic definition of requirements and their important role in systems building is recognized by us all, the exact timing of when requirements can be "specified" in the "real world" is a matter of some debate. So far in this text we have treated requirements gathering as a process covered in the first two phases of the process-model outline given in chapter 2—High-Level Context Analysis and Rapid Prototyping. Such practices are best suited for those systems in which the requirements have not yet been fully identified and perhaps are not even well thought out by prospective users. These processes are also useful in gaining a better understanding of the actual features of the system as desired by users, and are especially good for exploring possible user interactions. In this section I shall use the term *informal-requirements determination* to refer to this type of process.

There are those who would argue that a prerequisite for software development is a *complete* description of the requirements in some textual and diagrammatic form. Such a document is usually called a requirements specification, and is often used as an initial life-cycle document used to drive system development. It can also form the basis by which contracts for software development are drawn up between an organization and a contractor.

Detailed requirements specifications are typically found in domains where the system requirements have to be described in detail as a necessity right from the outset. Possible reasons include safety (e.g., medical systems where the system will play an important part in life preservation), and security (e.g., military systems where the access to certain controls by users is of paramount importance). I shall use the term *formal-requirements specification* in order to refer to the type of process whereby the development life cycle commences with a predefined requirements specification. Whether or not these requirements specifications are actually used during development is beyond this discussion, but it can be said that they offer a reasonable place with which to begin the analysis process.

Because many organizations do not have an object-oriented process in place yet, and are following a process of formal-requirements specification for now (for whatever reasons), we shall, in the next two subsections, show how a formal-requirements specification can be used in an object-oriented development, paying particular attention to tracking-and-validating requirements throughout the life cycle. In the subsequent subsection, however, we shall also look at some more informal activities discussed earlier in this book and examine what requirements traceability means in such a context.

8.3.1 Formal-Requirements Specification

There are a two different categories of requirements:

1. *Operational requirements*[2]: These are services that the system will provide for the users. They are generally described from a user's point of view, as the user is not concerned with how the services are provided, but merely that they are.

2. *System requirements:* These are constraints on the system within which it must operate. Examples include performance constraints, use of particular equipment, and conformance to international standards.

Requirements-specification documents do not always segregate operational and system requirements into different sections. The documents are commonly written using natural-language descriptions, broken into what sometimes seems to be arbitrary divisions. Although the use of natural language means that a specification can be easy to understand, it can lead to a couple of major problems.

---

[2]The term *operational* is preferred to *functional* because it has less leaning towards viewing the system from a functional point of view.

Namely, operational and system-level requirements are not clearly distinguished, and it is possible that several requirements may be encompassed in a single sentence (Sommerville, 1989).

The text below is an example of part of a typical requirements specification, taken from the insurance domain:

2.1.1   The system should support the ability to calculate the total fee due by a customer across all policies.

2.1.2   The system should be able to support the ability to integrate with a portable, PC-based system used by remote agents.

2.1.3   The system should hold customer address(es) independent from policy information.

2.1.4   Agent information to contain (among others): branch, accounts, account profiles, geographical territories, past performance, history, and progress patterns.

2.1.5   Agent terms to be displayed on an account-summary screen.

2.1.6   Once the system has associated a claim with a policy, it should only be able to associate it with a different policy if the original claim is notified in error.

We can see that this example text includes both operational and system-level requirements.

The operational requirements have been written such that the description is centered around the functions that the system must perform. In fact, the vast majority of formal-requirements documents written today could be classified as functional requirements. When conducting an object-oriented development based on such descriptions, there must be a mapping from the language of the functional-requirements specification to the object-oriented concepts used in the analysis. The mapping from analysis to design to development, if all within the object paradigm, is likely to be more uniform than the one from a functional specification to an object-oriented analysis.

Requirements specifications written using object-oriented concepts are few and far-between. The number of organizations that describe system requirements in terms of objects and related concepts can be counted on one hand. Often an object-oriented requirements description is the result of an initial object-modeling process (which may be the next step after reviewing a formal functional-requirements specification). This model is then typically used to further drive the object-oriented analysis and design.

Jacobson, Christerson, Jonsson, and Overgaard (1992), for example, develop a requirements model that describes how the system will be used from a user point of view. Their requirements model consists of use cases, a problem domain object model, and user-interface descriptions. The creation of these work-products is achieved through close cooperation with users and domain experts. The requirements model provides a lead in to further analysis, resulting in an analysis model—a total functional specification of the system without any reference to the implementation environment.

Shlaer and Mellor (1988) identify the analysis work-products as being a complete, consistent, unambiguous, verifiable description of the problem domain. Their work-products include a domain chart, an object-information model, object-state models, object-communication model, and process models. There is no formal requirements model constructed in this method, although one could argue that the object-oriented analysis (OOA) work-products constitute the requirements model. Much of the activities undertaken in arriving at such a description could be classified under the umbrella of requirements elicitation.

Most other methods are similar to Shlaer and Mellor in that they do not have a formal-requirements model. Most proponents of object-oriented methods would argue that the OOA process is closely related to requirements gathering, however, and that the OOA work-products provide a specification of the system, which is equivalent, and in some ways superior to a formal-requirements specification.

8.3.2 Tracking Requirements Through the Life Cycle

For the purposes of this section we shall assume that a formal-requirements specification has been produced and is of a similar form to the example shown previously. A key part of any system-development process is to validate that requirements are being met and also to be able to trace the requirements from the original specification through to the final code. In order to meet the above objectives in the context of an object-oriented development, there must be a mapping between the requirements specification and the object-oriented work-products that follow.

Figure 8.7 illustrates the development life cycle and the relationship each stage has to the original formal-requirements specification.

The first stage is to partition the requirements along the lines of the two categories: operational requirements and system requirements. I would recommend

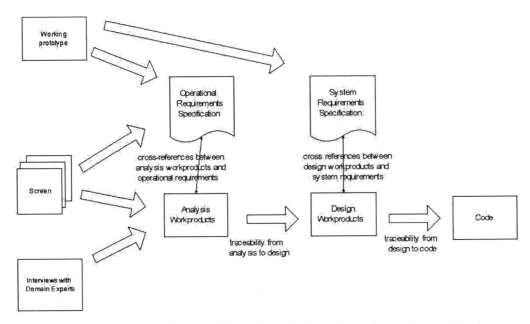

Figure 8.7. Relationship between life cycle and a formal-requirements specification.

separating the single requirements specification into two requirements documents: one for each category.

> Where using a formal-requirements specification, separate out operational and system requirements into two documents. There may be references between these documents.

Once this has been done the set of operational requirements can be further subdivided along the lines of subject matter. As described in earlier chapters, I have recommended partitioning a large problem along the lines of the subject matter (or domains) as an initial strategy with which to approach the analysis. We often find that many requirements can also be partitioned along lines of subject matter. For example: requirements relating to storing information over time can be addressed in a history domain, user-interface constraints can be assigned to the interface domain, communication requirements can be assigned to a communications domain, and so on. In the example specification extract, requirement 2.1.5 would be assigned to the user-interface domain, requirements 2.1.1, 2.1.3, 2.1.4, and 2.1.6 would be assigned to the application domain, and 2.1.2 would be assigned to a communication domain.

Following such a strategy means that a large single-requirements specification can now be appropriately partitioned into more manageable pieces. Not surprisingly, faced with a much more directed requirements document, the attitude of a team toward the whole issue of requirements documents also improves considerably.

As the analysis and design proceed, the operational requirements are mapped to modeling constructs, and many of the system requirements are mapped to object-design decisions. The mappings are recorded in the modeling work-products and become the key means of traceability back to the original specification. There is, of course, a more direct correspondence from the OOA to the OOD (object-oriented development), and the mapping from analysis to design should be more apparent than from the requirements to the OOA.

It is important to note that a requirements specification written in a functional way should not drive the analysis process because this may lead to a "functional-decomposition mind-set" (Firesmith, 1993). The OOA process should be similar to what I have described in earlier chapters, but the mapping back to the original requirements should be maintained.

Mapping Requirements. We have found that there are a number of types of requirements within the context of the operational requirements.

- *Data requirement:* The specification prescribes that some data must be stored, or at least provided by the system. Data requirements typically map to attribute(s) of object(s). Requirements 2.1.3 and 2.1.4 from the example are typical data requirements. They state that the system must be able to hold a variety of agent information and must also hold customer addresses separate from account information.[3]

- Requirement 2.1.3 could easily be satisfied by having a Customer object with address as an attribute, and a 1:M association with an object called Policy. Requirement 2.1.4 could be satisfied through a number of objects, attributes, and associations (e.g., Agent, AccountProfile, etc.).

- *Association requirement:* Not always as directly stated in a requirements specification as requirement 2.1.6 from the example, this type of requirement specifies that particular associations must be captured by the system.[4]

---

[3] It must be pointed out that these requirements are written from the perspective of the user and in no way prescribe a particular modeling or implementation construct. As long as the user has access to the data, the requirement has been met.

[4] As with the data requirement, this is written from the perspective of the user. It does not mean that there will necessarily be a direct association between two objects to support this requirement.

It typically maps to one or more relationships on the static-object model, and it is often the case that a data requirement will require an association requirement to support it.

- Requirement 2.1.6 could be supported by an association between an object Claim and another object Policy. There is also some constraint on this association in that the relationship between Claim and Policy can only be changed if there is some error. This may have implications on the behavior of one of the objects (say Claim) and thus now places an operational requirement on that object (see below).

- *Operational requirement:* This type of requirement describes one or more services that a system must provide, for example, requirement 2.1.1. An operational requirement typically maps to either a number of interactions between objects (represented by object-interaction diagrams) or to some aspect of the behavior of a single object (represented in the analysis models by an object's state change or an object performing some single task). The event schemas of Martin and Odell (1994) are a useful means of exploring the functionality required for operational requirements.

- Requirement 2.1.1 above could be met by the interaction of a number of objects used to calculate the total fee for a customer. Such an interaction could be initiated by the user, or by some periodic timer (monthly, say), or by some other process (e.g., policy renewal).

System requirements cannot be broken down into such neat divisions. They are either constraints that can be met at design time (e.g., performance, portability, etc.), or are system-level constraints that are closely related with physical aspects of the system (e.g., system size, memory constraints, physical connections, etc.).

Requirement 2.1.2 from the example specification is a system requirement that affects the physical aspects of the system, and will also affect the communication domain in the type of communication that is used with the remote PC.

Modeling. The existence of a formal-requirements specification does not lessen the need for any modeling to be undertaken. The process is iterative with new and misunderstood information being identified at all points in the process. The underlying principle when tracking requirements is to cross-reference all requirements in the analysis models, and vice versa. As new requirements are identified, which they will be, add them to the requirements specification.[5] As vague requirements are clarified or rejected, make the necessary changes to the specification.

---

[5] This is not to say that "scope creep" is allowed at this stage, but new (detailed) requirements can be added to the specification provided they fall within the scope of the application, or provided they are agreed to by all concerned.

Based on work-products identified in previous chapters, here are some suggestions as to how requirements can be traced to modeling work-products:

Object-structure model: This model typically satisfies data and association requirements. The description of each relationship or attribute on the object model should identify the requirements satisfied by that construct (if possible). As this is done, the original requirements specification should be annotated to indicate how each requirement is supported.[6]

Object-interaction diagrams: A single object-interaction diagram will represent the use of one or more services of the system. When finalizing the scenario, always identify which requirement(s) it supports and document this with the scenario. One operational requirement usually maps onto one or more interaction diagrams.

State models: A single object's state model will most likely correspond to the partial support of several requirements (because operational requirements are met by object interactions or a single object service), so there is no need to identify which requirements are supported by the state model as a whole. If a particular state of an object meets some requirement (preservation of some sequence of information over time, say), however, then this should be noted on the state model.

Validating Requirements at Analysis Time

Models should be reviewed against requirements. Both the original and the revised requirements specification should be available at the review. Each requirement should be checked off against the feature(s) in the model(s) that support it. Attention should be drawn to any requirements in the specification that have not yet been supported.

Validating Requirements at Design Time. The tracking of requirements through the design varies depending on whether you employ an elaborational or translational approach to design.

In an elaborational approach the scheme identified earlier should continue to be followed. Namely, annotation of documentation to indicate which requirements are being supported by which design constructs. For example, in order to meet particular performance constraints, there may need to be some reorganization of objects in the state models or there may be some extra design objects introduced. The documentation for such changes should cross-reference the requirements that gave cause for them to exist.

---

[6] Naturally, an original version of the requirements specification should be maintained.

> In an elaborational approach, design decisions satisfying require-
> ments should be noted as the model is changed. The documentation
> for such changes should cross-reference the requirements that
> caused them to exist.

In a translational approach to design the requirements are cross-referenced in
the set of rules. For example, a particular design rule may stipulate that two particularly closely cooperating analysis objects shall be merged into one class at
implementation time in order to meet performance requirements.

> In the translational approach a rule's documentation should identify
> which requirement has given cause for this rule to exist.

Design reviews, irrespective of the design philosophy, should review the design
constructs or rules against the system requirements that caused them to exist. Not
all rules or all design constructs will exist to meet specific requirements, however.
Some will simply exist to support the larger architectural scheme chosen for the
application.

8.3.3 Tracking Requirements Without a Requirements Specification

A key part of any system-development process is to verify that requirements are
being met and also to be able to trace the requirements from the original specification through to the final code. In order to meet the above objectives in the context of an object-oriented development, there must be a mapping between the
requirements specification and the object-oriented work-products that follow.

There are a number of key activities used in informal-requirements capture.
Namely, prototyping with end users, describing screens and screen flows, interviews with end users and domain experts, and task analysis of end users. These
activities are heavily used in RAD environments and any single activity can lead to
identification of requirements in multiple categories. For example, a prototyping
session with a group of end users may identify data, operational, and system
requirements. As a result, it is important that all identified requirements be captured and documented appropriately during the various sessions.

Prototyping. The prototype should be used to generate a set of system
requirements in conjunction with other activities. Prototypes used as the system
specification themselves are inadequate, as they may have large parts of function-

ality missing, may be used differently to the final system, may lead to ambiguities in the specification (due to the informal nature of a prototype), or may include extra functionality not to be included in the final system.

Prototyping with users typically identifies operational requirements that describe how the system is expected to behave from the end-user's viewpoint. The creation of a small executable prototype in Visual Basic, for example, can lead to the definition of a series of system events, data requirements, and functionality requirements. The operational and data requirements may themselves cover a number of domains: information on past data may be addressed by a history domain, behavior of a modem may be addressed by a communication domain, and so on. Therefore, as mentioned earlier, the specification of these requirements should be partitioned into operational and system requirements with operational requirements split across domains. A series of documents should be created that capture these requirements in a more formal manner.

Some system requirements may also be identified, for example, typical expected response times for system operations, system GUI conformance requirements, equipment interoperation requirements, usability requirements, and so on. These can be noted, and documented as they are identified.

Screens and Screen Flows. A key deliverable from a prototype is a series of window definitions and screen flows. These are valuable in capturing data requirements and requirements for the user-interface domain. The existence of a field on a window means that the data must either be an attribute of some object, the result of some operation on an object or series of objects, or be calculated from some object(s) attributes.

Buttons on a window typically trigger events sent either to subsequent windows or to the application. Each event sent to the system must have some data associated with it and some expected behavior. This is a key component in describing the events of a use case, which will subsequently tie in to the modeling of dynamic behavior (through object-communication scenarios and event traces, say). For each window one should specify the event(s) generated, their data, and the system behavior expected from sending that event. Figure 8.8 shows how fields and buttons can map to object concepts.

Object Modeling. The object-information model and its associated documentation (object description, attribute description, and relationship description) provides the formal documentation of the static requirements of a system. The inputs to the object modeling activity are:

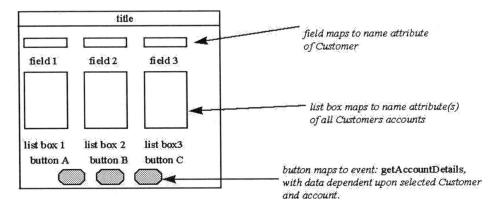

Figure 8.8. Window fields can map to object concepts.

- *Prototyping:* Key objects, attributes, and relationships can emerge from the prototypes. However, how they are represented on the screen may be radically different to the underlying conceptual model on which the object model is built. The analyst should use the prototypes as an input to understanding the system, not as a means of defining it.

- *Screens and Screen Flows:* These provide inputs to the definition of object attributes and relationships between objects. For example, a user examining a customer's details and their accounts could identify some attributes of the customer, an account, and a 1:M relationship between customer and account.

- *Interviews with domain experts:* These will identify objects, attributes, events, and relationships that may or may not have emerged from the previous two activities. They will also provide a thorough understanding of the "real" domain, and not just the user's perception of it.

The dynamic modeling, using object communication scenarios or something similar, will be heavily influenced by the prototype, especially in understanding the different steps in a scenario (through the screens and use of the system) or the sequence of scenarios (through the overall prototype).

A task analysis of users can provide input to the prototype. The prototype and the screen flows can lead to the definition of the scenarios. The screens can identify the events and the associated data. Thus these activities will provide input to the dynamic modeling and a means for validating the dynamics.

Figure 8.9 shows how the object-interaction diagrams can be tied together with the screens to trace user requirements to system functionality. Each screen in the flow can issue zero, one, or more events to the system. Each event generated can

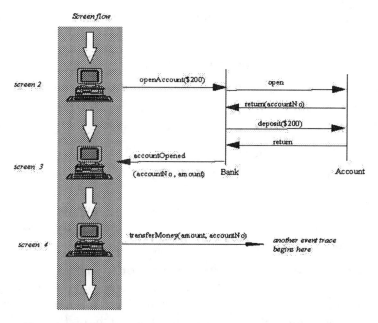

Figure 8.9. Flow of windows mapping to object interactions.

be modeled using event traces (or something similar depending on the method used). Thus, the flow of screens in a working prototype (indicated by the vertical shaded box) can be tracked to each event trace. Such a mapping should be documented and tracked throughout the life cycle. One way of documenting this is to place the relevant screen number(s) on the event trace at the appropriate place, as indicated on Figure 8.9.

Using an informal-requirements-capture process and documenting the identified requirements as described earlier, means that the requirements can be easily tracked throughout the development process. As a requirement is identified, write the source along with the requirement itself in the appropriate document.

8.4   Critical Success Factors for Object Projects

Chapter 1 outlined some of the lessons learned through the use of objects in constructing real-world applications. Based on those lessons and some of the more management-related experiences, I have tried to outline the critical success factors (CSFs) for an object-oriented development effort. These CSFs can be used as a checklist to ensure that any project you undertake pays attention to these issues. They are as follows:

- involvement of domain experts throughout
- a development life cycle that promotes iteration and incremental delivery
- ample education and training for the team
- involvement of someone (or some people) who has done it before
- a sound set of object models
- an architectural vision underlying the system

There are other important aspects that should be taken into consideration when ensuring a successful project, however, the above list represents the six most important. Let us look at each in turn:

Involvement of Domain Experts Throughout. The object models are central to an object-oriented project. Their validity is ensured by the involvement of domain experts in the creation of those models. We have already expressed the need for the involvement of domain experts throughout the development life cycle, but it is worth expressing that need once again because it is a critical success factor.

Domain experts ensure that object models are representative of the domain They do not just need to be involved up front but also need to be involved in the latter stages to ensure that the system design and implementation are also true to the domain.

A Development Life Cycle That Promotes Iteration and Incremental Delivery. Iterative and incremental are two words often used interchangeably when describing system development. To do so is incorrect. Iteration refers to repeating and changing work carried out a number of times, and as such an iterative approach allows for such repetition and change. Incremental delivery refers to the delivery of a system as a series of increments, with each increment building on top of the previous one.

Object models and object systems reflect a view of the problem domain, and as such they evolve as our understanding improves during the development process. Because the first object model you create for a system will undoubtedly be different than the final one, there is a need for a process that allows for change. Iteration, therefore, is a requirement of any development process. A one-time pass through the development life cycle is unsuitable for object-oriented developments, as it does not allow for evolution.

In an elaborational approach to development the iteration is inherent throughout all stages of the life cycle. In the translational life cycle, however, iteration is typically exhibited during the modeling. Once the modeling has gone through all its iterations, the code is generated from the design rules.

A big-bang approach to system delivery is inadvisable because of the difficulty that exists in delivering all functionality at one time; the potential sources of error, as many issues are not discovered until after the first release; and more important, the length of time this can take. It is far more advisable to deliver a system in increments. For each increment there should be some targeted functionality that delivers some system behavior that is meaningful to the end users.

It is important to note that iteration and incremental delivery do not exclude the use of a systematic development process that is "planned, measured and controlled" (Cook & Daniels, 1994).

Ample Education and Training for the Team. It is essential that all involved in a project understand the object paradigm and the impact it has on the life cycle. The popular just-in-time training that seems to pervade every development house is fine for tools and languages perhaps, but is far from adequate for those wishing to learn the fundamentals of objects. We have discussed the paradigm shift elsewhere in this book, and it is because of this that we must allow for the concepts of objects to settle in people's minds over a period of time. As Love (1993) points out: "Learning object-oriented software engineering is education; learning to program in C++ is training."

Involvement of Someone (or Some People) Who Have Done It Before. There is no substitute for experience. Masters in any field make their tasks look easy. Just as a master musician makes playing an instrument look easy, so it is with experienced system architects and object designers. A master jazz saxophonist typically practices for hours every day, and when it's time to perform, his or her playing seems effortless and simple. This is because the musician has years of experience on which he or she can draw when needed, and often does so without the observer realizing it. So it is with experienced architects and modelers.

> Objects cannot be learned overnight, and so it is worthwhile to use the expertise of someone who has experienced object development before. This utilization should be full time, especially if the experience of the team is very limited.

If you are a team with no object-oriented experience, then this expertise can be brought in from the outside using consultants or people from other parts of your organization. They do not need to be full-time team members but they can provide an objective viewpoint on your work as well as insights that will further your own experience

A Sound Set of Object Models. The set of object models created during the modeling process is the foundation on which the system is built. It is the codification of the knowledge of the domain through the representation of the key concepts of that domain.

I have seen a number of projects move to implementation too quickly, before they have gone into sufficient detail during the creation of the models. As a result, the subsequent implementation suffered from imprecise models, vagueness in how requirements were met, and so required a longer time to implement. These difficulties also manifested themselves through developers being unclear about the roles and responsibilities of each object;, lack of rigor in the use cases, resulting in rework of detail that could have been avoided;and excessive communication required between team members due to unclear or vague object models. Therefore, a set of coherent and precise object models are critical for success.

An Architectural Vision Underlying the System. As mentioned in chapter 1: "architecture is key." The importance of architecture and its relevance as a driving force in object projects is described by Booch (1996, p.21): "An architecture-driven style of development is usually the best approach for the creation of most complex software-intensive systems."

An object-oriented system with no underlying macroarchitectural vision is a system that will be lost in the software swamp, and may be inflexible and unscaleable. A system that has an architecture at its foundation is more likely to be stable, with a more resilient structure that allows for growth and flexibility. As identified in chapter 5, a sound architecture is a key component of any successful object-oriented development.

8.5 Summary

A number of different roles (both full and part time) for object-oriented projects were presented. They are as follows:

- domain experts
- reuse coordinator
- object modelers (senior and junior)

- end users
- designers
- application modelers/developers

Each role has distinct responsibilities in each phase of the project. We have found that projects that partition the work into small focused teams are more likely to succeed than those in which the team members work as a large single unit.

In organizing and managing the process a number of issues were addressed. The architectural focus of object projects affects project management and how the work is divided. Use cases are assigned to team members as a means for organizing their work. Progress can be tracked by monitoring how far people are with modeling their use cases.

Some strategies for running workshops were also introduced, including CRC cards, storyboarding, and building-block workshops. The use of the wall as a means of demonstrating progress and gaining feedback was also described.

When tracing a set of formal requirements in an object-oriented system one should consider the following:

- Map each requirement to the appropriate modeling construct(s). Annotate the requirements specification to indicate how each requirement is supported (which objects, attributes, use cases, etc.).

- Modeling can generate new requirements. Document these. Map them to the object models depending on the type of requirements.

- Depending on the route chosen for design, identify how each design requirement is to be satisfied. Where the decision is not obvious or the mapping is not simple, mark both the design document and the requirements document.

- Always use a two-way reference to trace requirements. Map modeling work-products to requirements and vice versa.

This chapter, and this book, concluded with six critical success factors for object-oriented development projects. They were as follows:

- involvement of domain experts throughout
- a development life cycle that promotes iteration and incremental delivery
- ample education and training for the team
- involvement of someone (or some people) who has done it before

- a sound set of object models
- an architectural vision underlying the system

References

Booch, G. (1996). *Object Solutions: Managing the Object-Oriented Project.* Menlo Park, CA: Addison-Wesley.

Cook, S., & Daniels, J. (1994). *Designing Object Systems: Object-Oriented Modeling With Syntropy.* Englewood Cliffs, NJ: Prentice-Hall.

Firesmith, D. (1993). *Object-Oriented Requirements Analysis and Logical Design.* New York: Wiley.

Gamma, E., Helm, R., Johnson, R., & Vlissides, J. (1994). *Design Patterns: Elements of Reusable Object-Oriented Software.* Reading, MA: Addison-Wesley.

Goldberg, A., & Robson, D. (1983). *Smalltalk-80: The Language and Its Implementation.* New York: Addison-Wesley.

Goldberg, A., & Rubin, K. (1995). *Succeeding With Objects: Decision Frameworks for Project Management.* Reading, MA: Addison-Wesley.

Gossain, S. (1995). Using client/server as a business strategy. *Object Magazine,* 5(*1*).

Jacobson, I., Christerson, M., Jonsson, P., & Overgaard, G. (1992). *Object-Oriented Software Engineering—A Use-Case-Driven Approach.* Reading, MA: Addison-Wesley.

Love, T. (1993). *Object Lessons.* New York: SIGS Books.

Martin, J., & Odell, J. (1994). *Object-Oriented Methods: A Foundation.* Englewood Cliffs, NJ: Prentice-Hall.

Martin, J., & Odell, J. (1996). *Object-Oriented Methods: Pragmatic Considerations.* Upper Saddle River, NJ: Prentice-Hall.

Shlaer, S., & Mellor, S. (1988). *Object-Oriented Systems Analysis: Modeling the World in Data.* Englewood Cliffs, NJ: Prentice-Hall.

Sommerville, I. (1989). *Software Engineering, Third Edition.* Wokingham, UK: Addison-Wesley.

Standish Group. (1995). *CHADS: An IT Report.* Standish Group Web Site.

APPENDICES

NOTATION

Object Structure

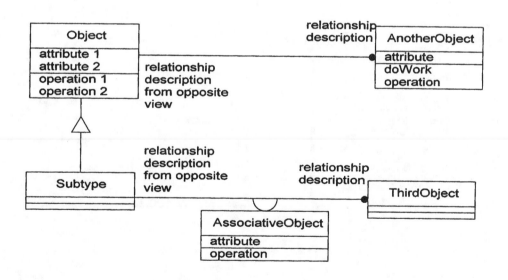

Object Relationships

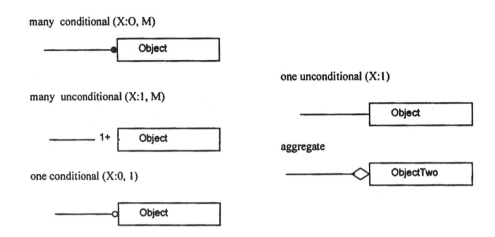

many conditional (X:O, M)

many unconditional (X:1, M)

one conditional (X:0, 1)

one unconditional (X:1)

aggregate

Object Interaction Diagram

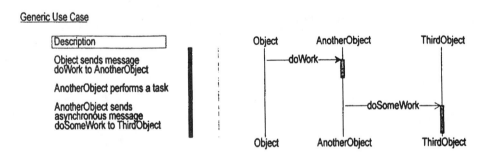

Generic Use Case

Description

Object sends message
doWork to AnotherObject

AnotherObject performs a task

AnotherObject sends
asynchronous message
doSomeWork to ThirdObject

Object State Model

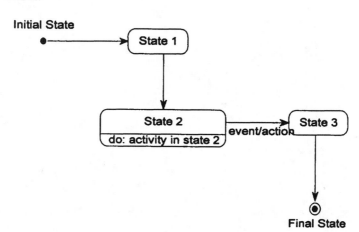

STRATEGIES SUMMARY

Lessons Learned

📖   There really is such a thing as a paradigm shift in moving to objects. People take varying amounts of time in going through this paradigm shift. Some people "get it" in days, for others it can take months; a few, sadly, never get it.

📖   Throughout the object-modeling process get as many different views involved in the process as possible—people from the business, domain experts, users, modelers, developers, and application support.

📖   Do not enter anything into a CASE tool until either the rate of change of the models begins to decrease, or the models begin to get too large to fit on a single large whiteboard. The best CASE tool early on is a whiteboard, some sticky yellow pads, and flip-charts.

📖   Reuse needs to be supported throughout the software life cycle. Before a project you need to look for potential reuse into the project.

287

During a project you need to constantly ask the question: "How can we build reuse into our objects?" After your project you need to identify reusable and potentially reusable components.

When making the transition, management education, and then buy-in, is essential. Managers at all levels need to be educated in order to fully appreciate the impact of objects.

When selecting your pilot project, choose one that has high visibility in the business community and one that will make a difference. Do not select a low-profile backroom project.

The method with most market share isn't necessarily the best one for your organization. Evaluate methods on their fitness for purpose, their support for a software process, and their fit into your organization.

Question methods—why, when, and why again. When using object methods, don't just blindly follow all the advice they provide.

Objects puts "bad" designs up front.

The Big Picture

For real-world objects, create system representations of these objects that respond to events rather than initiate them. They should be maintaining a representation of the object, rather than initiating activities.

Treat *extends* and *uses* as advanced features of use cases and do not use them until you feel comfortable working with simple use cases.

📖 Attempt to define 80% of the use cases that you will need to meet the systems functionality. Striving for the remaining 20% will take longer than the extra effort deserves. The remaining use cases will most likely be identified later in the design process.

📖 Involve users and domain experts equally throughout the system-development process.

📖 Translational approaches are probably best for creating similar medium-to-large applications in which the cost of creating architectures (translation rules) is offset by their repeated (re)use.

📖 A fully elaborational approach is very labor intensive and best used for smaller, highly optimized applications that require fine tuning at the class cluster, class, and attribute level.

Modeling System Structure

📖 In order to provide a useful conceptual picture of all the different subject matters in a system, construct a preliminary domain chart with key experts, analysts, and modelers.

📖 To find the domains in a system, hold a domain-storming session in which experienced designers, architects, and abstractionists sit with experts to identify candidate domains. Ask questions of each domain to determine if it really is a separate subject matter.

📖 To determine the interface between two domains, hold regular "bridge-definition workshops." These workshops need to be short, focused sessions held at regular intervals during the modeling. There needs to be a "sign-off" about 70% of the way into the modeling activity in which both parties agree to the interface and stick to it.

📖 Construct separate object models for each domain when modeling large systems, as they result in more reusable object-domain models. For smaller systems build a single-object model that can be geographically segregated into domains.

📖 Separate information of different domains from one another as long as possible. Don't show cross-domain relationships on the same object model until late in the process.

📖 When interviewing experts to elicit requirements, limit sessions to 1–2 hours' duration, ask questions continually, and summarize your understanding to verify information is being interpreted correctly.

📖 Provide a basic class in reading object models for your experts. A short class covering notation, how to read models, and understanding the issues should be given at the beginning of an expert's involvement in the process.

📖 When you have the luxury of experts on your modeling teams it can be a good idea to seed each team with an expert. Often, this can be the most effective use of his or her time and provide the maximum benefit to the modeling effort.

📖 If an expert would rather explore dynamics before structure, then this should be facilitated, and if he or she is more comfortable in looking at structure first then this should also be allowed. The analyst's role becomes that of facilitator and driver.

📖 When working with experts don't try to rename concepts they are familiar with, even if they seem to have incorrect names, unless you have buy-in. Remember you're constructing a model of the problem domain, and should use the language of that world.

📖 Hold a brainstorming session with domain experts and modelers to find objects. Use object categories as a means of getting started and follow up with scenario exploration.

📖 When you identify a role object, try to think of a tangible thing that may be acting in that role for a period of time. Or, if you identify a tangible thing, see if there are roles that it fulfills that may warrant being identified as a separate object.

📖 When you identify a tangible thing, see if there is a specification object that is necessary. To help do this, see if there are attributes that need to be captured but do not change with each instance of the tangible, but do change with a set of tangibles.

📖 Create a high-level event table derived from the use cases identified at the beginning of the modeling process. Use this table to further identify objects, with the assistance of domain experts.

📖 When deciding which attributes are important, consider the perspective you have of the object. Ask yourself: "What information pertaining to that object is important in the context of the system?" If in doubt, add the attribute to the object; it can always be removed later if it remains unused.

📖 In determining whether an attribute belongs to an object or not, take that object out of the model and consider it in isolation. If all the attributes still seem to make sense then it is likely they belong there. If not consider placing those out-of-place attributes elsewhere.

📖 Verify attribute names with domain experts. Use names that they are comfortable with, and that convey the meaning of the characteristic as understood by domain experts.

When assessing cardinality only look at the relationship at a moment in time, whereas when assessing optionality examine the relationship over the whole period covered by the analysis.

For each relationship on the object model consider the implications of the cardinality and optionality with respect to creating and deleting instances, by asking questions of the model.

Label relationships from the perspective of each participating object. It will aid in domain understanding and also may assist in identifying further relationships. This also leads to a more comprehensible model for all concerned, current and future. Remember the model will live long after the modelers have finished modeling.

Name relationships with phrases that provide the semantic context for the relationship. Don't just use the first phrase that comes to mind.

Examine each relationship in isolation to determine whether that relationship is really needed in the model. Ask yourself: "What value does this relationship bring in the understanding of the domain?"

Test the objects and relationships by ensuring that common questions (typical data queries, for example) asked of the model can be satisfied given the initial information, the objects, and the relationships. Use domain experts to provide you with typical examples.

As a guideline, try to create abstract objects when there is more than one subtype. An abstract object with only one subtype should always be justified, as it may be a solution looking for a problem.

Don't create extra objects on the model, in order to anticipate change, unless instances of them exist in the problem domain.

If an object has three or more states, each with at least one additional attribute or with at least one having a different relationship, use migrating subtypes on the object model instead of a using a state model.

Use an associative object when it is instantiated as a result of two other objects participating in a relationship. As a further test, see if the object's attributes are really capturing attributes of the relationship.

Simple rules that pertain to one attribute or one relationship can be captured through some diagrammatic annotation with a suitable description in the data dictionary.

Complex rules can be abstracted into an object such that they can be localized. The object that is a natural fit for the rules may already exist. If not, you may need to create one.

Where one rule applies across multiple instances but is dependent on an attribute of a specification object, capture that rule by annotating the attribute in question.

Complex rules that vary from instance to instance can be captured within an object. Look for rules that vary from one instance of a specification object to another.

In order to test your static-object model to see if the objects, attributes, and relationships are representative of the problem domain, ask questions of it and see if the answers correctly reflect the rules and policies of the problem domain.

Modeling System Behavior

Use future business-process models to identify system usage and create use cases. From these use cases one can define a number of scenarios to model using object-interaction diagrams.

Work with users to identify system events by asking them questions around objects that would be meaningful to them. For example, when is a new customer created, when is a customer deleted? when is a new account created? and so on.

It is important that when representing object interactions using event traces, or object-interaction diagrams, or some other model, that you notationally and semantically make a distinction between the two forms of communication.

When modeling interactions, do not just consider synchronous communication between objects, but also give consideration to the natural parallelism in the steps needed to perform a task. Model using asynchronous communication where necessary.

A CRC workshop requires a mix of people. Sessions with 6-8 people work best. An example would be 2–3 users, 2 domain experts, 1 business person, 1 facilitator, and 1 scribe. Keep sessions to 2–3 hours with a target number of scenarios to go through.

When the use of CRC cards seems too simple, and not detailed enough for the scenarios being explored, use a whiteboard to work with the participants to create detailed object-interaction diagrams. These will not be correct the first time around, but will begin to delve into the detail that CRC cards can miss.

When creating object-interaction diagrams, go into enough detail such that each task an object performs on receipt of a message can be written in pseudo-code. Doing so means that the level of detail is adequate for implementation and also ensures that the behavior required is understood sufficiently not to be open to interpretation.

Use object-interaction diagrams to provide a graphical indication of the "knowledge" an object has through its positioning on the diagram.

Hold object-interaction-diagram checkpoints and reviews regularly. Go through each object-interaction diagram, explore responsibilities of objects, cross-reference and update documentation to record them. Ensure that they are consistent across objects. Use of stereotypes can help in categorizing them.

Use the OCM to identify communication between objects that is inconsistent with the larger picture. Do this on a regular basis, say every week during the modeling of behavior.

Broadcast messages need not be systemwide. The notion of broadcast regions can be very useful if an object needs to broadcast messages only to a limited set of objects, perhaps those in the same subsystem or those in all other domains other than that in which the sender resides.

Use broadcast messaging very rarely in your design. Broadcasts are excellent for modeling the handling of system failures, major events, and alarm conditions.

Consider using the publish–subscribe messaging mechanism when a number of different objects are interested in receiving some pieces of information from another object, asynchronously.

📖   Consider expanding the conventional request–reply messaging mechanism to allow for requests with numerous replies, and requests with asynchronous replies. Doing so will ensure that the most flexible solution will be possible.

📖   If you have just started using object technology, use simple state models for your objects, such as Moore state machines. As you become more experienced you can begin to use more advanced features, such as nested states, and actions on multiple parts of the model (transitions, entry, exit, etc.).

📖   Whichever form of state model you choose for your modeling process, a key issue is to agree on the semantics of the constructs so that there is no room for ambiguity or vagueness in the models. Consistency and completeness are the keys to successful modeling.

📖   Create a state-transition table for every object with a state model. Doing so will ensure that all possible events have been considered for all possible states, thus reducing the possibility of error.

📖   During the object-interaction-diagram reviews, examine the semantics across objects to see if there are potential commonalities across objects that can be taken advantage of through the use of new higher level objects.

📖   When thinking about abstract objects early on in the process, try to visualize the principal objects in the domain at a generic level. Think of the behavior of the domain in terms of a set of interacting generic objects. These could be the initial set of abstract objects for the domain.

📖   Define test cases from the scenarios identified in the early parts of analysis. Use the high-level scenario table to step through each object-interaction diagram to ensure correct behavior. Also, prescribe sample test data for the test cases based on the different scenarios.

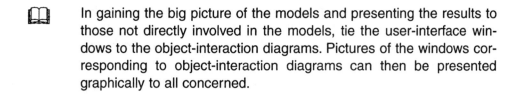 In gaining the big picture of the models and presenting the results to those not directly involved in the models, tie the user-interface windows to the object-interaction diagrams. Pictures of the windows corresponding to object-interaction diagrams can then be presented graphically to all concerned.

Architecture

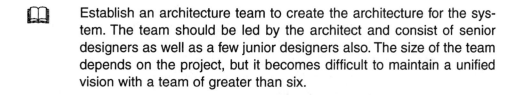 Establish an architecture team to create the architecture for the system. The team should be led by the architect and consist of senior designers as well as a few junior designers also. The size of the team depends on the project, but it becomes difficult to maintain a unified vision with a team of greater than six.

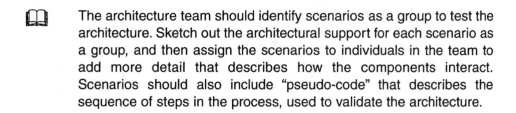 The architecture team should identify scenarios as a group to test the architecture. Sketch out the architectural support for each scenario as a group, and then assign the scenarios to individuals in the team to add more detail that describes how the components interact. Scenarios should also include "pseudo-code" that describes the sequence of steps in the process, used to validate the architecture.

If you wish to create an architectural framework, create the core abstractions first. Then examine other applications with similar architectures to create the reusable and extensible abstractions that will comprise this framework.

To find services, examine object-interaction diagrams to characterize similar functionality used by different clients. To judge their applicability to other applications, hold a group discussion with representatives from other applications and business units to present the service and its potential interface. Allow participants to present requirements, which should then be evaluated. Be very careful when broadening the applicability of a service as it will affect your project schedule.

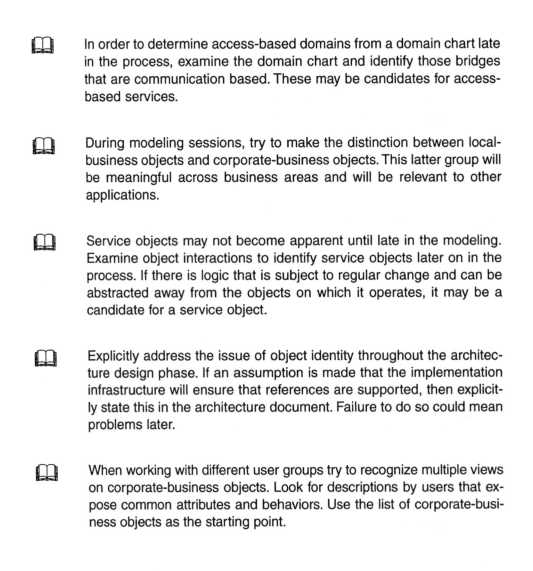

In order to determine access-based domains from a domain chart late in the process, examine the domain chart and identify those bridges that are communication based. These may be candidates for access-based services.

During modeling sessions, try to make the distinction between local-business objects and corporate-business objects. This latter group will be meaningful across business areas and will be relevant to other applications.

Service objects may not become apparent until late in the modeling. Examine object interactions to identify service objects later on in the process. If there is logic that is subject to regular change and can be abstracted away from the objects on which it operates, it may be a candidate for a service object.

Explicitly address the issue of object identity throughout the architecture design phase. If an assumption is made that the implementation infrastructure will ensure that references are supported, then explicitly state this in the architecture document. Failure to do so could mean problems later.

When working with different user groups try to recognize multiple views on corporate-business objects. Look for descriptions by users that expose common attributes and behaviors. Use the list of corporate-business objects as the starting point.

Designing Object Systems

When mapping one-to-one relationships, avoid the use of two-way references in design, as this can require extra overhead and introduces a greater chance of error. Review object-interaction diagrams to check if two-way access is necessary.

📖 Use one-way references where access is always from one side. Keep the reference from the side used in the search. For conditional relationships, keep the reference handle on the side of the instance that is always involved in the relationship.

📖 For one-to-many relationships do not use references on the many side if there are significant accesses from the one side. Examine the object-interaction diagrams to check.

📖 When designing associative objects, store references to each of the instances participating in the relationship. If there are frequent accesses from one of the sides of the relationship, consider adding in an additional reference from that instance to the associative object instance.

📖 When implementing migrating subtypes, use subtype hiding with delegation, rather than a direct mapping.

📖 Represent attributes as functions/operations in design where the value must be computed in real time.

📖 Consider using classes to represent multivalued attributes in a design.

📖 Map synchronous calls to simple-method invocations when instances are within the same processing boundary.

📖 If two objects in an object-interaction diagram communicate via an asynchronous message and are located in different process spaces, then the asynchronous message should be carried through to implementation.

📖 If two objects in an object-interaction diagram communicate via an asynchronous message, are located in the same process space, and are part of the same thread, then the asynchronous message should be implemented as a synchronous-method invocation.

    Broadcast messages need to be supported by the implementation environment if they are to be implemented as broadcasts. If not then the design needs to ensure there is a list of all instances available so that a number of asynchronous messages can be used as a means of simulating broadcast communication.

    For the most straightforward approach to designing state models, use a set of base-class libraries that provide much of the finite-state-machine functionality.

    Using sates as classes is a useful strategy for designing object-state models, especially when the object must be distributed across its state. It is especially useful for migrating subtypes with life cycles.

    When applying patterns, work on small clusters of objects in a small team or individually. Evaluate the models against the description of the pattern, the applicability, and the consequences. If appropriate use the pattern to reorganize the model accordingly. However, note any changes to potential changes to objects outside your cluster and discuss at the next team session. It may be necessary to undo the pattern's changes due to incompatibilities.

    If you are interested in applying design patterns, identify one person in the team to be the guardian of patterns whose responsibility includes determining if and when patterns are appropriate. The person should have a good understanding of patterns or at least the capacity for a good understanding.

    The pattern guardian should also be responsible for distributing knowledge about patterns to others in the team. Hold regular briefings to share such knowledge.

    When creating rules, go through all possible mappings for all constructs and determine under which circumstances each mapping would be used. The architect should be a key part of this effort.

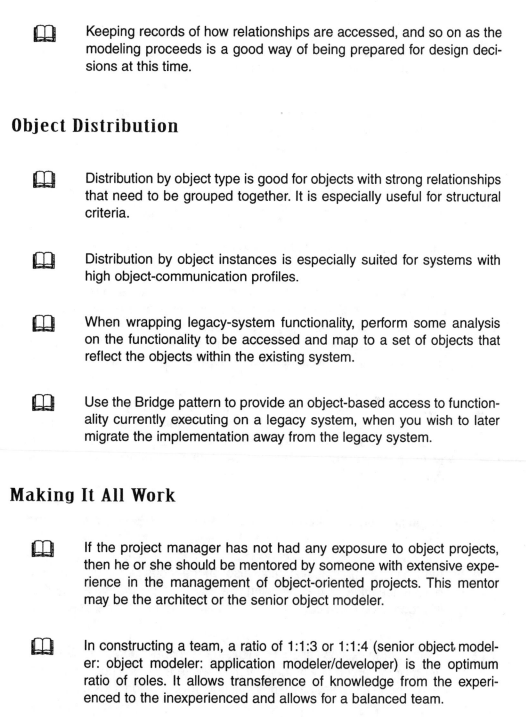

Keeping records of how relationships are accessed, and so on as the modeling proceeds is a good way of being prepared for design decisions at this time.

Object Distribution

Distribution by object type is good for objects with strong relationships that need to be grouped together. It is especially useful for structural criteria.

Distribution by object instances is especially suited for systems with high object-communication profiles.

When wrapping legacy-system functionality, perform some analysis on the functionality to be accessed and map to a set of objects that reflect the objects within the existing system.

Use the Bridge pattern to provide an object-based access to functionality currently executing on a legacy system, when you wish to later migrate the implementation away from the legacy system.

Making It All Work

If the project manager has not had any exposure to object projects, then he or she should be mentored by someone with extensive experience in the management of object-oriented projects. This mentor may be the architect or the senior object modeler.

In constructing a team, a ratio of 1:1:3 or 1:1:4 (senior object modeler: object modeler: application modeler/developer) is the optimum ratio of roles. It allows transference of knowledge from the experienced to the inexperienced and allows for a balanced team.

In order to fully leverage experienced resources, use small focused teams with a ratio of 1:1:4 for very experienced object person: mildly experienced object person: inexperienced object person.

Where only a few people have object experience in an organization, use the seeded-project-team model to effectively leverage their knowledge on a maximum number of projects.

The system architect who has overall responsibility for the architecture of the system must be regarded as a peer of the project manager and is responsible for the technical vision of the project. As a result, we find that project managers and architects must work closely together.

Allocate modeling of use cases and related scenarios to team members. Allow a team member to "own" a set of scenarios for modeling purposes. Ensure that objects do not become "fragmented" by holding periodic reviews of object models and scenarios, reviewing against roles and responsibilities defined earlier in the modeling process.

If the generic aspects of a system can be captured by an architecture, allocate your architecture team the responsibility of working on a set of architectural components that can be used by the core functionality. Other team members can model their interactions based on the generic definitions.

When tracking progress of a project make sure you keep a record of the number of use cases and objects. High-level reporting can then be carried out around these two concepts. For example: "We have completed modeling 12 out of 35 use cases" during the modeling, and "of the 195 objects identified in the modeling, we have completed implementation of around 55, which covers approximately 17 out of 35 use cases."

CRC card workshops should be limited to 2 hours each and it is worthwhile organizing a few of these workshops in a week. Focus each session around a few key scenarios that will provide insight into the domain.

📖 Use building-block workshops in the early stages of a project when aiming to gain the confidence of the users and domain experts in the process, and also to allow them some insight into the modeling process.

📖 Use storyboarding as a means of performing detailed analysis during modeling to validate models. Work with domain experts and object modelers to take a scenario step by step to conclusion.

📖 Use storyboards during workshops to demonstrate to users the "'secrets" of object modeling.

📖 Use a wall of the project room to display project work to date. Use it as a means of openly recording progress on the project and receiving feedback from all concerned. Encourage all (from business-project sponsor to end users) to review the wall, and provide open and honest comments. Update the wall periodically, the exact period should depend on the rate of the project.

📖 One evening a month (or every 2 weeks if preferred) invite people to come to the wall and take a look at the models. Provide "tours" and "viewings" for the guests. Take an art-gallery view of the models, explaining details and issues to those not involved in their creation (business sponsors, some domain experts, etc.).

📖 Where using a formal-requirements specification, separate out operational and system requirements into two documents. There may be references between these documents.

📖 Models should be reviewed against requirements. Both the original and the revised requirements specification should be available at the review. Each requirement should be checked off against the feature(s) in the model(s) that support it. Attention should be drawn to any requirements in the specification that have not yet been supported.

In an elaborational approach, design decisions satisfying requirements should be noted as the model is changed. The documentation for such changes should cross-reference the requirements that caused them to exist.

In the translational approach a rule's documentation should identify which requirement has given cause for this rule to exist.

Objects cannot be learned overnight, and so it is worthwhile to use the expertise of someone who has experienced object development before. This utilization should be full time, especially if the experience of the team is very limited.

INDEX

A

abstract objects, 94, 146
allocation of work, 254
archetypes, 216
architect, 153, 254
    position in the organization, 156
    responsibilities, 153
    role, 153
    role in object modeling, 164
    skills, 154
    system, 246, 254
architectural principles, 159
architectural vision, 158, 160–161, 278
architecture, 18
    as used in Shlaer/Mellor, 217
    awareness, 152
    components, 166
    definition, 152
    four-layer, 179, 180
    framework, 168
    initial model, 160
    mapping, 255
    object-oriented, 152
    preliminary model, 158
    preliminary sketch, 158
    prototype, 168

    relationship to work allocation, 255
    service-based. *See* service-based
        architecture
    specification, 164
    team, 153–159, 163
    three tier. *See* three-tier architecture
architecture design
    process, 156
    relationship to broader process, 156
associative objects. *See also* relationships:
    as objects
    mapping in design, 200
asynchronous communication
    definition, 123, 206
    example, 122
    mapping in design, 207
    use in request-reply messaging, 208
attributes, 84, 205
    adding, 145
    as classes, 206
    as functions, 205
    as values, 206
    dependencies between, 102
    finding, 84
    mapping to design constructs, 205
    modeling, 85
    naming, 85